International Socialism 152

Autumn 2016

Contributors

Talat Ahmed is lecturer in South Asian History at the University of Edinburgh. She is the author of *Literature and Politics in the Age of Nationalism: The Progressive Episode in South Asia, 1932-56*, and contributor to *Say it Loud: Marxism and the Fight Against Racism*.

Adrian Budd teaches politics at London South Bank University, where he is active in the UCU. He is the author of *Class, States and International Relations: A Critical Appraisal of Robert Cox and Neo-Gramscian Theory*.

Geoff Brown is a long-standing member of the Socialist Workers Party based in Manchester.

Céline Cantat is a Visiting Research Fellow at the Central European University in Budapest where she works on migrants' solidarity movements in Hungary and Central Europe. Previously, Céline completed her PhD at the University of East London, focusing on pro-migrant organisations and networks in France, Italy and the UK and their relationship to the EU and its border regime.

Martin Empson is the treasurer of the Campaign against Climate Change Trade Union group and the author of *Land and Labour: Marxism, Ecology and Human History*.

Mike Gonzalez is the author of *Che Guevara and the Cuban Revolution* (2004) and, with Marianella Yanes, *The Last Drop: The Politics of Water* (2015).

Charlie Kimber is the editor of *Socialist Worker*.

Philip Marfleet is a professor in the School of Social Sciences at the University of East London and the author of *Egypt: Contested Revoluion* (Pluto, 2016).

Chris Newlove is a member of Kingston Socialist Worker Student Society and is currently studying for an MA in Philosophy and Contemporary Critical Theory.

John Newsinger is a member of Brighton SWP. His most recent book is *On the Picket Line with the IWW: Big Bill Haywood's Revolutionary Journalism*.

Tony Phillips is a member of the SWP based in Walthamstow in London and is a Unison trade union branch secretary working in the fire service.

Michael Roberts blogs at thenextrecession.wordpress.com and his facebook site can be found at http://tinyurl.com/MichaelRobertsFB. His new book, *The Long Depression: Marxism and the Global Crisis of Capitalism*, is published by Haymarket Books.

Miriam Scharf is a socialist and activist in Newham, east London.

Roddy Slorach is the author of *A Very Capitalist Condition: A History and Politics of Disability*. He is a socialist activist based in east London and a supporter of Disabled People Against Cuts.

G M Tamás is a Hungarian philosopher and public intellectual. A dissident before 1989, he was a Member of Parliament (1990-94) and the Director of the Institute of Philosophy of the Hungarian Academy. His latest book is *Kommunismus nach 1989* (Vienna, 2015).

Martin Upchurch is Professor of International Employment Relations at Middlesex University, London.

Widening fractures

Alex Callinicos

The political situation in Britain is defined by the fractures that have opened up over Brexit and in the Labour Party. This journal supported a vote to leave the European Union on 23 June for two main reasons—first, and as a matter of principle, we oppose the EU as an engine for imposing neoliberalism in increasingly authoritarian forms, and, secondly, Brexit would cause a major crisis for British and, to a lesser degree, world capitalism. This latter judgement has been vindicated by developments since the referendum.[1]

It's important to understand the nature of this crisis. The issue isn't the impact of Brexit on economic growth in Britain—a subject of much argument among mainstream politicians and commentators in the past few months. The truth is that one can argue the toss about this: on the one hand, the surprise result had an immediate negative impact on what Maynard Keynes called "animal spirits"—ie confidence among consumers and investors—that might cut spending and growth; on the other hand, the sharp fall in the exchange rate of the pound seems to have boosted exports and growth (though it may push up inflation in the longer run).

No, the real problem lies in the disruption Brexit might cause to the global positioning of British capitalism and thereby to the dominant capitalist networks.

---

1 Callinicos, 2015 and 2016, and Choonara, 2016.

Britain's somewhat ambiguous location—in the EU but not in the eurozone, loyal junior partner to the United States and site of the biggest international financial centre—means that it has the capacity to send destabilising ripples across the world economy. The US is already feeling the effects of Britain's eclipse in Brussels. Within days of the vote, the EU's development of its own military capabilities was back on the agenda, a move hitherto blocked by London's opposition to any initiatives outside the ambit of NATO. And—contrary to the predictions of left Remain supporters, the Brexit vote may prove to be the final straw for the Transatlantic Trade and Investment Partnership (TTIP) being negotiated between the US and the EU.

As for the EU itself, as Susan Watkins puts it:

> at a stroke, it loses an eighth of its population, a sixth of its GDP, half its nuclear-arms cache and a seat on the UN Security Council—its diminution mocked in the Chinese media as the decline of the West. More alarming for the custodians of the Union is the example the English vote sets to other dissident electorates.[2]

Even Jean-Claude Juncker, the bibulous, bullying president of the European Commission, has admitted that Brexit represents an "existential crisis" for the EU.[3] But what path to take after Britain leaves will exacerbate the already profound divisions among member states. The dwindling band of federalists are pressing for further integration while the Eastern and Central Europeans are demanding cuts in Brussels' powers, the governments of the two key states, Germany and France, are running scared in the face of the Eurosceptic challenges from the Alternative für Deutschland (AfD) and the Front National respectively and Italy is increasingly restive over the Commission's efforts to control its fiscal policy.

Hard or soft Brexit?

No surprise then, that at her first major international outing, the G20 summit in Hangzhou in early September, Theresa May found herself under strong pressure, notably from Barack Obama and the Japanese government, to ensure that Brexit is as soft as possible—that is, that Britain's departure from the EU should change things as little as possible. This is a bit of a problem for May since, whatever else the more than 17 million people who voted to leave the EU on 23 June had in mind, they wanted things to change. Elsewhere in this journal Charlie Kimber analyses the reasons why Brexit triumphed on 23 June. But it's worth underlining the results of a detailed study of voting patterns conducted for the Joseph Rowntree Foundation by Matthew Goodwin and Oliver Heath.

---

2 Watkins, 2016, p27.

3 Brunsden, 2016.

Their main finding was that "the poorest households, with incomes of less than £20,000 per year, were much more likely to support leaving the EU than the wealthiest households, as were the unemployed, people in low-skilled and manual occupations, people who feel that their financial situation has worsened, and those with no qualifications". The strongest single predictor of how an individual voted was their educational qualifications, themselves largely a proxy for socio-economic position. Goodwin and Heath also found that highly qualified people in "low-skill areas" were much more likely to vote Leave than their counterparts in "high-skill areas", reflecting, they argue, how a sense of lack of opportunities can permeate entire communities. Brexit thus revealed "a country that is deeply divided along not only social but also geographical lines".[4]

The referendum rejected the EU, but it was also a vote of no confidence in the state of British society. Often this was articulated in reactionary, Little Englander and indeed racist terms. It's important to recognise that one impact of the Brexit vote has been to give confidence to racists and to cause widespread fear among Black and Minority Ethnic and Eastern European communities, particularly because of the uptick in racist attacks. But it's also important not to accept the conclusion drawn by the pro-Remain majority on the British left that the Leave victory was simply a racist vote. As Kimber shows, the consciousness behind the vote was far more mixed and ambivalent.

This argument isn't necessarily a comforting one. In one of his most important notes, "Analysis of Situations. Relations of Force", Antonio Gramsci argues that every situation can be analysed at a number of different levels, starting from the "organic movements (relatively permanent)" arising from the fundamental economic structure of the forces and relations of production and concluding with

> movements that may be termed "conjunctural" (and which appear as occasional, immediate, almost accidental). Conjunctural phenomena too depend on organic movements to be sure, but they do not have any very far-reaching historical significance; they give rise to political criticism of a minor, day-to-day character, which has as its subject top political leaders and personalities with direct governmental responsibilities.[5]

But, Gramsci goes on to argue, a key mediating dimension between structure and conjuncture is "the relation of political forces; in other words, an evaluation of the degree of homogeneity, self-awareness, and organisation attained by the various social classes".[6] The relation of political forces in the referendum was very

4 Goodwin and Heath, 2016.

5 Gramsci, 1971, p177.

6 Gramsci, 1971, p181.

unfavourable to the radical left. The majority, along with the bulk of trade union officialdom, offered more or less radical versions of the pro-EU case being put by the leaderships of all the major parties (with the exception of UKIP) and by most serious capitalist interests in Britain. The minority that called for a Leave vote largely waged a principled campaign, chiefly in the shape of Lexit, opposing the EU on an internationalist and anti-capitalist basis, but it was too weak to make its voice heard on the national stage. This allowed the Tory right and UKIP to pose as the spokespeople of the poor and marginalised, whom the left largely failed to represent. Rather than quarrelling over how we voted on 23 June, it would be more sensible to recognise this shared failure.

Does this mean that the effect of the referendum has been to push Britain sharply to the right, as many pro-Remain leftists claim? Not at all. To see this we have to move to the level of the "conjunctural", that of "top political leaders and personalities with direct governmental responsibility". David Cameron's abrupt exit from 10 Downing Street (followed last month by his retirement from the House of Commons) allowed May, who sat out the referendum as an almost silent Remain supporter, to seize the premiership. In this she was aided by the bungling of the leaders of the supposedly triumphant pro-Leave Tories—Boris Johnson and Michael Gove taking each other out like characters in the final scene of a Tarantino movie, and the equally hapless Andrea Leadsom blowing herself away in the space of a weekend. Further to the right, UKIP, which should have been well placed to capitalise on victory in a referendum it helped to achieve, has instead imploded.

May has sought to put her stamp on the new government, notably by clearing out the remnants of Cameron's Notting Hill set, headed by George Osborne. Her decision to expand grammar schools suggests that politically she is somewhat to the right of Cameron, though one probably shouldn't overstate this. She has scrapped Osborne's target of a budget surplus by 2019-20 (though the spending cuts he initiated continue to roll on).

Her joint chief of staff Nick Timothy offered a rationale for May's relentless invocation of "ordinary working class people" when, after Iain Duncan Smith resigned from the cabinet in March, he contrasted him with his opponent in government Osborne:

> The two men represent, in Tim Montgomerie's dichotomy, the two approaches of the modern Party: Easterhouse modernisation, which focuses on fighting the kind of poverty found on the Glasgow estate after which it is named, and Soho modernisation, which is all about social liberalism.
>
> Easterhouse and Soho are useful labels, but they represent a false choice for the Party... Instead of these polarising approaches, I have always felt we should have

> a different model, that might—to extend Tim's language—be called Erdington modernisation, named after the working class area of Birmingham. With this approach, of course we would still help the very poor and of course we would fight injustices based on gender, race and sexuality, but the Party would adopt a relentless focus on governing in the interests of ordinary, working people...
>
> These people have modest means, but they work hard, they want to stand on their own two feet, and they want to give their children the best start in life they can. They are natural conservatives for precisely the reason that the stakes they have are small. They want stability, certainty, and steady leadership by politicians who have their interests at heart. In particular, they are suspicious of politicians making big promises and dismissive of excitable talk about radical policies. To them, radicalism means risk, and they know they are the ones who lose out when radicalism turns to rot.[7]

So "ordinary working people" turn out to be the conservative section of the working class who, rejecting any kind of collective solution, have traditionally embraced individualism and voted Conservative with a capital C. One can understand how returning to grammar schools might appeal to this constituency, though it's hard to see it having much appeal to the Labour supporters for whom May's harping on about "ordinary working people" is sometimes interpreted as being a play.

In any case, it is very unlikely that May's personal political agenda will dominate her government. She is going to be preoccupied with managing the struggle unleashed by Brexit between antagonistic forces, crucially within the cabinet. Despite the self-immolation of the Leave leaders in the struggle to succeed Cameron, she confronts a Tory right reinvigorated by the referendum victory and pressing for a hard Brexit—as complete a break as possible from the EU, which will allow Britain to float free as a global free market trading power. For the likes of Nigel Lawson, Brexit offers "a historic opportunity...to finish the job which Margaret Thatcher started".[8] The hard Brexiteers have launched a pressure group called Change Britain, sponsored by Johnson, Gove, Lawson, and the Labour MP Gisela Stuart.

From this perspective, the EU is an obstacle to pressing ahead with further neoliberal "reforms". While in continental Europe, the EU, first with the Single European Act of 1986, then with Economic and Monetary Union (EMU), and most recently with austerity, has provided the mechanism through which neoliberalism has been imposed. In Britain, however, the shift in a free market direction

---

7 Timothy, 2016. Timothy is referring here to Montgomerie, 2005.

8 BBC News, 2016.

preceded these changes and took place at the national level, most decisively under Thatcher. During the 1990s, the role that the drive towards EMU, initiated by the federalist president of the European Commission Jacques Delors and confirmed by the 1992 Maastricht Treaty, played in Thatcher's downfall encouraged the Tory right to brand the EU as a bureaucratic corporatist monolith suffocating free enterprise.[9] The eurozone catastrophe served to reinforce this view, even though it is crystal clear that the debt crisis in Ireland and the Mediterranean has been used to extract further neoliberal socio-economic restructuring.

It is in any case crucial to understand that this ultra-Thatcherite conception is not shared by the dominant capitalist interests in Britain. They are in mourning over the referendum result and are determined to minimise the effects of Brexit. Already the lines of battle are becoming clear. One key issue is whether Britain will remain in the Single Market—whose introduction was very much a British project (Hugo Young called it "a fusion between the visions of Margaret Thatcher and Jacques Delors for the future of Europe").[10] Britain regularly tops the European league table for foreign direct investment because it offers corporate-friendly access to the Single Market. Fear that this access is under threat helps to explain the Japanese demarche in early September. The *Financial Times* explains:

> Before June, Japanese companies barely had to think about where they should set up in Europe. The answer, in most cases, was Britain.
>
> Over the past five decades, about 1,000 Japanese firms have used the UK in effect as a springboard into Europe... For Japan, it is not only future investments in the UK—in areas such as nuclear energy, autos, public transport, the internet-of-things and pharmaceuticals—that Brexit has put at risk. It has also hung a question mark over existing factories that employ some 140,000 British workers.
>
> Japan Inc's doubts were expressed in a 15-page memo published over the weekend that included a list of safeguards, including single market access and harmonised regulations, Tokyo is seeking in order to avoid an exodus.[11]

Many Japanese companies—for example, the car firms Nissan, Honda and Toyota—specialise in producing and exporting goods. But the Single Market is in services as well as goods. This is crucial to the British economy, which in the first quarter of 2013 ran a €10.2 billion surplus on intra-EU trade in services (while Germany had a €26.5 billion deficit) as well as an €89 billion surplus in extra-EU trade in services.[12] These surpluses, along with the profits of foreign investment,

9 Young, 1998.
10 Young, 1998, p333.
11 Harding, Campbell, and Noonan, 2016.
12 http://ec.europa.eu/eurostat/statistics-explained/index.php/International_trade_in_services

are crucial in helping to counter-balance Britain's chronic deficit in international trade in goods. British services exports are inseparable from the role of the City, since financial services and insurance play the predominant role.[13]

But now the City's pre-eminence in European finance is under multiple threats thanks to Brexit: it may lose access to the Single Market; banks based in London may be deprived of their "passport" rights to operate in the EU; and continental financial centres such as Frankfurt and Paris are certain to seek to topple the City's dominance of trade in the euro and poach some of its other business. According to the Financial Conduct Authority, nearly 5,500 UK-registered companies have passports issued by the European Commission to access the EU market. Interestingly, 8,000 companies based elsewhere in the EU have passports to operate in the UK. This reflects the centrality of London: in 2012 almost 80 percent of capital markets and investment banking activity in the rest of the EU was managed and executed in the UK.[14] But Nicolas Véron of the Bruegel think tank predicts that "the City is likely to decline in absolute size, and even more so in relative terms as global financial activity can be expected to keep expanding overall".[15]

As far as the EU is concerned, access to the Single Market is inseparable from free movement of labour. Thus Norway and Switzerland, non-EU states that participate in the Single Market, are required to give free movement to EU citizens (though Switzerland is trying to qualify this). The insistence on free movement is partly ideological and political—the so-called "four freedoms" of movement (goods, labour, services and capital) form the institutional substance of the EU, though of course, as Céline Cantat argues elsewhere in this issue, this doesn't stop the EU erecting more and more barriers to migrants.[16] But there are also economic arguments that free movement of services can't work without free movement of people.

Martin Sandbu argues that the Brexiteers' claim that it is in the EU's interest to offer Britain a favourable trade deal applies much less in the case of services than of goods (where Britain has a deficit with the rest of the EU):

> Information services will often have two important characteristics. First, they involve large economies of scale and benefit from geographic clustering which improves the flow of knowledge and know-how. Second, they will often exist in order precisely to serve the needs of a large market in goods (and the other types of services)—as is obvious with, for example, international banking

13 Norfield, 2016.
14 Noonan and Brunsden, 2016.
15 Véron, 2016.
16 Barnard, 2016.

> and commercial law. But that means the economies they serve will be at the mercy—both in terms of cost and in terms of the effects of the financial industry in particular—of geographically clustered service centres in which their own nationals' ability to work or set up shop is limited or zero.[17]

Nevertheless, the Brexiteers have been allowed to define the referendum result as the rejection of free movement of labour. Despicably, right-wing Labour MPs who campaigned for Remain are now selling the pass on free movement. Rachel Reeves, for example, has written: "Immigration controls and ending free movement has to be a red line post-Brexit—otherwise we will be holding the voters in contempt".[18] So politicians from both sides of the Brexit divide are mounting new attacks on the rights of millions of European workers in Britain, and thereby helping to legitimise the post-referendum surge in racist attacks on East Europeans. This underlines the importance of the anti-racist campaigning that Stand Up to Racism is increasingly driving. This must now include the new front of defending free movement.

The Tory Brexiteers don't seem to be too worried about losing the Single Market. International trade secretary Liam Fox has already called for Britain to leave the EU's Customs Union, which he says is a prerequisite for him to negotiate new trade deals with the United States, Canada, Australia, India and so on. But he is being opposed by chancellor of the exchequer Philip Hammond, who argues this could lead to the reintroduction of "hard borders" between Britain and the EU, at a high cost to British exporters.

Negotiating a new trade deal with the EU on whatever terms could take much longer than the two year lead-up to departure from the Union laid down in Article 50 of the Lisbon Treaty. The *Financial Times* expresses widespread ruling class concerns that

> there will be a hiatus between the point at which Britain formally leaves the EU and the point at which an EU Free Trade agreement comes into force... This would leave Britain in a dangerous position. The country would face, among other things, immediate tariffs on its exports to the EU, bureaucratic customs checks and loss of passporting rights for services. Some politicians compare it to falling off a cliff edge.[19]

Having bested them in the race to succeed Cameron, May gave three leaders of the Leave campaign plum jobs—in addition to Fox in a new Department for International Trade, Johnson in the Foreign Office and David Davies in another new Department, for Exiting the European Union. Handing over to

17 Sandbu, 2016.
18 Bennett, 2016.
19 Blitz, 2016b.

the Brexiteers responsibility for negotiating Britain's departure from the EU seems like setting a fairly obvious trap, and all three have enough form to suggest that they may fall out collectively and foul up individually. But it is a recipe for a divided cabinet. Reporting on the row over leaving the Customs Union, the *Financial Times* commented:

> The fact that the cabinet is still grappling with such a fundamental question—and that it remains unresolved—shows the depth of ministerial divisions over Britain's post-Brexit trading stance. But this debate also gives us some insight into Mrs May's position. After all, Mr Hammond and the Treasury are unlikely to be able to hold their ground on this matter if they did not have some backing from the prime minister.
>
> "There is one issue where the prime minister and chancellor do not see completely eye-to-eye and that is when to press Article 50," a senior government figure tells me. "She wants to press the button early next year while he is arguing that we should wait longer. But when it comes to the content of Britain's negotiating position, they both recognise—unlike others—the need to retain the fullest possible access to Europe's single market".[20]

Substantive negotiations with the EU may in any case have to await the outcome of next year's French presidential and German parliamentary elections. EU leaders will also be caught between contradictory pressures—to minimise the disruption caused by Brexit, to discourage any other member states from leaving, and to accommodate increasingly vocal anti-EU forces in their own domestic scenes.

But May has a particularly tortuous path to tread between the demands of big capital and the dreams of the Tory right. In the circumstances it's not particularly surprising that she has ruled out calling a snap election. The combination of May's honeymoon and Labour's troubles might deliver a big parliamentary majority for the Tories. But this would increase her difficulties, by swelling the number of Europhobic backbenchers striving for a free market Utopia beyond the EU. The fact that the present House of Commons has an anti-Brexit majority increases May's room for manoeuvre. Either way, the façade of stability she has imposed on an increasingly febrile Tory party is unlikely to last.

Dual power in the Labour Party

Brexit also figures in the second key feature of the political situation—the struggle between Jeremy Corbyn and the bulk of the Parliamentary Labour Party (PLP). The pretext for the "chicken coup" against him—first mass resignations from the Shadow Cabinet and a vote of no confidence, then a direct challenge

---

20 Blitz, 2016a.

to his position as leader—was his alleged failure to campaign sufficiently enthusiastically for Remain. A more rational political calculation might reckon that Corbyn's refusal to withdraw his criticisms of the EU in the lead-up to 23 June would position him well to reconnect with the millions of traditional Labour supporters who voted Leave. But many in the PLP may have feared that this stance, together with the implosion of the Tory party, might dangerously increase his credibility as an alternative prime minister. Certainly Corbyn's opponents must take the lion's share of the blame for Labour's subsequent slide in the polls.

The PLP seems to have relied on the mass resignations demoralising Corbyn into capitulation. Then, when this failed, they fumbled over who to run against him, ending up with the weaker of the two challengers. The sheer ineptitude of the revolt suggests that ideology played a big role. The vehemence with which Corbyn's opponents have challenged him over Syria, Trident and Brexit shows the extent to which the Labour right—which now extends beyond the Blairite hard core to incorporate followers of Gordon Brown (such as Tom Watson, the witch-hunting deputy leader) and elements of the soft left—have essentially chosen as their ground the defence of the New Labour legacy.

Their problem is that the ground is shifting under them. Arrogantly affirming their ownership of the Labour Party (see the endless declarations that "this is *our* party"), they resemble nothing more than Anglo-Irish absentee landlords during the War of Independence, blissfully unaware that their tenants are revolting and their country houses are in flames. Since the 2015 general election, Labour Party membership has grown from around 200,000 members to (in July this year) 515,000 members and affiliated supporters plus another 180,000 registered supporters.[21]

This influx, overwhelmingly of Corbyn supporters, has made the structures of the Labour Party the vehicle of a mass movement that, whatever the uncertainties about what it is in favour of, rejects the New Labour embrace of neoliberalism and imperialism. The Corbyn phenomenon has been compared with the new left parties elsewhere in Europe, and to Bernie Sanders's insurgency within the Democratic Party in the United States. The fact that Syriza in Greece and Podemos in the Spanish state have challenged social democratic parties like Labour does not undermine the comparison. The universal long-term decay of social democracy, thanks paradoxically to the Blairites' success in pressing for the party leader to be elected on a one person one vote basis, made Labour open to capture by a rebellion against the social liberalism that came to define the centre left in the Tony Blair era.

21 Keen and Audickas, 2016, pp11 and 13.

Watson's clumsy attempt at witch-hunting—"there are some old hands twisting young arms in this process, and I'm under no illusions about what's going on. They are caucusing and factionalising and putting pressure where they can, and that's how Trotsky entryists operate"—demonstrated the Labour right's complete incomprehension of how Labour has changed.[22] The best efforts of the Labour Party apparatus, egged on by Watson, to purge Corbyn supporters were insufficient to stop him overwhelming his inept opponent Owen Smith. Corbyn won an increased overall majority (62 percent compared to 59 percent the year before), with substantial majorities in the three categories of members, affiliated supporters and registered supporters. The hapless right-wing attempt to topple him has actually strengthened Corbyn, mobilising his base and thereby promoting Labour's transformation into a mass party of the left. After the result was announced the *Guardian* grudgingly conceded that "Labour is now unquestionably a changed party".[23]

Corbyn's re-election means, however, that the condition of disequilibrium created by the profound antagonism between him and the Labour right will continue. The old power structure, in which the axis between the PLP and the trade union bureaucracy could contain left-wing surges among the membership, has broken down. In its place we have a situation of dual power between Corbyn, legitimised by the support of a growing mass membership, and the PLP, with the trade union leaders hovering in the background as power brokers.

The disequilibrium will continue in part because the right has retreated from its earlier threats to split Labour. It was never clear where it would get the activists and money required for such a project, and May's defeat of the Brexiteers reduced to zero any chance of pro-EU Tories breaking away to form a new centre party. For some of the PLP, not splitting implies a limited truce with Corbyn. The *Telegraph* reported in the lead-up to the Labour Party conference:

> with polls suggesting that Mr Corbyn is on course to win next week's leadership election easily, a number of former shadow ministers are preparing the ground to return to work with him.
>
> They will demand a list of assurances from Mr Corbyn as a sign of his goodwill before pledging their support.
>
> These include allowing them greater say in the running of the shadow cabinet, giving his support to a return to shadow cabinet elections, and dropping the threat that MPs who opposed his leadership will face de-selection.[24]

---

22 Aitkenhead, 2016.

23 Asthana, 2016.

24 Ross, 2016.

According to the same report, the MPs would also insist on Corbyn dropping the so-called "McDonnell amendment"—ie the proposal by shadow chancellor John McDonnell to reduce the proportion of Labour MPs and MEPs required to nominate a leadership candidate from 15 to 5 percent. All in all, this is a funny kind of truce. The right seems hugely to overestimate its power, in the light not merely of Corbyn's victory over Smith but also the clean sweep of his supporters in the elections to the Labour National Executive Committee. It's as if, at the end of the American Civil War in April 1865, the defeated Southern army had insisted as a condition of surrendering at Appomattox that the North restore slavery. But some of the Blairites aren't prepared to offer even such a dubious truce. Luke Akehurst, general secretary of the right-wing camarilla Labour First, has said that, after Smith's defeat, "we will just have another leadership election again and we will carry on having leadership elections until we get a sensible result".[25]

It would therefore be potentially a fatal mistake for Corbyn to follow his re-election with substantial concessions to the right. It's clear that they are not open to genuine reconciliation. Wasting time trying to get the right onside carries a real danger that Corbyn will lose impetus and demoralise his own supporters. Fortunately, he has rebuffed Watson's attempt to restore the leadership electoral college dominated by MPs and trade union bureaucrats and to give back control over choosing the Shadow Cabinet to the PLP.

But, in the lead-up to the conference the Corbyn team was reported to be courting ex-shadow ministers such as Dan Jarvis. (The fact that the notably wooden Jarvis, whose only claim to fame is his service in Blair's wars as a Para officer, is widely touted as a future party leader is an indication of the extent to which New Labour is running on empty.) Corbyn explained: "I'm very confident we are as a party coming together. And I'm obviously having discussions with lots of colleagues. And there will be a full team in place to take on this government and provide very effective opposition".[26]

Instead of pursuing this kind of broad church approach, Corbynism needs to become a real movement with the ideological coherence and practical heft really to take Labour in a different direction. This won't be so easy. The obstacles are partly practical. I referred above to Corbyn supporters as a "mass movement" but in fact the picture isn't so simple. In the huge rallies he addressed all over the country during the summer, Corbynism certainly felt like a mass movement. But this movement so far has been most politically effective when taking part in the essentially atomised activity of voting for Corbyn online.

25 Clark, 2016.

26 Waugh, 2016.

Jean-Paul Sartre famously distinguished what he called the "series"—a social gathering such as a bus queue or a radio audience, where individuals are essentially isolated from one another, bound together by their passive dependence on something outside them—from the "fused group". Sartre describes the latter as "the sudden resurrection of freedom", when a change in the situation brings people together in a moment of collective action (he gives the example of the storming of the Bastille on 14 July 1789).[27] The Corbynites are more than a mere series—they share their support for Corbyn and (very importantly) they are aware that they share it. This sense of communality is reinforced through the very effective use of social media by the Corbyn team and by the rallies. But they certainly aren't a fused group.

This is a crucial point of difficulty for Corbyn. His traditional functions as leader of the Labour Party (and of Her Majesty's Opposition) are concentrated in Parliament and on the mass media. But these are two very hostile terrains, where he is relatively weak and surrounded by enemies. Where he is strong is in his support among the mass membership, but this is diffuse and atomised. Momentum is now making a serious effort to organise at least part of Corbyn's base through initiatives such as its fringe conference during the Labour Party conference in Liverpool, "A World Transformed".

This makes a lot of sense, but the question is how to turn even a successful conference into sustained organisation in working class communities that can widen support for Corbyn and his policies. The more Momentum tries to do this, the more the Labour right will attack it as a "party within a party", undercutting Corbyn's efforts at conciliation. Moreover, real organisation has to be built on struggle. But what should the focus of the struggle be? Against the right within the Labour Party, say by deselecting the most obnoxious MPs?

Even if the Momentum leadership were willing to take such a provocative approach, it's not clear how many Corbyn supporters are likely to be motivated to pursue the weary, highly bureaucratic struggle against the right in constituency and branch meetings. The alternative is a more outward looking orientation towards resistance to austerity, racism and war. Since these issues are what have drawn people behind Corbyn, this approach is far more likely to transform Corbynism into a real mass movement. But it won't avoid conflicts with the right. One obvious point of tension is the role played by Labour councils in implementing spending cuts.

It follows that building a mass movement can't be separated from giving Corbynism a more defined ideological profile. The renewed inner-party struggle has

27 Sartre, 1982, p401, and more generally, Book II.

forced Corbyn in this direction. In mid-September he gave a speech at Bloomberg that illustrated both the strengths and weaknesses of his policies:

> The overwhelming fact of the vote to Leave the EU is that the status quo is no longer an option... In voting Leave, in communities across the country [sic] rejected the status quo that had failed them.
>
> This is the failure of an entire economic model to provide the chances and opportunities to a generation of our people.
>
> It is an economic model that has discarded good jobs and stripped whole communities of their pride.[28]

So Corbyn refused to engage in the mainstream mourning over Brexit (epitomised in Owen Smith's ridiculous call for a second referendum). This is a potentially very powerful riposte to the Tory right's call to complete the Thatcherite revolution, one that argues instead that Brexit requires a break with neoliberalism. The same idea is expressed in Corbyn's call for a deal that keeps Britain in the Single Market but minus "state aid rules and requirements to liberalise and privatise public services". But the detail of his economic programme is standard post-crash social democratic fare—a £500 billion programme of infrastructure investment, an industrial strategy overseen by a new National Investment Bank, support for cooperatives, a National Education Service...

There's not much here that Owen Smith or Ed Miliband would dissent from. Even Theresa May is rehabilitating industrial strategy after the laissez-faire of the Thatcher, New Labour and Cameron years. Commenting on a speech by McDonnell calling for "new economics" at a conference earlier this year, Michael Roberts writes: "What was this new economics? Well, I'm afraid it was not new but really a rehash of old Keynesian arguments and policy proposals. As McDonnell said, the aim was to 'transform capitalism' with new rules and state intervention, not to replace it". Roberts argues that instead "Labour needs to develop a programme to replace capitalism by bringing into public ownership the major banks and business sectors under democratic control to be integrated into a plan for investment in people's needs not profit".[29]

Having been involved in Labour left politics for 40 years, Corbyn and McDonnell will be familiar with this kind of criticism—indeed they probably agree with it. The reason why they have adopted this much more timid programme is almost certainly a preoccupation with "credibility" and "electability". This is reflected in the very name McDonnell gave to his "Fiscal Credibility Rule", which commits a future Labour government to keeping current spending

---

28 Corbyn, 2016.

29 Roberts, 2016.

in balance over a five-year period and borrowing only to finance investment. When he announced it in March, the LabourList blog commented:

> While the economics of McDonnell's speech—deficit reduction and borrowing for investment in infrastructure—is not radically dissimilar to the Miliband and Balls approach, the most striking aspect of today's speech seems to be in rhetoric. By talking about "fiscal credibility" and "discipline", McDonnell is adopting the language of the existing economic narrative. Corbyn often speaks of wanting to "change the conversation"—but it appears the leadership are attempting to change the way we think about things, rather than how we speak about them.[30]

All of this underlines the simple fact that under Corbyn and McDonnell Labour remains an electoral party, competing in an arena where the political agenda is set by the neoliberal political elite and its interlocutors in the corporate media and big business more generally. Labour's left-wing leadership will be judged, like any other, by its success in winning votes. The support of the main trade union leaders (with the exception of the GMB) has been critical in allowing Corbyn to carry on in defiance of the PLP revolt.

This support no doubt reflects a number of factors—in the case of some unions (such as Unite and the Communication Workers Union) genuine political agreement, pressure from rank and file activists (among whom Corbyn is popular), and a sense that the Labour right has nothing very inspiring in the way of personalities or policies to offer. But it isn't a blank cheque. At the very minimum, the trade union leaders' need for an electorally successful Labour Party will push towards Corbyn the chimaeras of peace with the PLP and "credibility" in the bourgeois political scene.

All this begs the question of what would happen if Corbyn and McDonnell were to cross the electoral hurdle and make it to Downing Street—apparently an implausible prospect now, but something that can't be ruled out given the newfound propensity of British politics to produce the unexpected. Even their relatively modest economic programme would encounter formidable resistance from a capitalist class bruised by Brexit and geared to operating globally under minimal government constraint. Where would a left-wing Labour government get the strength to defy capital? This is an old question given fresh life by the depressing capitulation of the Syriza government in Greece to waterboarding by the EU. The answer can only come through the development now of a mass movement behind the Corbyn leadership. But, as we have already seen, this can only be achieved in defiance of the rules of the parliamentary game inside and outside Labour.

---

30 Pope, 2016. But see the interesting discussion of the post-Keynesian thinking behind the Fiscal Credibility Rule in Mason, 2016.

In other words, the Corbyn phenomenon—like Syriza before it—has not suspended the classic dilemmas of reform and revolution. This truth, and the vacillations of Corbyn and McDonnell, underline the need to maintain an independent revolutionary socialist organisation that is free from the compromises imposed by constitutional convention and intra-party manoeuvring. But this isn't a justification of bombastic flag-waving. On the contrary, the real test for revolutionary socialists will lie in the degree to which they are able to unite with all those who've rallied to Labour under Corbyn.

This means standing together against the common enemy of the Labour right. But probably more important is the promotion of struggles that transcend the conflict within Labour—above all against the rising tide of racism. The referendum result hasn't simply given more racists more confidence. It has created new fronts of struggle—above all to defend the free movement of labour after Brexit. One of Corbyn's most admirable stances has been his refusal to join in the anti-migrant rhetoric that hitherto has dominated all the mainstream parties. The development of Stand Up to Racism into a mass movement defending migrants and refugees will strengthen his hand. More importantly, it will help to ensure that it isn't the right that sets the agenda in Britain after Brexit.

References

Aitkenhead, Decca, 2016, "'I Want to Hug Him but Also Shout at Him': Tom Watson on Jeremy Corbyn and Labour Rifts", *Guardian* (9 August), http://tinyurl.com/je6c7qv

Barnard, Catherine, 2016, *The Substantive Law Of The EU: The Four Freedoms* (Oxford University Press).

Asthana, Anushka, 2016, "Corbyn Leadership Win Shows Labour is Now a Changed Party", *Guardian* (24 September), www.theguardian.com/politics/2016/sep/24/jeremy-corbyn-leadership-win-shows-labour-is-now-a-changed-party

BBC News, 2016, "Lawson: Brexit a Chance to Finish Margaret Thatcher's Work" (5 July), www.bbc.co.uk/news/uk-politics-36717050

Bennett, Owen, 2016, "Remain-Backing Labour MPs Call For An End To Freedom Of Movement As Part Of Brexit Deal", *Huffington Post* (19 September), www.huffingtonpost.co.uk/entry/labour-mp-freedom-of-movement-brexit_uk_57dfb7eae4b0d584f7f1b89b?

Blitz, James, 2016a, "May's Cabinet Faultline", *Financial Times* Brexit Briefing (14 September), www.ft.com/content/49309c1c-7a6b-11e6-ae24-f193b105145e

Blitz, James, 2016b, "Britain Risks Falling Off a Cliff Edge", *Financial Times* Brexit Briefing (15 September), www.ft.com/content/ef4d7b88-7b38-11e6-ae24-f193b105145e

Brunsden, Jim, 2016, "Juncker Uses State of the Union to Try to Heal EU Divisions", *Financial Times* (14 September), www.ft.com/content/8754dfb4-7a55-11e6-ae24-f193b105145e

Callinicos, Alex, 2015, "The Internationalist Case Against the European Union", *International Socialism 148* (autumn), http://isj.org.uk/the-internationalist-case-against-the-european-union/

Callinicos, Alex, 2016, "Brexit: A World-Historic Turn", *International Socialism 151* (summer), http://isj.org.uk/brexit-a-world-historic-turn/ (online only).

Choonara, Joseph, 2016, *The EU: A Left Case for Exit* (Socialist Workers Party).

Clark, Nick, 2016, "Inside the 'Moderates' Meet-Up': Vows to Keep Fighting to Oust Corbyn", *Socialist Worker* (13 September), https://socialistworker.co.uk/art/43380/Inside+the+Moderates+meetup:+Vows+to+keep+fighting+to+oust+Corbyn

Corbyn, Jeremy, 2016, "Reckless Tories Wandered Into Brexit—Now They Are Scurrying Away from the Mess", speech at Bloomberg (15 September), http://labourlist.org/2016/09/jeremy-corbyn-reckless-tories-wandered-into-brexit-now-they-are-scurrying-away-from-the-mess/

Goodwin, Matthew, and Oliver Heath, 2016, "Brexit Vote Explained: Poverty, Low Skills and Lack Of Opportunities" (31 August), www.jrf.org.uk/report/brexit-vote-explained-poverty-low-skills-and-lack-opportunities

Gramsci, Antonio, 1971, *Selections from the Prison Notebooks* (Lawrence & Wishart).

Harding, Robin, Peter Campbell, and Laura Noonan, 2016, "Japan Inc Rethinks Its Longstanding Bet on Britain", *Financial Times* (6 September), www.ft.com/content/e52af878-7418-11e6-bf48-b372cdb1043a

Keen, Richard, and Lukas Audickas, 2016, "Membership of UK Political Parties", House of Commons Library Briefing Paper, no. SN05125 (5 August), http://researchbriefings.parliament.uk/ResearchBriefing/Summary/SN05125

Mason, Paul, 2016, "The Thinking behind John McDonnell's New Fiscal Credibility Rule", *New Statesman* (11 March), www.newstatesman.com/politics/economy/2016/03/thinking-behind-john-mcdonnell-s-new-fiscal-credibility-rule

Montgomerie, Tim, 2005, "Editorial: Easterhouse and Soho Conservatism" (2 December), http://conservativehome.blogs.com/toryleadership/2005/12/editorial_easte.html

Noonan, Laura, and Jim Brunsden, 2016, "Banks Fear Chill Wind of EU 'Passport' Freeze", *Financial Times* (21 September), www.ft.com/content/f4519e4a-7f23-11e6-bc52-0c7211ef3198

Norfield, Tony, 2016, *The City: London and the Global Power of Finance* (Verso).

Pope, Conor, 2016, "McDonnell Promises to Balance the Books with Fiscal Credibility Rule", LabourList (11 March), http://labourlist.org/2016/03/mcdonnell-promises-to-balance-the-books-with-fiscal-credibility-rule/

Roberts, Michael, 2016, "Labour's New Economics—Not So New" (22 May), https://thenextrecession.wordpress.com/2016/05/22/labours-new-economics-not-so-new/

Ross, Tim, 2016, "Senior Labour MPs Draw Up Truce Plans to Return to Corbyn Cabinet if He is Re-Elected", *Telegraph* (10 September), www.telegraph.co.uk/news/2016/09/10/senior-labour-mps-draw-up-truce-plans-to-return-to-corbyn-cabine/

Sandbu, Martin, 2016, "Free Lunch: One Market, Indivisible", *Financial Times* (4 July), www.ft.com/content/1f009970-41c6-11e6-9b66-0712b3873ae1

Sartre, Jean-Paul, 1982 [1960], *Critique of Dialectical Reason*, Volume I (Verso).

Timothy, Nick, 2016, "What Does The Conservative Party Offer a Working-Class Kid from Brixton, Birmingham, Bolton or Bradford?" (22 March), http://tinyurl.com/ho7oslz

Véron, Nicolas, 2016, "The City Will Decline and We Will Be the Poorer for It" (14 September), http://bruegel.org/2016/09/the-city-will-decline-and-we-will-be-the-poorer-for-it/

Watkins, Susan, 2016, "Casting Off?", *New Left Review*, II/100, https://newleftreview.org/II/100/susan-watkins-casting-off

Waugh, Paul, 2016, "Dan Jarvis Among 'Moderate' Figures Tipped To Join Jeremy Corbyn's Shadow Team", *Huffington Post* (16 September), http://tinyurl.com/gm4uymc

Young, Hugo, 1998, *This Blessed Plot: Britain and Europe from Churchill to Blair* (Macmillan).

Coming soon from Bookmarks

1917: THE RED YEAR

★ A Graphic Novel by Tim Sanders and John Newsinger ★

This stunningly illustrated graphic novel follows the lives of Natalia and Peter, two young people who found themselves at the centre of a revolutionary storm.

In 1917, Russian women workers poured out of their factories on International Women's Day and sparked a revolution. Defying Cossacks armed with whips, they took control of the streets and pelted other factories with stones and snowballs, calling on other workers to join them.

The government brought in the troops to restore order. But soldiers' anger at the war, at food shortages and at the injustice of a rotten system exploded on the streets of St Petersburg. They mutinied and joined the marchers.

That is where Natalia and Peter's story begins. We know where it ends: in weeks the Tsar was gone, followed a few months later by the government that replaced him. By October, workers had taken control. But what happens in that momentous year changed those who lived it forever and has inspired millions since.

Bookmarks—the socialist bookshop
1 Bloomsbury Street, London WC1B 3QE
020 7637 1848
www.bookmarksbookshop.co.uk
publications@bookmarks.uk.com

Why did Britain vote Leave?

Charlie Kimber

The British vote on 23 June 2016 to leave the European Union was a bitter blow for the establishment, big business, the international financial institutions, the rich and the politicians.[1] With only minor exceptions they had united to support a Remain vote. Tory prime minister David Cameron had been very sure that he would win the referendum. That serene complacency lies in tatters. Just a year after his unexpected general election success, the EU vote destroyed Cameron.[2] Chancellor George Osborne, the hitman of austerity, was also forced out and contrary to much expectation, Boris Johnson did not become the Tory leader. The Leave vote tore apart the Tories and, although there will be a brief period of calm after the insertion of Theresa May as prime minister, there will be further trouble ahead. But the Leave vote also revealed a much deeper bitterness and alienation from traditional political forces. Remain had the support of most of the Tory leadership, Labour, the Scottish National Party, Plaid Cymru, the Lib Dems, the Greens and Sinn Féin, parties that make up 97 percent of the House of Commons. But Remain lost.

There have been real fears expressed that the vote was motivated mainly by racism—and there were people who voted Leave for racist reasons. But this was

1 An instant, and powerful, analysis of the vote by Alex Callinicos was published online by this journal—Callinicos, 2016.

2 Parker and Barker, 2016.

certainly not the most important factor that explains why 52 percent voted Leave (on a 72 percent turnout). The central issue is that it was a revolt against the establishment. People who are generally forgotten, ignored or sneered at delivered a stunning blow against the people at the top of society; this was a rejection of the governing class.

The vote was partly driven by bitter anger at the grinding and relentless attacks on working class people since the onset of the financial crisis. A month after the referendum the Trades Union Congress produced research showing that British workers have suffered the biggest fall in real wages among leading OECD countries. Between 2007 and 2015 real wages in Britain fell by 10.4 percent—a drop equalled only by Greece. During a similar period the richest 1,000 people in Britain have seen their wealth more than double to £576 billion.[3] But the vote also reflected a deeper political rejection of the people at the top of society. A few days before the referendum the *Financial Times* reported on research carried out by Professor Will Jennings of Southampton University. Jennings has studied British attitudes towards the political establishment since the 1940s. The paper concluded:

> Trust has eroded steadily over decades, but is now running alarmingly low. The UK's Mass Observation archive, which collects diaries and other private correspondence, shows that people today write about doctors, the clergy and lawyers in more or less the same way as they did back in 1945. That is not the case with politicians: "Citizens now described their 'hatred' for politicians who made them 'angry', 'incensed', 'outraged', 'disgusted' and 'sickened'." Among the words used for politicians are arrogant, boorish, corrupt, creepy, devious, loathsome, lying, parasitical, pompous, shameful, sleazy, slippery, spineless, traitorous, weak and wet. As Prof Jennings says, "whatever measure you use political mistrust is rising—you see a generalised malaise".[4]

The Leave vote was that feeling made flesh. It was driven by such factors as the MPs' expenses scandal, the decades-long sense that the political parties are now all the same, the widespread contempt for the "pillars of society", the lies told to launch the Iraq war and the resentment that comes from sensing that a tiny group at the top of society are making millions while you're suffering—and they are also laughing at you. It's a mood that the right seek to channel, but it is also potentially subversive in a very radical way. Labour former prime minister Gordon Brown reflected the fear that engulfed the ruling class. He wrote: "An ugly EU referendum campaign has led to an even uglier aftermath. Historians will see the largest popular revolt against political, business and financial elites

3 TUC, 2016.
4 Buck, 2016.

as the nearest Britain has come in centuries to a revolution".[5] He overstated the closeness to revolution, but he was right to detect the whiff of insurgency that escaped the control of all the normal containing factors.

The reasons for that rebellion are contradictory, and the fallout from the vote is uncertain. But that does not change the essential character of what has taken place. We should welcome this development. Liberals fear turmoil, revolutionaries should not. We are not going to get to the British revolution without some complicated and many-sided developments that require the left to grasp the moment—and if they don't then the right can grab that feeling of anger instead. The year of the referendum also saw meetings in many places to remember 100 years since the Easter Rising in Dublin. Many in the audience would have nodded sagely at Lenin's understanding of what happened:

> To imagine that social revolution is conceivable...without revolutionary outbursts by a section of the petty bourgeoisie with all its prejudices, without a movement of the politically non-conscious proletarian and semi-proletarian masses against oppression...to imagine all this is to repudiate social revolution. So one army lines up in one place and says, "We are for socialism", and another, somewhere else and says, "We are for imperialism", and that will be a social revolution!... Whoever expects a "pure" social revolution will never live to see it. Such a person pays lip-service to revolution without understanding what revolution is.[6]

Of course the Leave vote was not the Easter Rising. But Lenin's method is important.

Labour MP Diane Abbott was right to say the referendum result was a "roar of defiance against the Westminster elite". Labour leader Jeremy Corbyn said that a clear message from the vote was "that millions of people feel shut out of a political and economic system that has let them down". The Bagehot column in the bosses' magazine *The Economist* said: "The vote for Brexit looks like—and to some extent is—a cry of fury by those who have borne the burden of European integration without benefiting proportionally from its advantages".[7] Elsewhere in the same edition the magazine editorialised: "Proponents of globalisation, including this newspaper, must acknowledge that technocrats have made mistakes and ordinary people paid the price".[8]

John Hilary, the executive director of War on Want, who has taken a leading role in the fight against the neoliberal Transatlantic Trade and Investment

5 Brown, 2016.
6 Lenin, 1916.
7 *Economist*, 2016a.
8 *Economist*, 2016b.

Partnership (TTIP), said: "The Leave vote is a rejection of the political caste in this country, as most commentators already agree. The fact that voters in many traditional Labour strongholds came out for Brexit must be seen as a call for a new kind of politics based on decisions that benefit the many, not the few".[9]

The Socialist Workers Party called for a Leave vote. We did so for three main reasons. Firstly, the EU is an openly pro-capitalist institution which in recent years had shed any pretence of delivering social protection and instead has emerged as the enforcer of austerity across a continent. This was most vividly demonstrated by the brutal financial waterboarding of Greece in 2015 which broke the challenge of Syriza. Secondly, the EU, through its Fortress Europe structures, acts to repel migrants and refugees from outside Europe. The EU's much-vaunted freedom of movement has always been highly limited: some freedom for those inside the EU; barbed wire fences, detention camps and a panoply of security forces to push back those from outside. As migrants poured from the war zone of Syria and elsewhere, such a policy turned the Mediterranean into a mass graveyard as thousands of people died in the desperate attempt to find safety. Internal barriers went up and border controls were reintroduced. The EU imposes racist laws. This was further underlined by the EU's deals with the repressive Turkish regime to restrict refugees attempting to come to the EU and then to deport refugees in Greece to Turkey. Thirdly, the EU is part of the imperialist world order that, along with NATO, delivers important support for the United States and provides reliable partners in its murderous actions. That is why since the late 1940s the US has promoted European integration to secure a stable junior partner for managing global capitalism.[10]

Many radical parties in the rest of Europe shared our position, and celebrated the result. On 24 June the Portuguese Left Bloc held an international rally to launch its convention. Eric Toussaint from Belgium, a long-time campaigner against the imposition of debt on the Global South, said Leave had "made me wake up in the best of moods". He added: "It is a rejection of the neoliberal EU and shows that it can be defeated and lays the basis for future exits around Europe on a radical left basis." Zoe Konstantopoulou, former Syriza president of the Greek parliament, compared the Leave vote to the Oxi ("No") referendum in July 2015 that rejected an EU austerity deal. "This is a day that proves that people write history," she said, "a day that proves that people are more courageous than their leaders." Left Bloc leader Catarina Martins said that reducing the Leave vote to racism or xenophobia was wrong and that the EU's policies had strengthened racism and xenophobia. She urged the left to oppose the EU to

9 Hilary, 2016.
10 A full analysis of the EU is provided in Callinicos, 2015.

cut across UKIP's Nigel Farage, Front National leader Marine Le Pen and other racist forces.[11]

In Ireland the socialist grouping People Before Profit supported Leave and after the result said it was "chickens coming home to roost for corporate and increasingly undemocratic Europe". Brid Smith TD said: "This vote should be seen as an opportunity for an alternative Europe. I welcome this blow to the EU project. The EU has never been about a workers' Europe and its recent treatment of Greece and Ireland shows its primary concern is not the welfare of citizens or refugees but the welfare of the banks and the bond holders".[12]

Gerry Carroll, a member of the Northern Ireland assembly said:

> There are "reasons to be cheerful" about the outcome... David Cameron—one of Europe's biggest austerity mongers—is gone. The British establishment, from top to bottom is in turmoil, and Britain may well be facing its biggest constitutional crisis for a century or more. The Tory party, who seemed to be in a position of unquestionable strength just months ago, is split. And the neoliberal project of the EU...is in a deep crisis.[13]

Eamonn McCann, another member of the Northern Ireland assembly, said: "There is no need for the pessimism and near panic which seems to have descended on many. There is no inevitable outcome here. It's all to be fought for".[14]

The EU played a key role in stopping anti-austerity policies in Greece. To put it more accurately, 2015 in Greece showed that genuine and consistent anti-austerity policies require breaking from the EU, a possibility that Syriza refused to countenance. This was part of its more general approach of "playing by the rules" of capitalism. The EU would play the same role if a Labour government under Jeremy Corbyn were elected in Britain. For example, it would be impossible to renationalise the entire rail network under EU rules.

The SWP believes socialists had to tell the truth about the EU and support a Leave vote. But the campaign had to eschew any element of racism and British nationalism. That meant it had to break completely from the official Leave campaign, dominated by right-wing Tories such as Boris Johnson and Michael Gove. The Left Leave campaign ("Lexit") involved the SWP, the Communist Party, Counterfire, the Indian Workers Association (GB), the Bangladeshi Workers

---

11 See the videos of the sessão internacional on the EsquerdaNet Youtube channel—www.youtube.com/user/EsquerdaNet/

12 People Before Profit Alliance, 2016 (a TD is a member of the Irish Parliament).

13 People Before Profit Alliance, 2016.

14 People Before Profit Alliance, 2016.

Council of Britain and some leading trade unionists. There was also a Scottish Left Leave campaign and a tour of more than 20 cities for a left exit campaign by the Trade Unionist and Socialist Coalition (TUSC). These put forward a case against the EU that was the polar opposite to the one that came from the Tories, UKIP or for that matter the Labour Leave campaign. The significance of Lexit was not in moving millions of votes—its influence was relatively marginal—but in the demonstration of how to mount a principled anti-racist, anti-capitalist, internationalist campaign.

But this is hugely contested territory. Many on the left saw the vote as simply an affirmation of reaction and racism. Socialist Resistance, the British section of the Fourth International, is a very small organisation but it spoke for a considerable part of the left when it said, "The vote to leave the EU is a victory for the right-wing xenophobes and a disaster for the struggle against austerity in Britain".[15] It is a serious argument, but it is wrong, pessimistic and demobilising.

There is a good deal of contemptuous dismissal of Leave voters as stupid and reactionary and racist. Much of it is based on myth. To take a small example, one popular story immediately after the referendum was that people had frantically started searching on Google for "What is the EU?" in the hours after the result was announced. The numbers, we were told, had tripled. The implication was that the uneducated masses had voted Leave without any basis and now, after the event, were trying to find out what they had actually done. It's true there was a spike in the numbers searching this question, but from an extremely low base. In the month before the Brexit vote, 8,100 Britons googled "What is the EU?" That's around 261 a day. If the numbers did indeed triple, that's still fewer than 1,000 the day after the vote.[16] We don't know if they were voters or not, or if they had voted Remain or Leave. The story was, like many, a slur designed to demonise Leave voters.

Who voted Leave?

In this article I have made much use of the survey produced by Lord Ashcroft and his team. The source is not perfect, but it is the most comprehensive one that is publicly available. Ashcroft says: "On referendum day I surveyed 12,369 people after they had voted to help explain the result—who voted for which outcome, and what lay behind their decision".[17] What do his results show?

15 *Socialist Resistance*, 2016.

16 McGoogan, 2016.

17 Ashcroft, 2016. The "I surveyed" reminds us of Bertolt Brecht's "Questions from a Worker Who Reads": "Caesar defeated the Gauls. Did he not even have a cook with him?"

Table 1: Social class and the referendum

<table>
<tr><th>Social class</th><th>Description</th><th>Percentage of population</th><th>Votes for Leave (percentage)</th></tr>
<tr><td>A</td><td>Higher managerial, administrative and professional</td><td>4</td><td rowspan="2">A and B: 43</td></tr>
<tr><td>B</td><td>Intermediate managerial, administrative and professional</td><td>23</td></tr>
<tr><td>C1</td><td>Supervisory, clerical and junior managerial, administrative and professional</td><td>27</td><td>C1: 51</td></tr>
<tr><td>C2</td><td>Skilled manual workers</td><td>21</td><td>C2: 64</td></tr>
<tr><td>D</td><td>Semi-skilled and unskilled manual workers</td><td>16</td><td rowspan="2">D and E: 64</td></tr>
<tr><td>E</td><td>State pensioners, casual and lowest grade workers, unemployed with state benefits only</td><td>9</td></tr>
</table>

Source: National Readership Survey, 2015; Ashcroft, 2016, table 2, p5.

Class

There was a very strong class element to the Leave vote. The Ashcroft poll uses the National Readership Survey (NRS) social classification grades. These are based on occupation and are widely used in market research. They are not the same as class divisions but they do paint a very broad picture of class and the vote.

Every group except A includes large numbers of workers. The B group, for example, includes some lecturers, teachers and healthworkers. Ashcroft's survey found that the AB social group were the only one where a majority, 57 percent, voted to Remain. The C1 group had a small Leave majority, the C2 and DE groups voted 64 percent Leave.[18] There is also a clear correlation between income and the Leave vote; the poorer you were, the more likely you were to vote Leave. The woman who told the *Guardian*'s John Harris: "If you've got money, you vote in, if you haven't got money, you vote out,"[19] might have been speaking about her local area and obviously making a very broad generalisation. But it has a glimpse of the truth.

Given these figures it seems strange that Ashcroft also found that most people in full time or part time work voted Remain. But this is because the survey weighting reflects actual turnout in the referendum and ABs were more likely to take part in the referendum than other groups. The survey used the views of 5,111 ABs, who, according to NRS, make up 27 percent of the population. But it used only 4,846 C1s and C2s combined, groups that make up 48 percent of the population.

YouGov found similar links between a Leave vote and social categories;

18 Ashcroft, 2016, table 2, p5.

19 Harris, 2016.

according to their figures the AB group voted 39 percent Leave, C1 46 percent Leave, C2 63 percent Leave, DE 66 percent Leave.[20] This survey also found that those with a household income of less than £20,000 voted 62 percent Leave, those with a household income of £60,000 or more voted 35 percent Leave.

There is plenty of other evidence showing that most working class people voted Leave. Ashcroft found, "around two thirds of council and housing association tenants voted to leave".[21] Just three of the top 50 areas with the highest share of people from DE class backgrounds voted to Remain.

Data from the *Guardian* shows that in areas where a lower proportion of residents had formal qualifications (an indicator of class rather than intelligence) people tended to vote Leave. Leave voters also tended to live in areas where people earn less.[22]

The *Daily Mirror*'s analysis showed that the areas voting Leave had an average weekly wage of £410.47 compared with £459.52 for Remain.[23] None of this proves the vote was necessarily progressive. But it should surely give some pause to those on the left who see the 17 million Leave voters as just a racist horde.

There is deep bitterness and anger inside the working class. The referendum provided an outlet for it. The hatred of the elite, unaccountable power, the sense you are regarded as worthless and irrelevant—and the dislike of the undemocratic EU—combined in the Leave vote.

Unlike a general election there was no argument about "vote for us or you'll let the Tories in". Both the official Leave and Remain campaigns were led by Tories. The Remain argument about the positive effects of the EU and the disaster that awaits if you departed from it utterly failed. It doesn't work to tell people who rarely have holidays, let alone foreign holidays, that a Leave vote might make it harder for their flights abroad. As Satyajit Das pointed out, "the inconvenience of the non-EU line at immigration or the ability to own a holiday retreat on the continent does not concern those who have never had those opportunities".[24]

As Ralph Fevre argues:

> For 40 years—as union membership declined and inequality increased—Britons were told that education and the labour market were level playing fields on which those with talent and application could shape their own futures. Employers

20 YouGov, 2016.

21 Ashcroft, 2016.

22 Go to www.theguardian.com/politics/ng-interactive/2016/jun/23/eu-referendum-live-results-and-analysis

23 Grant, 2016.

24 Das, 2016.

> concurred as they promised material rewards and self-fulfilment for those who took advantage of the new individualism. But many Britons were excluded from this neoliberal settlement from the start and their descendants still aren't getting degrees or good jobs.[25]

This fury can be directed even more clearly against the bosses and the rich if it is given a clear lead. But that means welcoming it, not disparaging it.

Place

London was the only English region to vote for Remain, although even in the capital over 1.5 million people voted Leave.

Every other English region backed Leave—by 58 percent in Yorkshire and Humberside, 54 percent in the North West, 59 percent in the West Midlands and the East Midlands, and more than 50 percent in both the South East and South West. Wales voted by 53 percent for Leave, Scotland voted by 62 percent for Remain.

Taking the analysis to a city and town level is very revealing. There is a close association between areas that suffered particularly badly from the Thatcherite assault of the 1980s and a Leave vote. Almost 70 percent of people in Doncaster voted Leave, and 57 percent in the steel and former mining area of Neath Port Talbot in Wales also voted Leave. In Hartlepool 70 percent voted Leave along with 61 percent in Sunderland. Blaenau Gwent voted 62 percent Leave, despite quite large amounts of EU funds being deployed in the area.

These are areas that were ripped apart by the global pioneers of neoliberalism three decades ago, and they have never recovered from it. Did anyone attempt to go to the areas where the mines closed or where the steelworks rust and tell people that their prosperity was at risk if they voted Leave? If so they would have been laughed at. The former mining area of Bolsover, where the main warehouse of Sports Direct, recently lambasted for its "Victorian working practices", is situated, voted 71 percent for Leave.[26]

A small majority of those who voted Remain thought that for most children growing up today, life will be better than it was for their parents. Leavers thought the opposite by 61 percent to 39 percent. Nearly 60 percent of Leave voters thought life in Britain is not better today than it was 30 years ago—and for many that reflects the reality of their lives and their children's lives.[27]

---

25 Fevre, 2016.

26 See also Higgins, 2016: "Wigan's Road to Brexit".

27 Ashcroft, 2016.

Age

According to the Ashcroft poll, 73 percent of 18 to 24 year-olds voted to remain, falling to 62 percent among 25-34s. The 35-44 age group split almost equally between Remain and Leave. A majority of those aged over 45 voted Leave, rising to 60 percent of those aged 65 or over. This shouldn't be translated into "only the old voted Leave", and we should remember the median age of the British population is over 40 and the median age of potential voters is 46. One study suggested that 87 percent of eligible students in universities voted in the referendum, and 85 percent of them voted Remain. For many this was an expression of support for migrants and refugees, backing for some sense of internationalism, and a vote against UKIP and the reactionaries who headed the official Leave campaign. In the SWP we don't think the EU has anything to do with real internationalism or anti-racism, but we know that lots of young people were motivated by positive reasons to vote Remain. This is a good sign for the future.

A reactionary vote?

Racist attacks, and hate attacks in general, increased in the immediate aftermath of the Leave vote. Some 6,193 incidents were reported across England, Wales and Northern Ireland in the four weeks after 16 June 2016, according to the National Police Chiefs' Council. The most common offences reported were harassment, assault, verbal abuse and spitting. This includes homophobic, transphobic, racial, religious and disability hate crime.

There were 3,001 offences reported between 1 and 14 July. This was a 6 percent drop compared to the two weeks before, which saw 3,192 reports. But the figure is a 20 percent rise on the same period in 2015. There were many other reports of a similar nature. It is undoubtedly true that some racists were emboldened because they, wrongly, believed the Leave vote meant voters supported them. Many migrants to Britain and many black, Asian and Muslim people felt fear as the news of racist attacks spread. We should not dismiss it. The murder of Jo Cox MP during the referendum campaign by an alleged Nazi enraged by her pro-refugee views, is a reminder of the high stakes involved.

Some people argue that the Leave vote was fundamentally reactionary. Commentator Omer Aziz wrote: "Since the results were finalised, there has been a stubborn refusal among the commentariat and the political class to acknowledge the role that racism played in the vote. Racism not as a peripheral cause. Racism not as a tertiary cause, but rather racism as the *central* factor in determining who won on June 23".[28]

---

28 Aziz, 2016.

Table 2: "Do you think of multiculturalism as being a force for good, a force for ill, or a mixed blessing?"

	10 (good)	*9*	*8*	*7*	*6*	*5*	*4*	*3*	*2*	*1*	*0 (ill)*
Leave voters (percent)	2	2	6	8	8	26	9	10	8	6	14
Remain voters (percent)	14	11	18	16	11	19	9	6	5	3	3

Source: Ashcroft, 2016, table 27, pp112-113.

Racism *was* an issue in the Leave vote. It was the dominant aspect for some people (a minority) and a factor for others. But it was not the central component. Half of Leave voters told Ashcroft's pollsters that the biggest single reason for wanting to leave the EU was "the principle that decisions about the UK should be taken in the UK". A third said the main reason was that leaving "offered the best chance for the UK to regain control over immigration and its own borders." Just over one in eight said remaining would mean having no choice "about how the EU expanded its membership or its powers in the years ahead." The reasons most people gave for a Leave vote were, at least in large part, democratic and anti-elitist, not racist. But the Ashcroft poll has been systematically misinterpreted to provide spurious evidence of reactionary Leave voters.

Sayeeda Warsi, a Conservative member of the House of Lords, for example, tweeted that "around 75 to 80 percent" of Leave voters believed multiculturalism, social liberalism, immigration, and feminism were "a force for ill". Her misunderstanding (if that is what it was) of the statistics was frequently followed by left-wingers on social media. It is true that, for example, 81 percent of those who think multiculturalism is a force for ill voted Leave. But that is not the same as 81 percent of Leave voters thinking that multiculturalism is a force for ill.

People were asked to rank how they felt about multiculturalism on an eleven point scale where a score of ten means it is "very much a force for good" and zero "very much a force for ill". In this survey Remain voters were, overall, more favourable to multiculturalism that Leave voters. But it is also true that 52 percent of Leave voters thought multiculturalism was a force for good or a mixed blessing. This is a very long way from the oft-repeated claim that 81 percent of Leave voters were against multiculturalism.

To take another example, 74 percent of those who thought feminism was a force for ill voted Leave. But 44 percent of Leave voters thought feminism was a force for good and only 23 percent a force for ill (33 percent were in the "mixed blessing" neutral category).[29]

---

29 Ashcroft, 2016, table 29, pp128-129.

Nearly a third of both Leave and Remain voters thought capitalism was a "force for ill", a cheering statistic for socialists given that there is so little discussion of alternatives to it in the mainstream and no major political party (including Labour) actually declares that it is hostile to capitalism.[30]

The figures for immigration are more disturbing. Just 14 percent of Leave voters thought immigration was a force for good, 62 percent a force for ill (24 percent in the "mixed blessing" category). Remainers saw immigration 57 percent a force for good, and 17 percent a force for ill (26 percent "mixed blessing"). Partly this reflects the fact that people in the lowest three social class categories C2, D and E were much more likely than A, B or C1 to admit that they thought immigration was a force for ill, and nearly two-thirds of C2, D and E voted Leave.

There is a serious battle to be fought over immigration, but the weaponisation of the issue occurred well in advance of any EU referendum. Huge numbers of people have been convinced over a long period that immigration is a problem and must be brought down. The 2016 British Social Attitudes report says:

> The proportion of respondents favouring some reduction in migration rose from 63 percent in 1995 to 72 percent in 2003 and 78 per cent in 2008, just before the onset of the economic crisis. Since then, there has been a small decline, with 75 percent of respondents in 2011 advocating a reduction in immigration overall and 51 percent wanting a large reduction. Most of the increase in demand for reduction thus dates to the late-1990s/early-2000s, and the balance of public concern has remained broadly stable since 2003.[31]

Such figures are worrying, but utterly unsurprising. All the main political parties (including Labour) have spent years telling everyone who would listen that there are "too many" migrants coming to Britain and that they cause problems for housing, jobs, wages and public services. Labour's infamous "Controls on Immigration" mug produced for the 2015 general election is an example of such a push.[32] One of the most refreshing aspects of Jeremy Corbyn's leadership is that he has bucked this trend. But not a day goes by without a newspaper running a story about the supposed bad effects of immigration, with hundreds of stories a year about the threat to the NHS, the criminal nature of migrants, the threat to "our culture" and so on. Such saturation coverage has an effect.

Politicians and the media have systematically sought to link the issue of immigration to the very real questions of a declining NHS, a lack of affordable

30 Ashcroft, 2016, table 33 pp160-161.
31 NatCen, 2016.
32 This pledge also appeared on the "Edstone".

and good quality housing, low pay and insecure work. It is particularly poisonous when people's anger is directed away from the actual culprits—the rich, the bankers, the corporations—towards migrants. It substitutes an illusory enemy for the real one. It also tells people that if they want to improve their services and living standards they need to take action over immigration. This is what much of the polling data reflects: angry people who want change and imbibe some anti-migrant myths in the absence of collective struggle.

Neoliberal society says that if there are problems in your life then the root is individual failing and the way out is atomised, individual and competitive action. If you don't have a house or a good job it is because you didn't try hard enough at school or won't work hard enough now. The solution is to trample on others. If the area where you live is crumbling then don't try to act collectively, try to protect your own piece of turf and don't worry about the rest. Such an ideology is fatally undermined if people start to realise that their personal experiences are not finally about their individual efforts but about the collective organisation of society. The ruling class has every interest in peddling the idea that instead of addressing that question you should turn on your neighbour. For decades racism has been deliberately employed in this way.

An important report about racism after the Leave vote, based on social media groups and analysis and with the support of the Institute of Race Relations, was unsparing in its description of the racist attacks that occurred.[33] But it gave a central role to events before the referendum and in particular the role of former home secretary and now prime minister Theresa May (who supported Remain). The report, "Post-referendum racism and xenophobia", said that May had helped create the "hostile environment" that paved the way for post-referendum attacks: "If a hostile environment is embedded politically, it can't be a surprise that it takes root culturally." Singling May out as one of those who helped create such a "hostile environment", the report recalls that in 2012, she used a newspaper interview to declare: "The aim is to create here in Britain a really hostile environment for illegal migration".[34] The report said: "This was brought to fruition in July 2013 when the Home Office deployed mobile ad-vans in six London boroughs telling people to 'GO HOME or face arrest'." It adds, pointedly, "Around a quarter of the incidents recorded in our database specifically use the words 'Go Home' or 'Leave'." It concludes that the politics dominating the official Leave campaign were "a continuation of this politically mainstream, hostile stance towards immigration and xeno-racist narratives".[35]

33 Komaromi and Singh, 2016.

34 Kirkup and Winnett, 2012.

35 Komaromi and Singh, 2016, p9.

During the referendum campaign Nigel Farage unveiled a vile poster with a picture of a queue of mostly non-white migrants and refugees with the slogan "Breaking Point: The EU Has Failed Us All." It clearly incited racism. Unison union leader Dave Prentis reported the poster to the police and even Douglas Carswell, UKIP's only MP, called it "morally indefensible".

Immigration was the main issue for the official Leave campaign for the final weeks before the vote, but the heads of Remain also used racism. David Cameron ran a brutally Islamophobic campaign against Labour's Sadiq Khan in the London mayoral battle in May. He had previously called migrants a "swarm" and had denounced Corbyn for meeting a "bunch of migrants" in Calais. Other official Remain figures made similarly racist comments. Cameron launched the referendum on the basis of a deal to cut in-work benefits to migrants from the EU, a measure that would have meant one section of the working class was effectively paid less than another. This was overtly rooted in the idea that migration was an evil.

So both the official Leave and Remain campaigns used racism. The exception was Scotland where the Remain campaign was dominated by the SNP, and did not use racism as part of its argument.

The remarkable fact is not that anti-immigration views have percolated into substantial sections of the population but that millions reject the myths. These include a substantial number of working class people. Most workers are not racists, and neither are most Leave voters. A poll in September 2015 found that nearly a third of people in Britain had personally backed the refugee relief and solidarity effort. More than six million people, 12 percent of the population gave money to a refugee charity appeal, a further 10 percent donated food, clothes or other goods, and another 9 percent volunteered their time or backed social media campaigns supporting refugees.[36] A major international poll taken in the immediate aftermath of the referendum showed that the percentage of people in Britain who were positive about immigration was 35 percent, the fourth highest figure of the 22 countries surveyed, and the highest figure in Europe. It was well up on the 28 percent in 2015 and the 19 percent in 2011. Similarly the percentage in Britain saying there were "too many immigrants in our country" was 49 percent, down from 60 percent in 2015 and 71 percent in 2011.[37]

If Leave was solely or predominantly an anti-immigrant and racist vote, we would not expect those most directly targeted by racism and Islamophobia to be part of it. It's true a majority of black and Asian people voted Remain, but about a third of those describing themselves as Asian voted Leave, as did over a quarter

36 Travis, 2015.

37 Ipsos-Mori, 2016a.

of black voters; nearly a third of Muslims voted Leave.[38] Of course there are a few black UKIP members, and some black and Asian people might have opposed the EU because, for example, they think it has allowed too many Eastern Europeans to come to Britain. But it's far from the whole explanation of these figures.

Such findings undermine the view that the racists and fascists will be in the vanguard after the Leave vote. If the racists were really roaring ahead we might expect UKIP to advance in confident form. After all, it has secured its declared main aim of winning Brexit and it made some advances in the May elections before the referendum. But certainly UKIP did not benefit in the immediate aftermath of the vote. Nigel Farage resigned as leader, which he was unlikely to have done if he thought there was a clear path to future victories. Paul Nuttall who had been tipped as his successor (and regarded as "worse than Farage" by some on the left in case we thought there was anything to be celebrated about Farage's departure) then ruled himself out of the contest. Nuttall also said he would be standing down as UKIP's deputy leader after their next conference, although he would continue as an MEP, with all its attendant luxuries and bounties.

Then it got worse for UKIP. The second favourite after Nuttall, Steven Woolfe, was banned from standing by the party's national executive as he didn't get his application in on time. The ruling led to bitter infighting among UKIP members and three executive members resigned. The declared candidates recalled the odd, horribly reactionary and weirdly obsessive people who are normally found only in the contest to be Republican candidate for US president. So UKIP now has a completely unknown and untested leader in Diane James—unless Farage once again reverses his pledges and returns.

UKIP stood in 20 council by-elections between the Leave vote on 23 June and 11 August. In 11 its percentage of the vote fell, in eight it was standing for the first time and in just one its vote increased. The fall in the vote happened even in areas that had voted heavily for Leave. For example, the Bexley St Michael's by-election of 30 June saw UKIP's vote fall by nearly 15 percentage points. This is an area (Bexley) that voted 63 percent Leave.[39]

Nor have the British fascists, fragmented and broken by the campaigning work of Unite against Fascism and others, seen an increase in their numbers. Many stories of post-Leave racism were illustrated by a picture of the Nazi demonstration in Newcastle the weekend after the result. But the demo wasn't some novel reaction to the vote, it was one in a series of tiny Nazi mobilisations that have taken place across Britain over the last few years since the defeat of the

38 Ashcroft, 2016.

39 See the spreadsheet at https://docs.google.com/spreadsheets/d/1X85PgCqavImGZPGdbrEfQc6uzNP98KXwZcf-8JsKZto/edit#gid=1194771573

English Defence League and the Nazis were easily outnumbered by anti-fascist protestors. The local anti-fascist group, Newcastle Unites reported:

> Nazis from the EDL, North East Infidels and National Front descended on Newcastle with the aim of spreading hatred and dividing our community. 20 fascists, who lived as far as Dover, arrived with their "Stop immigration, start repatriation" and "refugees not welcome" banner hoping they would be heard in the city. Unfortunately when they arrived at the Monument hundreds of antiracists were there waiting for them. Considering the EDL had this planned for months, their grouping could be only described in one word: PITIFUL! Throughout the demonstration many members of the public doing their shopping were joining us. By the end of our demonstration we had almost 300 people of all ethnicities and religions standing as one condemning them and their ideology. After three hours the fascists left sodden and demoralised. They could not be heard over the "Refugees Welcome" and "Nazis out" chants.[40]

Not exactly a warm welcome. In early July the Nazis went to Southampton. They mustered 16 on their side and were met by over 1,000 anti-fascists, the city's biggest such mobilisation for decades. There is, of course, no room for complacency, but it is not true that the Nazis are on the march. They must be kept down.

Labour

The entire referendum debate, and the future of British politics, would have been transformed if a Corbyn-led Labour Party had argued for a left Leave vote. It would have meant the campaign would have been much less about immigration and much more about anti-austerity and workers' unity. It would have won over large numbers of young people to the reality that there is a progressive and internationalist case against the EU.

Ashcroft's survey says that nearly 40 percent of Labour voters at the 2015 general election (quite a low base) voted Leave anyway. If Labour had backed Leave it would have meant an even bigger defeat for Remain. It would have been Corbyn who was photographed celebrating the morning afterwards, not Farage. Labour would have connected with a much wider section of working class people who voted Leave, and offered a left focus for their anger at the world rather than abandoning them to reactionaries. Labour would have been in a better position to attack the new May government and to define the Brexit negotiations in terms of internationalist and working class concerns.

It didn't happen. During his battle for the Labour leadership in 2015, Corbyn hinted he might support leaving the EU. He said he had "not closed his mind"

40 Newcastle Unites, Facebook post 25 June. Go to http://tinyurl.com/jukys45

to exit and was opposed to giving David Cameron a "blank cheque". At one hustings he said, "I think we should be making demands—universal workers' rights, universal environmental protection, end the race to the bottom on corporate taxation, end the race to the bottom in wage protection." In this he was entirely in line with his history of opposition to the EU and the Maastricht and Lisbon treaties. Corbyn said the Maastricht Treaty "takes away from national parliaments the power to set economic policy and hands it over to an unelected set of bankers who will impose the economic policies of price stability, deflation and high unemployment throughout the European Community".[41] Corbyn's political mentor was Tony Benn, a wholeheartedly anti-EU figure.

It turned out the way to make Corbyn back the EU was to elect him Labour leader. He compromised to keep at least some of the right within his own party vaguely and, as it turned out, temporarily on side. Corbyn campaigned for Remain but certainly without any of the enthusiasm and verve that he generally brings to his political activity. He often gave the impression that he was doing it as a duty. But crucially Corbyn did not campaign alongside the Tories. Regrettably Sadiq Khan, Labour's new mayor of London, took to the streets for Remain alongside Cameron, the man who had savaged him in a foul Islamophobic way just weeks earlier. Former shadow chancellor Ed Balls sat smiling at a Remain event next to axe-man George Osborne. Former Labour leader Neil Kinnock joined a Remain phonebank with Cameron and former Lib Dem leader Paddy Ashdown. These people were replaying a horror film—the Labour campaign alongside the Tories during the Scottish referendum. This resulted in a wipeout at the subsequent general election, with Labour suffering a fall in Scotland from 41 MPs to one.

Meanwhile the union leaders seemed determined to undermine the reasons for their existence by insisting that workers' rights, in the past and today, derived from the benevolent largesse of the EU. The EU tore into Greek workers and cheered on the French government as it battled to introduce a new Work Law stripping away rights. The EU made not a whimper as the Tories pushed through their new anti-union laws in the run-up to the referendum. Nevertheless the union leaders (except for the RMT, ASLEF and BFAWU unions) loyally trooped behind Remain. Len McCluskey of Unite recognised that "voting for the status quo is not exactly a popular option" but he still called for his members to do it.

This abandonment of working class interests by the Labour Party and most trade union leaders risked directing those who rightly opposed the EU towards the racists and reactionaries. This was pushed further when a string of Labour figures, obviously believing that the way to win the working class is to be more racist, began pushing for further restrictions on freedom of movement. Tom

41 Moseley, 2016.

Watson, Labour's deputy leader, said EU immigration rules would have to be revisited, saying "woe betide" the party if it ignored public concerns. Ed Balls said: "We need to press Europe to restore proper borders, and put new controls on economic migration". Even shadow chancellor and Corbyn ally John McDonnell was reported to have said that Labour would "look again at the free movement of labour". To his credit, Corbyn refused to go along with this shift.[42]

Contradictory ideas

Workers' ideas are not fixed. Socialists should seek to direct the rebellion of 23 June further in a positive direction and squash any reactionary elements. Those on the left who see only a further spiral downwards are turning their back on an opportunity to connect with and broaden working class revolt.

The Italian Marxist Antonio Gramsci argued that workers have contradictory consciousness. He wrote that a worker has "two theoretical consciousnesses (or one contradictory consciousness): one which is implicit in his activity and which in reality unites him with all his fellow workers in the practical transformation of the real world; and one, superficially explicit or verbal, which he has inherited from the past and uncritically absorbed".[43] The experience of collective work and society is pitted against the individualist pressures and ideologies of capitalism.

The idea of contradictory consciousness is not the same as describing uneven consciousness—that, for example, some workers vote Tory and others back Jeremy Corbyn. Nor is it an attempt to link particular ideas to different sections of the class—the false idea that manual workers and white collar workers will have different ideas because their experiences in the workplace are not the same in some respects. Instead the term contradictory consciousness seeks to engage with the reality that workers as groups or even individuals may *simultaneously* have brilliant anti-racist instincts but may be opposed to strikes. Others may be for very militant struggles over pay and conditions but be wholly signed up to an agenda of aggressive British nationalism. Even this description (which anyone who has argued for socialist ideas will immediately recognise) underplays the level of contradiction.

The Social Attitudes Survey has asked people over many years whether they would describe themselves as very prejudiced or a little prejudiced against people of other races. The number who say they are very prejudiced is tiny (around 3 percent), and the total who say they are very or a little prejudiced has fallen by around 10 percent since the 1980s to around 30 percent. This is far lower than the numbers who think immigration is negative in some respect.

42 BBC News, 2016.
43 Gramsci, 1971, p661.

Opposition to immigration is rooted in racism, but it does not mean that people are wholly wedded to racist ideas.

Karl Marx famously said that it is "social existence that determines consciousness"[44] and this is very powerfully borne out by a poll taken just before the referendum. It found that 42 percent of voters overall, and 65 percent of those intending to vote Leave, thought immigration had a bad impact on Britain as whole. But asked about the area where they lived, only 24 percent overall thought that immigration had a bad impact. Well over half of Leave voters said immigration was either a good thing for where they lived or had no impact. When it came to individual experience, 78 percent of voters overall, and 62 percent of Leave voters, said immigration had been either good for them personally or had no impact. So the view that was based most on what the media and politicians say (the effect of immigration on Britain as a whole) was the most hostile to immigration. The one that involved the most direct material experience (personal impact) saw just one in five people say immigration was a bad thing.[45]

The most powerful factor shaping ideas is struggle. During a period of big strikes workers tend to see each other as partners in a fightback rather than competitors. When strikes are low the rotten ideas of division are more likely to find an echo. It's worth looking at UKIP's polling figures over the past five years. In January 2011 UKIP was polling at 5 or 6 percent nationally. After a year that saw the biggest trade union demonstration in British history (March 2011), a strike by two million workers over pensions (November 2011) and a series of inspiring international battles, UKIP was down to just 2 or 3 percent in the polls—a negligible number. It is when the struggle stopped from 2012 onwards, choked off by the union leaders, that UKIP support rose steadily to reach nearly 14 percent in the 2015 election. This underlines the criminal effect of the union leaders' and Labour leaders' failure to organise resistance.

Conclusion

The SWP believes the Leave vote will benefit the working class across the world and the struggle against racism. It is a further blow to the coercive neoliberal power of the EU and its racist laws. The dismantling of the pro-capitalist EU must begin with revolts at a national level. But we do not think the question of how someone voted in the referendum is a supremely defining question. We recognise that we have more in common with an anti-racist, or a striker or a Corbyn supporter who voted Remain that we do with a racist or a Tory who voted Leave. It matters for us all to understand what happened on 23 June.

---

44 Marx, 1977.

45 Ipsos-Mori, 2016b.

There is a very important political task for all socialists after the Leave vote. However we voted on 23 June, we have to unite against racism, austerity, the Tories and the anti-Corbyn Labour MPs. We have to come together over the general issues but also the specific ones that are raised in the negotiations about Brexit. For example, Theresa May has repeatedly refused to guarantee the future rights of all EU citizens who are presently in Britain. This is a very important issue, directly affecting the three million EU citizens in Britain (two million of them workers) but indirectly affecting all of us who benefit from the contribution these people make. Over 100,000 EU nationals work in the education sector, and 80,000 in healthcare. Over a quarter of food business workers are EU nationals, and there would not be nearly enough skilled construction workers without EU nationals. For anti-racist reasons and for the unity of the working class we need a strong campaign from Remain and Leave voters together to win cast-iron commitments to the full rights of EU citizens in Britain—and to defend and extend the free movement of labour.

That has to be backed up by a wider programme raising issues that can engage with workers angry at the political elite and austerity—a major programme of council house building, higher taxes for the rich and the corporations, an end to the perks and expenses of elected officials, £10 an hour minimum wage, the repeal of all the anti-union laws, cancelling Trident and using the money for the NHS and education, stopping the privateers, no more powers to snoop on and police us, real action to stop climate change and so on. We need to define more clearly what we want from a possible Labour government and what we demand in policy terms from a Corbyn leadership. We need to move from generalities to campaigning specifics.

Mobilisations by Stand Up to Racism will be very important because issues like refugee rights, the defence and celebration of migrants, opposition to state racism and support for and participation in Black Lives Matter are going to be constant features of the political scene. Agitation for more strikes and protests, and building the People's Assembly will also be crucial.

The class anger, and the class issues underlined by the Leave vote need to be addressed by the left. That doesn't mean bending to racism, it means bringing together the battle against racism and the fight for social change and real improvements in workers' lives.

British politics has seen big shifts in recent years. UKIP emerged as a populist racist party that could mobilise millions of votes. In Scotland the independence referendum became a focus for class resistance to the Tories and a way that people believed they could fight for a better world and produced a radical social movement. Independence lost (quite narrowly) but the SNP all but eliminated Labour parliamentary representation in Scotland at the 2015 general election. A radical challenge to austerity politics then emerged around Corbyn, but unexpectedly this challenge emerged within the structures of the Labour Party rather than taking the form of a new party. We should expect more shifts and lurches. We are not (or at least should not be) spectators. We must be participants in the outcomes, and that means intervention, innovative thinking, and organising. After the Leave vote the battle is on. Socialists should gladly embrace and shape it.

References

Ashcroft, Lord Michael, 2016, "How the United Kingdom Voted on Thursday... and Why, Full Tables" (24 June), http://lordashcroftpolls.com/wp-content/uploads/2016/06/How-the-UK-voted-Full-tables-1.pdf

Aziz, Omer, 2016, "Brexit Wasn't About Economics. It Was About Racial Hatred", Huffington Post (29 June), http://tinyurl.com/hjose23

BBC News 2016, "Jeremy Corbyn says EU Free Movement Means No Immigration Limit" (19 June), www.bbc.co.uk/news/uk-politics-eu-referendum-36570383

Brown, Gordon, 2016, "Leaders Must Make the Case for Globalisation", *Financial Times* (17 July), www.ft.com/content/a0849e08-4921-11e6-8d68-72e9211e86ab

Buck, Tobias, 2016, "Middle England Drives Brexit Revolution", *Financial Times* (15 June), https://next.ft.com/content/63beb670-321f-11e6-ad39-3fee5ffe5b5b

Callinicos, Alex, 2015, "The Internationalist Case Against the European Union", *International Socialism 148* (autumn), http://isj.org.uk/the-internationalist-case-against-the-european-union/

Callinicos, Alex, 2016, "Brexit: A World-historic Turn", *International Socialism 151* (online only), http://isj.org.uk/brexit-a-world-historic-turn/

Das, Satyajit, 2016, "Brexit has Exposed how Ignorant the Educated and Cosmopolitan have Become about Modern Britain", *Independent* (3 July), http://tinyurl.com/z6mh3uj

Economist, 2016a, "Brexitland versus Londonia" (2 July), www.economist.com/news/britain/21701540-britain-increasingly-looks-two-countries-divided-over-globalisation-brexitland-versus

Economist, 2016b, "The Politics of Anger" (2 July), www.economist.com/news/leaders/21701478-triumph-brexit-campaign-warning-liberal-international-order-politics

Fevre, Ralph, 2016, "More in Hope, Less about Immigration: Why Poor Britons Really Voted to Leave the EU", The Conversation, (4 July), http://tinyurl.com/h2vu9uk

Gramsci, Antonio, 1971, *Selections from the Prison Notebooks* (Lawrence & Wishart).

Grant, Rob, 2016, "Areas with Lowest Paid Workers Voted for Brexit while Highest Paid Backed Remain", *Mirror* (24 June), www.mirror.co.uk/news/uk-news/areas-lowest-paid-workers-voted-8275990

Harris, John, 2016, "If You've Got Money, You Vote In...If You Haven't Got Money You Vote Out", *Guardian* (24 June), www.theguardian.com/politics/commentisfree/2016/jun/24/divided-britain-brexit-money-class-inequality-westminster

Higgins, Andrew, 2016, "Wigan's Road to 'Brexit': Anger, Loss and Class Resentments", *New York Times* (5 July), http://tinyurl.com/zvsctyk

Hilary, John, 2016, Brexit is a Rejection of the EU, TTIP and the Political Caste", War on Want (24 June), http://waronwant.org/media/brexit-rejection-eu-ttip-and-political-caste-0

Ipsos-Mori, 2016a, "Global Views on Immigration and the Refugee Crisis" (July), www.ipsos-mori.com/Assets/

Docs/Polls/ipsos-global-advisor-immigration-and-refugees-2016-charts.pdf

Ipsos-Mori, 2016b, "Just One in Five Britons say Immigration has had a Negative Effective on them Personally" (20 June), http://tinyurl.com/zd5g6qn

Komaromi, Priska, and Karissa Singh, 2016, "Post-Referendum Racism and Xenophobia" Institute of Race Relations (29 July), www.irr.org.uk/wp-content/uploads/2016/07/PRRX-Report-Final.pdf

Kirkup, James, and Robert Winnett, 2012, "Theresa May Interview: 'We're Going to give Illegal Migrants a Really Hostile Reception'", *Telegraph* (25 May), http://tinyurl.com/bvh9qaeLenin, V I, 1916, "The Discussion on Self-determination Summed Up", www.marxists.org/archive/lenin/works/1916/jul/x01.htm

Marx, Karl, 1977 [1859], Preface to *A Contribution to the Critique of Political Economy* (Progress Publishers), www.marxists.org/archive/marx/works/1859/critique-pol-economy/preface.htm

McGoogan, Cara, 2016, "Were Brits Really Googling 'What is the EU?' After Voting to Leave?", *Telegraph* (27 June), www.telegraph.co.uk/technology/2016/06/27/were-brits-really-googling-what-is-the-eu-after-voting-to-leave/

Moseley, Tom, 2016, "In Quotes: Jeremy Corbyn and the EU Referendum", BBC News (14 April), www.bbc.co.uk/news/uk-politics-eu-referendum-35743994

National Centre for Social Research (NatCen), 2016, Social Attitudes Survey (33rd Annual Report), www.bsa.natcen.ac.uk/latest-report/british-social-attitudes-33/introduction.aspx

Parker, George, and Alex Barker, 2016 "How Brexit spelled the end to Cameron's career", *Financial Times* (24 June) https://next.ft.com/content/4b0222f0-317c-11e6-bda0-04585c31b153

People Before Profit Alliance, 2016, "Press Statement on Brexit Vote" (25 June), www.peoplebeforeprofit.ie/2016/06/people-before-profit-alliance-press-statement-on-brexit-vote/

Socialist Resistance, 2016, "The Vote to Leave the EU is a Victory for the Right-wing Xenophobes, But the Struggle Goes On" (24 June), http://socialistresistance.org/8534/brexit-vote-is-a-disaster-but-the-struggle-goes-on

Trades Union Congress, 2016, "UK Workers Experienced Sharpest Wage Fall of Any Leading Economy, TUC Analysis Finds" (27 July), http://tinyurl.com/hv6dgny

Travis, Alan, 2015, "One Third of Britons Have Helped Refugees in Some Way", *Guardian* (24 September), http://tinyurl.com/ohfcnex

YouGov, 2016, "How Britain Voted" (27 June), https://yougov.co.uk/news/2016/06/27/how-britain-voted/

The ideology of Europeanism and Europe's migrant other

Céline Cantat

Europe is more present than ever in the media and in political discourse.[1] The recent decision by Britain to leave the European Union (EU) is perhaps the most serious blow to the European project yet. However, it is in continuity with a long series of popular consultations through which the EU project and its institutions have been repeatedly heavily criticised or outright rejected by people of its member states. In 2015, the Greek people rejected the EU's bailout conditions en masse. But as early as 1992 and the Danish vote against the Maastricht Treaty, referendums suggested that the EU triggers at most a very weak sense of identification—and often downright hostility. In 2005, in both the Netherlands and France, people voted against the European Constitution. To avoid similar results, a referendum that should have been held in Ireland was cancelled. Yet a few years later, in 2008, the Irish rejected the Lisbon Treaty by 53 percent.

In spite of this clear democratic pitfall, crucial questions regarding the nature of the EU project, and the ideologies animating its trajectory and setting its goals, hardly ever seem to be raised. Official accounts of European integration by its architects and pro-EU politicians insist on presenting "Europe" as an internationalist or a post-national project, confining to the past the excesses of

1 Many thanks to Camilla Royle, Alex Callinicos, Joseph Choonara, Philip Marfleet and Prem Kumar Rajaram for their valuable comments on earlier drafts of this article.

nationalism and national rivalries and promoting cooperation and friendship among its member states and their people. In turn, criticisms and rejections of the EU are only ever explained through accusations of nationalist insularism. Not only do these discourses betray profound class contempt, they also fail to acknowledge the persistent resonance of race and territory in the project and idea of "Europe."

A political economy of the origins and process of European integration can help deconstruct official accounts of the European project. It reveals the complex and contradictory relationship between the EU and its member states and calls into question ideas of an "internationalist Europe". It allows for an understanding of how official narratives of Europe and European identity have been constructed and mobilised in order to produce popular identification towards an unpopular European project. This ideological operation becomes particularly visible when assessing discourses of Europe from the perspective of the forms of marginalisation that they produce. I argue that official narratives of Europe have been based on a notion of European belonging premised on the idea of a distinct and recognisable European character that could set aside Europeans from non-Europeans. This is what I call the ideology of Europeanism. This narrative has led to the production of new figures of otherness at the regional level, among which the "migrant" has played a central role.

Post-war capitalist crises and the origins of the EU

Recently, the negative outcome of the Syriza-led government's attempt at negotiating anti-austerity policies within the framework of the EU clearly demonstrated that the Union would not allow the implementation of a programme challenging the prerogatives of neoliberal capitalism. This temporarily opened up space for a much needed debate on the capitalist ideologies at the heart of the EU. Yet left-wing critiques of the European project have overwhelmingly called for "Europe to be fixed" and have formulated a narrative whereby the European project was hijacked by forces of neoliberal capitalist globalisation sometime in the 1980s.[2]

Indeed, according to official accounts, the process of European construction was initiated and pushed forward in the post-war period by its benevolent founding fathers: "visionary leaders" who offered "their energy and motivation" so that European citizens could enjoy a "climate of peace and stability".[3] The European project thus started from the dream of a "peaceful Europe" to reach

2 See for example Yanis Varoufakis (Häring, 2015) but also a range of left wing commentators including grassroots movements eg Cooper, 2015.

3 From the EU website. Go to http://europa.eu/about-eu/eu-history/index_en.htm

a "Europe without frontiers" by the 1990s.[4] The Jean Monnet and the Robert Schuman Foundations, as well as political organisations including the European Movement and Christian Democrat parties, have participated in the elaboration and the diffusion of this dominant historical account.

Accordingly, one of the dominant explanations put forward to account for the ruthlessness demonstrated by the EU, and more particularly Germany, towards both Greece and the people of the member states who have been subjected to severe austerity measures since 2010 has been the idea of a shift—a turning point when the utopian project of a Europe of peace and prosperity was seized by forces of neoliberal capitalism.

However, an examination of its origins rather shows that the European project has always been shaped by, and has shaped, modes of capitalist development in the region and beyond. The European Community (EC) was established to restore European capitalism and contain the cyclical crises caused by capital's tendency to internationalisation in the post-war period. Its evolution into the EU and its growing association with the neoliberal project was not caused by a sharp shift away from its original objectives, as much as it reflected the embeddedness of the European project, since its inception, into global capitalist processes.

Alan Milward convincingly argues that the origins of the European Community have been one of the most "ill-understood aspects of recent history and present political life".[5] This is, he suggests, because of the commonly held assumption that the EC was in antithesis to the nation-state. Quite the opposite, the establishment of the EC was central to the reassertion of the post-war capitalist state in Europe—this was, in Milward's words "the European rescue of the nation-state".[6] Western European economies emerged from the Second World War devastated, with severely decreased levels of industrial output in Germany, Austria, Italy, Greece, France and the Netherlands, and growing social agitation due to high levels of unemployment and inflation.[7] The instability of Western European capitalism was all the more worrying for the European bourgeoisie because Moscow had made clear its intention to incorporate Eastern Europe.

These concerns were shared by the US administration of the time, who wanted to restructure European economies on a regional basis so as to avoid the resurrection of rivalries between nationally-tied firms and capital of the inter-war period. The first building block of the European project, the Organisation for European Economic Co-operation (OEEC), came about as a conditionality

4 Go to http://europa.eu/about-eu/eu-history/index_en.htm
5 Milward, 2000, p2.
6 Milward, 2000.
7 Harman, 1971.

attached to the 1947 European Recovery Program (better known as the Marshall Plan after then-US secretary of state, George Marshall). In 1949, NATO was established as another pillar of the US post-war vision of a capitalist West to which the EC/EU was central.

In other words, the origins of the European project reflect the changing nature of the post Second World War international system dominated by the US and the realisation by the ruling classes of capitalist nation-states that they needed to internationalise some of their economic activities in order to remain competitive. This also means that the EC (later EU) has been marked from its very beginning by tension, reflecting the relation between the national organisation of capital and the tendency towards its internationalisation. The EC was used as an arena for cooperation but also for competition by Europe's national politicians and as a means to pursue domestic agendas. This resulted in endless disputes about the distribution of subsidies or the definition of European common standards for production, reflecting the conflicting national interests at stake in the EC. Bernard Connolly, a key Eurocrat, described this as "the rotten heart of Europe".[8] As a result, the EC structure was highly unstable.

The neoliberal turn: building the European Union

In 1957, the Treaty of Rome created the European Economic Community (EEC) which established a European common market. One of the aims of the EEC was to overcome this instability by encouraging cross-border mergers, supported by the establishment of a form of supra-state and further integration of the European capitalist classes at the European level. However, this proved a difficult task and the desired Europeanisation of capital kept clashing with national state boundaries.[9] Though the trend of systems of production was to exceed national boundaries, the majority of firms continued to be owned and to operate from particular national bases.

As global capitalism kept internationalising, the contradiction between national and international organisation became increasingly problematic for European capitalist classes. In particular, the movement of capital had to be deregulated so as to promote intra-European investments. This also required that the investment environment across Europe be harmonised. Throughout the 1970s, several attempts at fixing exchange rates among European currencies failed due to member states' resistance. It is only in 1986 that the project of a monetary union succeeded: the Single European Act (SEA) was signed in order to create a Single Market by 1992. The governors of the central banks of

8 Connolly, 2013.

9 Harman, 1991.

the twelve EEC member states set out a plan to establish the Economic and Monetary Union (EMU), which paved the way for the adoption of a single currency—the euro. The agreement around the EMU essentially emerged as a compromise reflecting the interest of the two dominant economic powers in the EEC—France and Germany.[10]

Shortly after, the Maastricht Treaty created the European Union (EU), which replaced the EC. The establishment of the EU reflected the need for further integration between European member states at a time when the global economy was changing. It mirrors the global shift towards neoliberalism in the late 1970s and 1980s.

Indeed, by the 1970s, the post-war Keynesian compromise was quickly losing ground to neoliberal approaches and the so-called "golden age" of capitalism seemed to be coming to an end. In the US, the hundred-year period of rising wages was permanently over, while privatisation of production and deregulation of markets were reaching unprecedented levels. In the UK, the 1979 appointment of Margaret Thatcher as prime minister inaugurated a programme of privatisation, market deregulation, liberalisation and trade union marginalisation. The reorganisation of traditional economic sectors (and complete dismantlement of others) in the UK was paralleled by similar restructuring processes in other Western European countries.[11] With the relaunch of the single market project and the Maastricht Treaty, neoliberalism became firmly embedded into the structure of the European project.[12]

Since the late 1970s the EU has actively embraced neoliberalism. Yet rather than a sharp turning point, the shift towards neoliberal capitalism mirrored the dialectical relation of the European project to global processes of capitalist accumulation and reproduction. In this sense, the racialised, capitalist and territorial ideologies that have been central to the constitution of the European nation-state have always been embedded in the ostensibly supra-national figure of "Europe."

"You don't fall in love with a single market"

A consequence of its capitalist nature and class violence, the European project has been the object of popular hostility. This has constituted a major challenge for pro-European politicians. One of their responses has been to engage in the production of discourses of European identity and belonging in the aim of legitimising the European project and triggering identification among the people of its member states.

10 Callinicos, 1997.
11 Marfleet, 1999.
12 Gill, 2003, p63.

The issue of popular mistrust towards the European project became an object of growing concern in the mid 1970s. At the time, the EC became the target of rising hostility from people of the member states and segments of national capitalist classes.[13] Yet European politicians, such as Helmut Kohl and Jacques Delors, remained firmly convinced that more integration was needed for European economies to survive. The idea of a "legitimacy deficit" of the Community gained currency and attention started being paid to "European public opinion". As further economic and political integration was encouraged by leading European politicians, a fear emerged that it would be limited unless people started feeling "more European".

As Delors put it, "you don't fall in love with a common market; you need something else".[14] Indeed, as observed by Philip Marfleet:

> The EC was not a nation-state in which an ideology of "belonging" could be mobilised during periods of instability or crisis. It lacked a framework for nationalism: myths of common origin, a national religious community, a monarchy. The Community had been constructed upon nation-states which had emerged from centuries of local rivalry: there could be no reference point for an EC patriotism, no European Jeanne d'Arc.[15]

The issues of mistrust towards the European project and of its lack of democracy have furthered over the last two to three decades. Since its "neoliberal turn", the EU has indeed been increasingly associated with authoritarian modes of governing—as happened elsewhere in the neoliberal world. As state functions once dominant in the context of Keynesian, developmental and socialist national states (such as welfare provision and social support) have been rolled back, other state interventions geared towards preserving the market-driven, neoliberal global order have gained precedence.[16]

This has been particularly visible since 2008 and the advent of the economic crisis in Europe. The neoliberal structural reshaping of the state has been led with virtually no democratic deliberation under the banner of "austerity". This lack of popular consultation illustrates the anti-democratic and increasingly authoritarian nature of the neoliberal state and of the European project; it also indicates the overall inability of neoliberalism to garner popular consent and support. Where resistance movements and social struggles have erupted to oppose austerity, European states have engaged in intensified repression,

---

13 Most notably in the British Conservative Party.

14 Quoted in Laffan, 1996, p95.

15 Marfleet, 1999.

16 Jessop, 2002, p454.

including police deployment and the passing of laws criminalising protest.[17] This is in line with Loïc Wacquant's observation about the neoliberal state, which has become increasingly "liberal at the top and paternalistic at the bottom".[18] This new formation "presents radically different faces at the two ends of the social hierarchy: a comely and caring visage toward the middle and upper classes, and a fearsome and frowning mug toward the lower class".[19] Those at the bottom of the class and ethnic structure are faced with an increasingly punitive logic, coupled with particular forms of "disciplinary philosophy of behaviorism and moralism".[20]

The politics of Europeanism

As popular hostility towards the EU grew, a key strategy deployed by Europe's architects has been to insist on the need for a cultural European identity to emerge. Yet, in a formation as contradictory as the European Union, what are the available ideological resources that can be mobilised in order to produce a sense of unity?

As of the 1970s, a set of symbols aimed at signifying a common European history and culture, and at triggering affection towards Europe among the people of its member states, was introduced. These include a European flag, adopted in 1983, a European anthem (the prelude to the "Ode to Joy" from Beethoven's ninth symphony chosen in 1972), a motto ("Unity in Diversity") as well as "Europe Day", adopted in 1985. In addition, a range of cultural activities supposedly related to Europe were implemented and a number of cultural institutions aimed at promoting European ties established.

This new European culture brought together an odd mix of populist initiatives, with little anchorage in the region's history, and symbols of high culture, with little chance of triggering popular attachment. Gerard Delanty describes such attempts at producing European cultural identity as: "pathetic exercises in cultural engineering: the Eurovision Song Contest, Euro-Disney, the Ecu, the Annual European City of Culture and the cultural apparatus of the new institutions was not the stuff out of which new symbolic structures could be built".[21] Delanty observes that the mobilisation of emblems inspired from the traditional appendage of nationalism is largely inadequate. What this indeed reveals is the lack of meaningful material and popular ideology within the European Community which could generate an emotional response or a sense of belonging towards "Europe".

---

17 See Wearden, 2012, and www.aedh.eu/Spain-repressive-laws-that-also.html

18 Wacquant, 2010, p217.

19 Wacquant, 2010, p217.

20 Wacquant, 2010, pp202-203.

21 Delanty, 1995, p208.

Europe's existential quest for meaning also took on the form of historical narratives keen on tracing back the roots of the European Community/Union to ancient times. These would draw on a putative European past to present the current EU project as the logical continuation, in fact the culmination, of a European historical and cultural spirit in motion. Such accounts also tend to sanctify Europe, upholding it as a desirable model with universal validity. In the UK, no group expressed better the mythology of Europeanism than New Labour. In *Why Europe Will Run the 21st Century*, Mark Leonard, a close friend and adviser to Tony Blair at the time, claims that:

> Europe represents a synthesis of the energy and freedom that come from liberalism with the stability and welfare that come from social democracy. As the world becomes richer and moves beyond satisfying basic needs such as hunger and health, the European way of life will become irresistible.[22]

Such or similar claims have been made by most mainstream parties across member states. They present Europe and its history as characterised by enlightenment, attachment to liberties and social justice. The European Union is then the logical and desirable expression of the values of an identifiable European cultural space. These narratives attempt to identify common historical and cultural features bringing together Europeans and produce a discourse of "Europeanity". They form dominant discourses of Europe or, in other words, the ideology of Europeanism.

This narrative routinely features in political discourses and the media. It translates into widespread references to "European values", "European culture", to the idea of a "European way of life" or the notion of a specific form of "European solidarity". On the left side of such liberal arguments, a discourse embracing the putative cosmopolitanism offered by the European project is also commonplace. The idea of "Europe" being a cosmopolitan project relies, on the one hand, on an attachment to rather prosaic initiatives developed by the European Union in order to buttress a sense of European identity among people of its member states. These include the Erasmus student exchange schemes and town twinning projects, designed in the hope that cross-border interactions between citizens of EU member states would form the basis from which familiarity, trust and a collective European identity would emerge and translate into support for European integration.

Student mobility programmes are an interesting case in point. EU policy makers have claimed that education was "one of the key elements in European integration"[23]—again in a move mimicking one of the key strategies of nation-building processes at the pan-European level. Yet, even enthusiastic pro-EU

22 Quoted in Anderson, 2011, p47.

23 Neave, 1991, p37.

advocates have questioned the potential of these short student mobility programmes to constitute the basis for a consistent feeling of "being European" to emerge.[24] Besides being limited in scope and time, they only concern a small elite of university-educated students. They are thus far from providing a conduit for workers and less privileged people to experience and identify with "Europe". The shallow nature of such efforts has been likened to a "balloons and flags" strategy by Ole Weaver and Morten Kelstrup.[25]

More importantly, the argument according to which the European project promotes progressive cosmopolitanism reveals a lack of understanding of the relationship between the European project and the nation-state. As seen, the EU may be "more than the nation-state but [it is] never detached from it".[26] The EU operates from the top down, and works through the structures and ruling classes of its member states. In this sense, there is no place within the EU project for internationalist ideas promoting forms of cross-border solidarity from below. Rather than a cosmopolitan project with the potential for the emergence of internationalist solidarities, the EU operates as a supra-national apparatus ruling from above and based on national structures that are hierarchically linked to one another.

The limited mobility permitted within the Schengen Area may resemble the manifestation of a progressive right to movement when exercised by privileged EU citizens. Yet freedom of movement within Schengen was above all designed —and expresses—capital's need for cheap labour and the exploitative labour relation linking Western and Northern European countries to their Southern and Eastern counterparts. As argued by Czech economist Ilona Švihlíková, Eastern and Central post-communist economies have entered into a neoliberal/neo-colonial relationship with their Western European counterparts (and more particularly Germany), characterised by economic dependence and the exportation of cheap human labour.[27] The dismantlement of Eastern and Central European welfare systems under the auspices of the World Bank and the IMF during the transition to a market economy in the region (a prerequisite to enter the EU) also means that the local labour force lacks the basic means for its social reproduction and is pushed into exploitative forms of westward mobility. As will be discussed, this also reveals the extent to which "Europe" is characterised by and produces inequalities and uneven development, and is based on complex intra-EU hierarchies.

Far from progressive cosmopolitanism, the process of forging "European identity" has in fact relied on mechanisms of exclusion inspired from national

24 See for example Sigalas, 2009.
25 Waever and Kelstrup, 1993, p67.
26 Marfleet, 2001, p86.
27 Švihlíková, 2015.

identity projects and on the production of enemies and Others, in order to set "Europe" apart from its imagined outside.

Europe and its Others

The idea of Europe has a long history of producing Others. Gerard Delanty claims that defining and representing Europe has always relied on representations of what it is not and of its boundaries and borders. "Europe" has always been characterised by its lack of unity besides that achieved through adversity. Europe's cultural and political identity has historically been articulated in relation to Others, and through a process of constant reconstruction of "ins" and "outs" reflecting particular sets of power relations at given points in time. Ideas of Europe have thus been characterised by their production of differences, on both geographical and "mythological" terms.[28] Delanty's conclusion is that these dynamics of exclusion are more than ever at work in the project of the EU:

> Who is a European is largely a matter of exclusion, and in the dichotomy of self and Other which constitutes the discourse of European identity, Europeanity is constructed in opposition with the non-European, in particular Islam. This sense of the uniqueness of the European is today emerging as a basis for a kind of supranational identity and citizenship which European integration does not have.[29]

Philip Marfleet looks back at the history of the notion of European civilisation and identifies the Enlightenment in the 18th century as a turning point, when ideas of Europe started to take a specific political and cultural shape. These new ideas resulted from the experience of European bourgeois classes in the world and were hence closely related to colonial expansion, of which merchants were the prime beneficiaries. The idea of a superior European civilisation provided a moral legitimisation for their colonial ventures and the oppression of people seen as inferior. Marfleet concludes that "to this extent, the idea of Europe was one generated by those who wished to assert a universal mission for capitalism".[30]

Early forms of "Europeanism" already bore heavy contradictions in the context of the intense rivalries opposing European colonial powers. In effect, different ideas of Europe were mobilised by national ideologies in order to serve their own national interests. Delanty refers to colonial France's concept of Europe as "a thoroughly French affair...proclaim[ing] 'the superiority of the European religion, the white race and the French language.'"[31] In the first half of the 20th century, it is the fascist

28 Delanty, 1995.
29 Delanty, 1995, p9.
30 Marfleet, 1999.
31 Delanty, 1995, p71.

vision of a culturally uniform, unified European continent that gained prominence over other visions of Europe. Adolf Hitler's "European New Order", which would be imposed on the world by Nazi Germany, entailed the supremacy of the "master race" and the physical annihilation of those considered "racially inferior".

Europe's migrant Other

Throughout the Cold War, Europe's obvious Other was the Soviet system; the notion of Western civilisation bringing together Europe and the US against the Communist enemy was a crucial part of Western propaganda. With the collapse of the Soviet Union, which constituted its key ideological counterpoint, "Europe" yet again had to reinvent its Other so as to define itself.

As seen, the contradictions characterising the European project and the centuries of national rivalries opposing the states that now constituted its "core" members made it difficult to come up with a unifying ideology. In this context, the "migrant" emerged as a key figure around and against which European cooperation was pushed forward. Immigration and asylum became central policy areas for joint action between highly divided member states. Accounts inspired by Samuel Huntington's theory of a "clash of civilisations" started playing a key role in the construction of a new sense of Europeanity.[32] The "clash theory" relies on a primordialist reading of history and of the world, which is seen as divided into closed and homogeneous areas of "culture". In an era of decreasing influence by nation-states, it is these cultural blocks that shape global relations. In Huntington's view, those belonging to other "civilisations" are constructed as absolute Others. It is in the mirror of these Others from non-Western "cultural areas" that European politicians have tried to anchor an ever-fleeting sense of a European identity.

Liz Fekete also evidences the intrinsic relation linking practices of racism against migrants in Europe, and the strengthening of a shared sense of European belonging and identity. She speaks of "xeno-racism" to describe:

> a racism that is not just directed at those with darker skins, from the former colonial territories, but at the newer categories of the displaced, the dispossessed and the uprooted, who are beating at Western Europe's doors, the Europe that helped to displace them in the first place.[33]

This demonstrates the centrality of racism to the idea of Europe and to the ideology of Europeanism, bringing to mind reflections by Étienne Balibar and Immanuel Wallerstein, who observe that racism, while a persistent mechanism of control and exclusion, evolves in its objects and articulations depending on

---

32 Marfleet, 1999, 2003.

33 Sinavandan quoted in Fekete, 2001, p24.

historical, social and political conjunctures.[34] But the shift towards forms of "cultural racism" does not mean that older forms of racism have disappeared, nor that the fundamental structure and functions of racism have changed.

This broad definition of racism looks beyond the specifically "ethnic" and "biological" forms taken by racism at particular points in history and analyses the origin and genealogy of the "race myth". It helps in evidencing the persistence of deeply racist ideologies in contemporary official discourses of Europe. As argued by Mike Haynes, "it is here, in both the ideas and practice of immigration control, perpetuated both at the intergovernmental level and at the level of the EU, that the new 'Europe' is being forged, as much as in the debates and celebrations of internal unity".[35] European identity is thus created at its external and internal borders—in its regime of visa and residence permits, detention centres and discrimination towards migrants in member states.

Mitteleuropa and Europeanity

Another civilisational myth of and in Europe in the post-1989 era revolves around the revival of the notion of *Mitteleuropa*. These discourses, which prepared for and underpinned so-called eastern enlargement processes, claimed that Central and (some) Eastern European countries had been "kidnapped, displaced and brainwashed"[36] by Soviet Communism and needed to return to their natural "European home". A notorious expression of the *Mitteleuropa* narrative was Milan Kundera's essay "The Tragedy of Central Europe"—published a few years before 1989. Kundera conjures the image of a Western-oriented *Mitteleuropa* rooted in Roman Christianity and democracy. The tragedy of *Mitteleuropa*, Kundera claims, was to be "culturally in the West but politically in the East".[37] For Kundera, Western Europe must be sharply distinguished from its oriental parts—an eastern European space of Byzantine heritage centered around Orthodox Russia and culturally incompatible with the West.

The *Mitteleuropa* narratives develop a homogenising and essentialist view of Europe and the West. They are based on the assumption that there exist shared socio-cultural and historical characteristics that define those belonging to Europe and set them apart from (and above) non-Europeans. This produces a strict separation between what is perceived as (Western) Europe and its imaginary outside. As noticed by cultural theorist Dino Murtic, discourses of Europe in post-Yugoslav and Central European spaces have activated "a chain of othering". In Serbia, Muslim

34 Balibar and Wallerstein, 2010.

35 Haynes, 1999, p25.

36 Kundera, 1984, p33.

37 Kundera, 1984, p33.

Bosnians and Kosovars are the Others against which Christian Europe has to be defended. In turn, Serbia is deemed chaotic, corrupted and of Byzantine heritage by its Croatian neighbour, itself a threat to the peaceful *Mitteleuropa* in the eyes of Slovenia. Yet ultimately, for Western European countries, Central and Eastern European states (and perhaps even more, former Yugoslavia) are all seen as "not quite European" yet.[38] Moreover, the discourse of *Mitteleuropa*, with its insistence on identifying distinctively European cultural traits associated with Christianity and certain imaginations of the West, has revived millennial figures of internal otherness, most prominently the Roma and the Jew. Again, this shows that the notions of belonging and identity underpinning discourses of Europe have borrowed from processes of inclusion/exclusion mobilised in the construction of national ideas. This is far from what a real internationalism from below could look like.

The idea of *Mitteleuropa* belonged to an elite discourse, circulated by politicians and intellectuals such as Milan Kundera and Václav Havel, and recycling Western European ideological representations of a superior European culture. Yet it did echo forms of popular enthusiasm in Central and Eastern Europe towards the prospect of joining the EU in the 1990s. More than a call to return to a long lost cultural home,[39] joining "Europe" was perceived by some as a potential way out of economic difficulties and a distancing from the legacy of Stalinism. Nowadays, although support for the EU is relatively higher in Central and Eastern European countries than in Western and Southern member states, distrust is also growing across the region. For example, in 2015 63 percent of Czechs, 51 percent of Slovaks and 61 percent of Slovenians reported that they did not trust the EU.[40] As elsewhere in Europe, such rejection can be associated with aggressive forms of nationalism, on the erroneous basis that "Europe" and the nation-state are antithetical. Yet, as shown, the exclusionary narratives of European belonging, and particularly the notion of *Mitteleuropa*, which gained currency in the late 1980s and 1990s, in fact prepared the ground for the forms of conservative Europeanism and nationalism that have recently spread across Central and Eastern European countries.

Core and peripheries in the EU

The process of separating "Europe" from its alleged "outside" has implications "inside" Europe itself illustrating that "Europeanity", while a transnational claim, is in fact always understood and articulated locally—in relation to specific

38 Murtic, 2015.

39 Mikhail Gorbachev referred to a "common European home".

40 According to data from Eurobarometer, 2015, http://ec.europa.eu/COMMFrontOffice/PublicOpinion/index.cfm/Survey/getSurveyDetail/instruments/STANDARD/surveyKy/2098

social, political, economic and historical contexts. As seen with the notion of *Mitteleuropa*, different discourses of Europeanity produce different geographies, hierarchies and imaginations of Europe. This is particularly striking in relation to the "east" of the EU, an uncertain space where the borders of Europe and the boundaries of Europeanity are questioned and reshaped.[41]

In the summer of 2015, in the context of the so-called migrant crisis, a particular articulation of the tension and contradiction generated by different discourses of "Europeanity" was manifested. A number of Western European media and political commentators developed a narrative opposing, on the one hand, the compassionate and progressive Western member states trying to find "collective solutions" to receive migrants in respect of "European values", and on the other, nationalist and xenophobic Central and Eastern EU countries and most notably Hungary (as well as other countries of the V4[42]).

This narrative reacted to such atrocious images as the Hungarian police containing groups of exhausted migrants with water cannons, or the infamous footage of a journalist from a Jobbik-affiliated TV channel tripping up a Syrian man carrying his young son in his arms.[43] They also came in the context of a government-orchestrated anti-immigrant campaign of which some of the most shocking manifestations were billboards carrying messages such as "If you come to Hungary do not take the jobs of Hungarians" and a national consultation on immigration and terrorism featuring questions such as: "We hear different views on the issue of immigration. There are some who think that economic migrants jeopardise the jobs and livelihoods of Hungarians. Do you agree?" or "Do you agree with the view that migrants illegally crossing the Hungarian border should be returned to their own countries within the shortest possible time?".

It is therefore in a context of particularly spectacular physical and symbolic violence against migrants that French Foreign Affairs Minister Laurent Fabius claimed that Eastern European countries "did not respect Europe's common values"[44] and that Angela Merkel called on their governments to "[show that] Europe...is a continent of values, a continent of solidarity".[45] Yet these accusations, that Eastern European countries lacked solidarity and were not being "genuinely European" in their treatment of migrants, betray a particular cynicism

41 De Genova, unpublished.

42 The Visegrad 4 or V4 is an alliance between the Czech Republic, Hungary, Poland and Slovakia.

43 Jobbik—"Movement for a Better Hungary"—is Hungary's radical far-right party.

44 Go to www.euractiv.com/section/justice-home-affairs/news/fabius-calls-eastern-europe-s-reluctance-to-receive-migrants-scandalous/

45 Quoted in Macdonald, 2015.

considering that the borders of these very countries have been reinforced over the past ten years with EU money and through Frontex joint operations.[46]

Moreover, the bordering practices enacted over the summer of 2015 by and in Central and Eastern Europe have been in large part justified precisely in the name of Europe and the preservation of "Europeanity". Hungarian prime minister Viktor Orbán has repeatedly stated that Hungary was defending "Hungarian and European culture" against "an invasion of outsiders".[47] Of interest here is the distinction made by Orbán between Europe, whose identity and culture he claims are based on its Christian roots, and the EU, which he recently stated was in the "grip of madness" over immigration.[48] Orbán indeed represents Hungary and Eastern EU member states as being in between two fires: migrants coming "from the outside" and the "troublesome and inadequate" policies coming from Brussels.[49] This has allowed Orbán to position the V4 countries as the "vanguard" in leading Europe back to its "true", genuine origins and values, which have to be protected against outsiders and more particularly Muslims.[50]

Discourses around migration and "Europe" produced by Hungarian authorities can thus be looked at as attempts at challenging intra-European hierarchies. Also at stake is the preservation of an economic relationship based on exporting cheap labour to Western and Northern member states. While understandably shocking to many, nationalist-like narratives of a white and Christian Europe that have emerged from Central and Eastern Europe over the last couple of years are largely consistent with the *Mitteleuropa* narratives celebrated by EU supporters in the 1990s. Again, claims to European identity are articulated around racialised, anti-migrant discourses.

Operationalising difference

Such racist discourses targeting particular groups on the grounds of "civilisational difference" and "cultural incompatibility" are premised on the idea of fundamental differences between putative Europeans and non-Europeans.

This is reminiscent of Edward Said's remarks on orientalist discourses and the way in which they construct people as being of different value based on essentialist,

---

46 Legally: the "European Agency for the Management of Operational Cooperation at the External Borders of the Member States of the European Union", Frontex is the EU's border agency. Established in 2004 and with (tellingly) headquarters in Warsaw, Poland, Frontex's main mission is to manage the cooperation between national border guards to secure the EU's external borders.

47 *Hungarian Free Press*, 2015.

48 Traynor, 2015.

49 Van Baar, 2015.

50 *Al Jazeera*, 2015.

racialised representations. Importantly, Said shows that such discourses naturalise inequalities, strikingly demonstrating how the discursive construction of the "Orient" by the West was a political tool of domination. Orientalist representations lent themselves to European imperialist ambitions in the East and legitimised European control. The discourse of Orientalism, Said contends, was essential to the way European culture "was able to manage and even produce the Orient, politically, sociologically, militarily, ideologically, scientifically and imaginatively".[51]

Today, the structural marginalisation of particular groups is justified in the name of insurmountable cultural and civilisational differences. This has implications both inside and outside the territories of Western nation-states. On the one hand, this new Orientalism has paved the way for and been mobilised in support of (global) military campaigns, including George W Bush and his allies' so-called "War on Terror". These military interventions, portrayed as landmarks of a new era of global governance in the post-Cold War "new world order", have served the purpose of neo-imperialist expansion.[52]

On the other hand, in an era of intense international migrations where the geographical separation between East and West is blurred by people's mobility and global integration, the new Orientalism has mobilised new representations which naturalise the exploitation and oppression of certain groups.[53] The figure of the migrant, endowed with a range of characteristics pointing to the impossibility of her cultural assimilation into a supposedly consistent set of European values, is a key image of this new Orientalism. Since the end of the Cold War, one of the main features of this revamped "oriental" Other—whether in a faraway land that requires Western intervention or inside Western territory as a migrant—has been its association with representations of Islam. This Islam is framed as dangerous, ubiquitous and homogenous and functions as the antithesis to Western and European "civilisation".

The operationalisation of Europe's racist discourses is also visible in another way. Increasingly, nationalist xenophobic discourses are framed around notions of Europeanity or European civilisation. Marine Le Pen, the leader of the French Front National, recently took a position in favour of Russian president Vladimir Putin over the crisis in Ukraine, on the basis that he was "a defender of the Christian heritage of European civilisation".[54] Similarly, UKIP leader Nigel

---

51 Said, 1978, p3.

52 In the postcolonial, post-cold war era, imperialism is characterised, as Alex Colás and Richard Saull put it, by US hegemony "in a world of open doors (capitalist markets) and closed frontiers (territorially sovereign states)"—Colás and Saull, 2006, p2.

53 For further reading see for example Samman and Al-Zo'by, 2008, and Alam, 2007.

54 The Front National also sought funding from Russia to finance its election campaign, see www.uawire.org/news/france-s-far-right-national-front-asks-russia-for-27-million-loan

Farage, in the wake of the *Charlie Hebdo* attacks in which several French cartoonists were killed in January 2015, argued that there was a need to defend "Europe's Judeo-Christian culture".[55] In a similar vein, Viktor Orbán has called for "Europe to be preserved for the Europeans".[56] Such racist discourses also routinely target groups such as children of migrants and European Muslims.

As seen, the EU project does not only erect external borders of absolute otherness. It also creates different shades of valuation against the formation of "Europeanity" and produces internal borders. The use by mainstream media of the derogatory acronym PIGS (Portugal, Italy, Greece and Spain) to refer to the Mediterranean countries of the EU is illustrative of an operation of marginalisation of the peripheries of the new Europe.[57] Similarly, if Europe's new racism primarily targets migrants coming from outside the EU, it also identifies "internal enemies". Roma people, who were the victims of aggravated persecution in the 1920s and 1930s, and of Nazi oppression in the 1940s, have faced new forms of extreme marginalisation in the last two decades. In Central and Eastern Europe, the post-1989 transition has led to heightened racism and violence against Roma communities, and pogroms and mob attacks have multiplied. In Western Europe, Roma migrants have also been subject to incredible levels of media hostility as well as physical abuse. Many Roma people coming to Western Europe have been expelled, in spite of many of them being EU citizens. France in particular has engaged in a policy of deportation of Romani communities, under the pretext of removing "illegal camps" across the country.[58]

Europe, borders and territoriality

The founding treaties of the European Community do not contain rules concerned with the harmonisation of border control. This was perceived as being exclusively the responsibility of nation-states. During the so-called "guest-worker" epoch,[59] the industrial needs of Western European economies meant

55 BBC News, 2015.

56 http://hungarytoday.hu/news/pm-orban-europe-preserved-europeans-47390

57 See for example Dawber, 2015 or BBC News, 2010.

58 See for example www.bbc.co.uk/news/world-europe-11310560

59 This refers to the period between 1958 and 1973 during which around eight million work permits were issued to migrant workers by member states of the EEC (Belgium, France, Italy, Luxembourg, the Netherlands and West Germany). One-third of the so-called "guest-workers" came from within the EEC (mainly Italy) but many were recruited through bilateral agreements for example between Germany and Turkey or Algeria and France. Workers were deemed "guests" insofar as they were expected to leave once their work permits had expired or if they were no longer considered able to work in the physically demanding and dangerous sectors usually reserved for guest-workers (mainly in building, mining, factories and transportation).

that large numbers of migrant workers were encouraged to come and work in Europe. At the time, the legal status of working migrants was not a salient political issue. Internally, the idea of the free movement of people remained secondary to the project of market development.[60]

In the late 1960s and 1970s, as the post-war boom came to an end, the situation started changing. In Western European countries there was a surge in political and media concern about immigration. Policies shifted from relatively permissive approaches to being increasingly restrictive and control-oriented.[61] This move partly aimed at institutionalising and controlling migrant mobilities that exceeded Western states' formal regimes of labour.

Simultaneously, as the European Economic Community pushed for further integration, the idea emerged that a framework for the convergence and harmonisation of immigration policies[62] and border control policies[63] across European member states was necessary. While the EC was still marked by tension and competition between national economies, immigration and border policies became a key area within which member states could further cooperate.

Since the mid-1980s, the task of harmonising immigration policies and of commonalising border control has been the rationale behind the creation of a vast number of European bodies—from research and experts groups to specialised agencies such as the aforementioned Frontex agency. In 2002, Spanish prime minister José María Aznar stated that common migration policy in the EU was "the most important question in European politics at the moment". One of the key justifications behind the reinforcement of the EU's borders has been the claim that it is essential to maintain free circulation within the Union. The (partial and incomplete) suspension of intra-EU national borders through the Schengen Treaty has been heralded as the ultimate illustration of the progressive potential of the Union. Yet, from the perspective of its external borders, Schengen is far from the embodiment of postnational cosmopolitanism that it is claimed to be. In fact, the Schengen area operates as a single state for international travel and has matched the elimination of internal borders with a reinforcement of Europe's external borders (those with non-EU member-states).

European politicians have also argued that the move towards the supranationalisation of border management was necessary to match the new realities of globalisation—including new forms of mobility resulting in new "global threats".

60 Huysmans, 2000.

61 Fielding, 1993, p43; Huysmans, 2000, pp754-755.

62 Conditions of admission and stay of so-called "third country nationals".

63 The implementation of immigration rules via visa management, identity checks, police borders and so on.

The rationale here is that in a world in flow, the material definition and functioning of the border as physical demarcation becomes obsolete. It is time to move away from traditional understanding and to adopt a globalised and dynamic view of space and territories. To address the new "challenges" facing states, borders must change into more diffuse webs of regulations, better able to anticipate and apprehend undesirable and potentially dangerous mobilities. In this sense, customary understandings of borders as physical lines clearly delimiting the boundaries of states and their sovereignty are argued to be increasingly irrelevant.[64]

The EU is presented as a case in point to show the obsolescence of traditional concepts of territory, sovereignty and identity. A complex matrix of rules and regulations concerned with the right to enter the Union has been developed. It is matched internally by an equally intricate topology of residence permits, with associated rights and restrictions. The borders of the EU are also continuously reshaped, both through successive enlargements and through subtler processes of reconfiguration.

In fact, the EU border regime is centred around two complementary processes. On the one hand, Europe is increasingly projecting its borders outside its territory and geographical delineations. This is in large part done through European authorities' intervention in the policies of border and migration controls of peripheral countries. Provisions for "extra-territorial processing" of asylum claims, whereby transit camps are set up in strategically located sites in order to assess asylum applications before allowing potential refugees to enter Europe, are also an example of this externalisation of Europe's borders. On the other hand, the borders of Europe are increasingly reproduced inside its territories, including through the multiplication of detention centres for migrants. As pro-migrant activists have claimed for some time, these camps are no longer exceptions or anomalies. Rather, they have become key institutions of the EU and its migration policies.

Europe's rebordering processes have been so brutal that the notions of "a war against migrants" and "Fortress Europe" have been coined. Although a powerful metaphor for those meaning to highlight the dynamics of exclusion in the EU and at its borders, "Fortress Europe" does not, however, fully capture the complex developments taking place at the EU's borders and beyond. Rather than hermetically closing the space of Europe and strictly keeping migrants out, the borders of the EU operate a process of differential and subordinated inclusion.

But in spite of the changing form and deterritorialised nature of Europe's borders, their legitimising rationale and representations very much echo traditional views on the border.[65] They mobilise bounded understandings of territories and identities

64 Carrera, 2007, p6.

65 Carrera, 2007, p3.

that show striking continuity with national imaginaries. The border remains a territorial and symbolic demarcation between "inside" and "outside"—that is, between what is constructed as European and what is considered as not. The discourse of the EU with respect to borders and migration reinvests the traditionally national idea of securitising the territory as one of the main prerogatives of sovereignty. It also recycles the old national dichotomy between an "us" and a "them". Capitalist territorial imaginations and geographies have thus remained central to the European project and to ideas of Europe.

Securitising migration and neoliberal blame shifting

The focus on border and "immigration management" and on providing "integrated" responses to "threats" coming from migrants reflects a larger trend at work since the late 1980s, and in particular since 9/11: the securitisation of migration. This refers to a tendency to problematise the phenomenon of people moving across borders within a security framework calling for security responses.[66] It is underpinned by the assertion of an increasing connection between migration and the destabilisation of public order.

A set of tensions is at play in the emergence of this global security agenda against migration and migrants. On the one hand, global migrations are rendering internal and external borders less definite: it is precisely around this claim that the idea of a global threat calling for and legitimising the securitisation of borders crystallises. At the same time, the intensification of migratory movements is closely linked to an increase in the economic, political and social pressures faced by the populations of many countries of the Global South. This is in part a consequence and an outcome of the failure of the world development agenda produced in parallel to neoliberal globalisation and neo-imperialist ventures.

The "global threat discourses" thus rely on a process of displacement of blame underpinned by a double logic of "personification" and "geographisation" of blame. The causes of various political and economic processes are displaced and pushed towards the imaginary outsides of the Western world. In turn, migrants originating from these very areas are considered as embodying and literally carrying various forms of danger. This logic is used as a rationale for the global securitisation of migration controls. It is framed through a new semantic field around the idea of an obscure, lurking menace, characterised by "tribalism", "warlordism", "sectarianism", "ethno-nationalism" and so on. Regions of the world that are perceived as "producing migrants" are represented as alien, backward hinterlands, plagued by scarcity and anarchic wars, violence and terrorism.

66 See Huysmans, 2000; also Bigo, 2002; Bigo and Jeandesboz, 2009.

Robert D Kaplan's 1994 article, "The Coming Anarchy",[67] is a striking illustration of this development. Kaplan relies on "personification" of blame and argues that the dangerous and backward features of "dark" Southern and Eastern societies will be brought into the civilised, advanced Global North through migratory movements. This argument is widespread in the mainstream press and media, which produce and project the figure of a deviant and dangerous global migrant threatening Western civilisation and culture.

This discourse has called for a security response to people's mobility. As a result, states' capacities to exclude and deport have developed and taken on new forms.[68] These include pooling together their national resources at a supranational level (as is the case in the EU) and an increased reliance of surveillance technology and externalisation and privatisation of border controls. Externalisation relies primarily on the system of visas, which must be applied for and are issued in the country of origin, but also, for the EU in particular, on a much more comprehensive and complex set of regulations that tend to push the external borders of the Union outwards towards the East and the South, in order better to repel migrants. Increasingly, controls on migration now take place outside the borders of the EU and many are conducted by private companies. For example, European consulates across the world increasingly subcontract the visa selection process to a multinational firm.

The discursive mobilisation of the forced migrant as an absolute Other against which territories and identities have to be defended, and in the name of which a series of restrictive measures must be deployed, is a global practice. It is one that nation-states (and blocs of states) readily utilise in order to neutralise social and political tensions including those emerging in response to the mutation of the local state into a manager of global neoliberal capital.

As argued by Fran Cetti, the increasingly deterritorialised and securitised borders of the European Union have been a key location for the production of the forced migrant as a figure of fear. Cetti shows that this operation relies on but also goes beyond the "quotidian social production of marginal and excluded figures". Rather, she claims, the migrant, often pushed into the global circuits of "survival migration" by global capitalism and exclusionary border and immigration policies, has become a central ideological resource in the attempt to naturalise and depoliticise neoliberal capitalism.[69]

---

67 Kaplan, 1994. The article, later published as a book (Kaplan, 2000), was originally subtitled: "How Scarcity, Crime, Overpopulation, Tribalism, and Disease are Rapidly Destroying the Social Fabric of Our Planet".

68 Nyers, 2010, p414.

69 Cetti, 2012.

To come back briefly to the example of Hungary: recent moves towards further securitisation and authoritarianism have been justified in relation to the migrant global figure and in the name of preserving the country from "outsiders", particularly "Muslims". Yet the processes of militarisation, securitisation and criminalisation of the Hungarian society, which have targeted primarily Hungary's minorities and poor, including Hungarian Roma and homeless people, must be understood in longer-term dynamics. To quote but a few, since the arrival to power of Orbán's Fidesz party in 2010, the Hungarian Constitution has been rewritten, the powers of the Constitutional Court curtailed, welfare has been eroded in favour of compulsory and disciplinary workfare schemes (targeting primarily Roma and the poor) and an environment has been established within which racist speech and prohibited far-right paramilitary activities are tolerated, particularly in the villages where the Roma live.[70]

These developments come in the wake of the process of so-called Europeanisation of Hungary and Central Europe, which has relied on a brutal transition from communism to capitalism—from a command economy to a market economy and into an integrated global economy—under the auspices of the World Bank and the IMF, which were prerequisite to Hungary entering the EU in 2004. In spite of a very specific historical trajectory, largely different from core Western EU states and marked both by its experience of USSR state socialism and by the absence of a global colonial past, Hungary has adopted a neo-Orientalist discourse similar to that articulated by key European ideologues and Western nation-state politicians. In this sense, Hungary is largely in tune with the process of production, marginalisation and exclusion of racialised non-European Others against which the image of Europe as an homogenous entity is being produced and reproduced in the aim of stabilising the EU as a key locus of neoliberal globalisation.

Conclusion

The European Community was a tool to manage the tendency to internationalisation of capital and to contain the cyclical crises of capitalism in the post-war era. Its evolution into the European Union reflected the shift towards global neoliberalism in the 1970s and 1980s. Where dominant accounts of European integration put forward by Eurocrats and pro-Europe politicians describe an internationalist project of peace and reconciliation, it has always been marked by tension and contradiction. In this context, an ideology of Europeanism aimed at triggering popular support towards the European project has been developed. It has produced particular visions of "Europe" and "Europeanity" underpinned by racialised figures of otherness.

70 Fekete, 2016.

Migration, which is in part a result of the intensification of neoliberal capitalist relations on a global scale, has been framed as a security threat in need of containment. A harmonised European border regime has been put in place in order to "deal" with migratory movements and to proceed to the selective inclusion of people within segments of European societies and labour markets. This process has gone hand in hand with the formulation of ever more racist discourses, targeting both non-European migrants and those deemed as "less European" within the EU.

The recent surge in racism following the Brexit vote in the UK has been presented as in antithesis to the idea and values of the European Union. In reality, discourses of Europe and Europeanity produced by the EU have participated in the racialisation and marginalisation of various groups over the last three to four decades, including people coming from the peripheries of the EU and beyond. Rather than an aberration in full opposition to Europe, these racist reactions can be better understood precisely by looking at them in relation to the European Union and to dominant narratives of European belonging.

Europeanism cannot be the basis for the development of a real internationalism from below. However, since the establishment of a coordinated European border regime in the 1990s, a range of grassroots movements in solidarity with migrants and refugees has emerged across the EU and beyond. Their opposition to the EU border regime and its appalling human consequences has been underpinned by the formulation of new political discourses that challenge the geography of separation and the false cosmopolitanism of the EU. They put forward new forms of internationalism, based on notions of world citizenry and solidarity without borders, and open up the way for new forms of radical cosmopolitanism from below.[71]

71 See Cantat, 2015.

References

Alam, Shahid, 2007, *Challenging the New Orientalism: Dissenting Essays on the "War Against Islam"* (Islamic Publications International).

Al Jazeera, 2015, "Hungarian PM: We Don't Want more Muslims" (4 September), www.aljazeera.com/news/2015/09/refugees-hungary-train-station-150903064140564.html

Anderson, Perry, 2011, *The New Old World* (Verso).

Balibar, Étienne and Immanuel Wallerstein, 2010, *Race, Nation, Class: Ambiguous Identities* (Verso).

BBC News, 2010, "Europe's PIGS: Country by Country" (11 February), http://news.bbc.co.uk/1/hi/8510603.stm

BBC News, 2015, "UKIP's Nigel Farage Urges

'Judeo-Christian' Defence after Paris Attacks" (12 January), www.bbc.co.uk/news/world-europe-30776186

Bigo, Didier, 2002, "Security and Immigration: Toward a Critique of the Governmentality of Unease," *Alternatives: Global, Local, Political*, volume 27, number 1.

Bigo, Didier, and Julien Jeandesboz, 2009, "Border Security, Technology and the Stockholm Programme", Centre for European Policy Studies: INEX Policy Brief Number 3 (November).

Callinicos, Alex, 1997, "Europe: the Mounting Crisis", *International Socialism* 75 (summer), www.marxists.org/history/etol/writers/callinicos/1997/xx/europe.htm

Cantat, Céline, 2015, "Contesting Europeanism: Discourses and Practices of Pro-migrant Organisations in the European Union", PhD thesis, University of East London.

Carrera, Sergio, 2007, "Frontex and the Challenges of Irregular Immigration in the Canary Islands", CEPS Working Document Number 261 (22 March), http://tinyurl.com/h23wr5l

Cetti, Fran, 2012, "'Europeanity', the 'Other' and the Discourse of Fear: the Centrality of the Forced Migrant as 'Global Alien' to an Emerging European National Identity", PhD thesis, University of East London.

Colás, Alejandro, and Richard Saull, 2006, *The War On Terror and the American "Empire" after the Cold War* (Routledge).

Connolly, Bernard, 2013, *The Rotten Heart of Europe: The Dirty War for Europe's Money* (Faber and Faber).

Cooper, Luke, 2015, "EU Debate: We Need to Stay in Europe to Change Europe", *Red Pepper* (December), www.redpepper.org.uk/eu-debate-we-need-to-stay-in-europe-to-change-europe/

Dawber, Alistair, 2015, "While Greece Flails, are the Rest of the Stricken Pigs Taking Off?", *Independent* (20 February), http://tinyurl.com/htkmfco

Delanty, Gerard, 1995, *Inventing Europe: Idea, Identity, Reality* (Palgrave Macmillan).

De Genova, Nicholas, unpublished, "Introduction", in Nicholas De Genova (ed), *The Borders of "Europe": Autonomy of Migration, Tactics of Bordering*.

Fekete, Liz, 2001, "The Emergence of Xeno-Racism", *Race and Class*, volume 43, number 2.

Fekete, Liz, 2016, "Hungary: Power, Punishment and the 'Christian-national Idea'", *Race and Class*, volume 57, number 4.

Fielding, Anthony, 1993, "Migration, Institutions and Politics: The Evolution of European Migration Policies", in Russel King (ed), *Mass Migration in Europe: The Legacy and the Future* (Belhaven).

Gill, Stephen, 2003, "A Neo-Gramscian Approach to European Integration", in Alan W Carfuny and Magnus Ryner (eds), *A Ruined Fortress? Neoliberal Hegemony and Transformation in Europe* (Rowman and Littlefield).

Häring, Norbert, 2015, "Yanis Varoufakis: 'Europe Is Our Home, We Need to Fix It'", *Handelsblatt* (30 October), http://tinyurl.com/hk7n8s4

Harman, Chris, 1971, "The Common Market", *International Socialism* 49 (first series, autumn), www.marxists.org/archive/harman/1971/xx/eec-index.html

Harman, Chris, 1991, "The State and Capitalism Today", *International Socialism* 51 (summer), www.marxists.org/archive/harman/1991/xx/statcap.htm

Haynes, Mike, 1999, "Setting the Limits to Europe as an 'Imagined Community'", in Gareth Dale and Mike Cole (eds), *The European Union and Migrant Labour* (Bloomsbury Academic).

Hungarian Free Press, 2015, "Viktor Orbán on Defending Europeans and 'The Invasion of the Outsiders'" (18 November), http://hungarianfreepress.com/2015/11/18/viktor-orban-on-defending-europeans-and-the-invasion-of-the-outsiders/

Huysmans, Jef, 2000, "The European Union and the Securitization of Migration", *Journal of Common Market Studies*, volume 38, issue 5.

Jessop, Bob, 2002, "Liberalism, Neoliberalism, and Urban Governance: A State-Theoretical Perspective", *Antipode*, volume 34, issue 3.

Kaplan, Robert D, 1994, "The Coming Anarchy", *The Atlantic* (February), www.theatlantic.com/magazine/archive/1994/02/the-coming-anarchy/4670/1/

Kaplan, Robert D, 2000, *The Coming Anarchy: Shattering the Dreams of the Post Cold War* (Random House).

Kundera, Milan, 1984, "The Tragedy of Central Europe", *New York Review of Books* (26 April).

Laffan, Brigid, 1996, "The Politics of Identity and Political Order in Europe", *Journal of Common Market Studies*, volume 34, number 1.

Macdonald, Alastair, 2015, "EU, Balkan Leaders Agree Migration Plan", *Reuters* (26 October), http://tinyurl.com/gkoko6t

Marfleet, Philip, 1999, "Nationalism and Internationalism in the New Europe", *International Socialism 83* (summer), www.marxists.org/history/etol/newspape/isj2/1999/isj2-084/marfleet.htm

Marfleet, Philip, 2001, "Europe's Civilizing Mission", in Janet Fink, Gail Lewis and John Clarke (eds), *Rethinking European Welfare: Transformations of European Social Policy* (Sage).

Milward, Alan, 2000, *The European Rescue of the Nation-State* (Routledge).

Murtic, Dino, 2015, *Post-Yugoslav Cinema: Towards a Cosmopolitan Imagining* (Palgrave MacMillan).

Neave, Guy, 1991 "On Programmes, Universities and Jacobins: Or, 1992 Vision and Reality for European Higher Education", *Higher Education Policy, supplement: Leverage and Change*, volume 4, number 4.

Nyers, Peter, 2010, "Abject Cosmopolitanism: The Politics of Protection in the Anti-Deportation Movement", in Nicholas De Genova and Nathalie Peutz (eds), *The Deportation Regime: Sovereignty, Space, and the Freedom of Movement* (Duke University Press).

Said, Edward, 1978, *Orientalism* (Random House).

Samman, Khaldoun and Mazhar Al-Zo'by, 2008, *Islam and the Orientalist World-System* (Paradigm).

Sigalas, Emmanuel, 2009, "Does ERASMUS Student Mobility promote a European Identity?" Webpapers on Constitutionalism and Governance Beyond the State, www.wiso.uni-hamburg.de/fileadmin/sowi/politik/governance/ConWeb_Papers/conweb2-2009.pdf

Švíhlíková, Ilona, 2015, *Jak jsme se stali kolonií* [How we became a colony] (Rybka).

Traynor, Ian, 2015, "Migration Crisis: Hungary PM says Europe in Grip of Madness", *Guardian* (3 September), www.theguardian.com/world/2015/sep/03/migration-crisis-hungary-pm-victor-orban-europe-response-madness

van Baar, Huub, 2017, "Evictability and the Biopolitical Bordering of Europe", *Antipode*, volume 49, issue 1.

Wacquant, Loïc, 2010, "Crafting the Neoliberal State: Workfare, Prisonfare, and Social Insecurity", *Sociological Forum*, volume 25, number 2.

Waever, Ole, and Morten Kelstrup, 1993, "Europe and its Nations: Political and Cultural Identities", in Ole Waever, Barry Buzan, Morten Kelstrup and Pierre Lemaitre (eds), *Identity, Migration and the New Security Agenda in Europe* (Palgrave Macmillan).

Wearden, Graeme, 2012, "Europe's day of anti-austerity strikes and protests turn violent—as it happened", *Guardian* (14 November), www.theguardian.com/business/2012/nov/14/eurozone-crisis-general-strikes-protest-day-of-action

Food, agriculture and climate change

Martin Empson

Scientific evidence of the deepening environmental crisis is growing.[1] Climate change is happening faster than scientific models had predicted. At the same time, despite rhetoric at the COP21 climate conference in Paris at the end of December 2015, we are seeing little, if any, action to reduce emissions.

So it is not surprising that hundreds of thousands of people demonstrated during COP21. These protests were part of a reinvigorated and growing climate movement that used the opportunity presented by COP21 to return to the streets. In Britain, as well as elsewhere, this movement has brought together wide social forces, from environmental campaigners and NGOs, to trade unions and left wing organisations. The movement is increasingly taking up wider political demands and, with the popularity of the slogan "System Change not Climate Change", it bears a striking resemblance to the anti-capitalist movement of the early 2000s.

Within the movement important debates are being raised about what needs to be done. The dominant tone of these discussions is left wing, epitomised by the popularity of Naomi Klein's book *This Changes Everything: Capitalism Versus the Climate.*[2] The book is in part a product of the environmental movement,

---

1 I'd like to thank Alex Callinicos, Esme Choonara, Sarah Ensor, Suzanne Jeffery, Ian Rappel and Camilla Royle for their comments on drafts of this article.

2 Klein, 2015.

particularly what she calls "Blockadia", movements that have emerged out of resistance to attempts by fossil fuel corporations to build pipelines, extract shale gas and exploit tar sands. The book has also helped shape the movement itself, leading to debates among activists about the nature of capitalism and its fossil fuel imperative.

But other debates are re-emerging. One that has manifested with renewed force is the question of agriculture, food and climate change. On both the London and Paris climate demonstrations around the COP21 conference, activists organised blocs calling for veganism to become a significant part of the fight against climate change. These blocs were often marked by calls on other activists to change their personal lifestyles to "save the planet". In London several hundred vegan activists held placards with slogans including "Want to Change the Climate? Change Your Diet Go Vegan!" or "Vegan Diet will save the Planet". The Bristol based vegan campaigning organisation Viva! produced placards reading "There's no such thing as a meat eating environmentalist". Such demands contrast with the slogans that have dominated the movement more recently, which demand large-scale state action on climate change, such as the call for "One Million Climate Jobs".

This focus on animal farming has been dramatically fuelled by the popularity of the 2014 film *Cowspiracy: The Sustainability Secret*. Directed by activist Kip Andersen and filmmaker Keegan Kuhn, *Cowspiracy* has become enormously influential, and after it was updated by executive producer Leonardo DiCaprio and streamed online by Netflix, it has been watched thousands of times. The 90-minute documentary argues that animal agriculture is responsible for 51 percent of global emissions and the systematic destruction of rainforests, as well as wider environmental problems. As the title suggests, it implies a conspiracy involving government bodies, agricultural corporations and environmental NGOs to avoid discussing the role of animal farming in the environmental crisis.

The conclusion of the film is that only a vegan lifestyle can save the planet. And this argument is entering the mainstream of the environmental movement, as one banner on the London march for Climate, Justice and Jobs had it, "The No 1 Cause of Climate Change is Animal Agriculture". Demands to reduce meat eating aren't limited to activists either, with governments and even the UN making similar calls.[3]

But by emphasising individual behavioural changes as a way of tackling climate change this approach fails to challenge the systemic problems with the food system under capitalism, which are the real source of the problem. *Cowspiracy* rightly highlights many problems with modern farming. Its focus, however, is not on the nature of agriculture under capitalism, but one particular aspect of it.[4]

3 Graham-Leigh, 2014, pp7-8.

4 It is worth noting that *Cowspiracy* never mentions any agricultural corporations, nor does it investigate food production outside of the United States so there is no attempt to discuss the

Modern agriculture is enormously destructive to the environment. This is the result of a food system driven by profit and dominated by supermarkets and multinationals. As a result the system causes enormous quantities of waste, and holds up a "Western diet" as the ideal. Consumers are then blamed for their bad food choices, with little regard for the context in which those choices are made.

The solution is not individual dietary changes, but a radical transformation of the food system itself. In this article I will explore the environmental impact of agriculture under capitalism, particularly its contribution to climate change. I hope this can strengthen the anti-capitalist aspect of the climate movement, and in turn the wider revolutionary challenge to capitalism.[5]

Agriculture and climate change

Cowspiracy's headline figure is that "livestock and their by-products account for...51 percent of all worldwide greenhouse gas [GHG] emissions". This figure is based on a report for the Worldwatch Institute by Robert Goodland and Jeff Anhang who argue that:

> The life cycle and supply chain of domesticated animals raised for food have been vastly underestimated as a source of GHGs...replacing livestock products with better alternatives would be the best strategy for reversing climate change. In fact, this approach would have far more rapid effects on GHG emissions and their atmospheric concentrations—and thus on the rate the climate is warming—than actions to replace fossil fuels with renewable energy.[6]

But these dramatic figures are contradicted by other studies. The United Nations Food and Agricultural Organisation (FAO) acknowledges that "the livestock sector plays an important role in climate change" but suggests that the emissions figure is much lower. In their 2013 report, *Tackling Climate Change Through Livestock: A Global Assessment of Emissions and Mitigation Opportunities,* the FAO argue that livestock represents 14.5 percent of human-induced GHG emissions.[7] This is a reduction on an earlier study by the FAO which concluded that livestock was responsible for 18 percent of GHG emissions.[8] The earlier

---

question of livestock agriculture in the developing world, or the role of animals (such as for ploughing or transport) in agriculture outside of their use for meat, milk and eggs.

5 Because this article focuses on the question of agriculture and climate change, some of the wider debates are only touched on or omitted entirely. There are many books that take these further including my own—Empson, 2014. Other books that are useful include Magdoff and Tokar, 2010, Lymbery, 2014, Graham-Leigh, 2014 and McMahon, 2013.

6 Goodland and Anhang, 2009, p11.

7 Gerber and others, 2013, pxii.

8 Steinfeld and others, 2006.

study was considered flawed by some as it compared the full life-cycle of the livestock sector (including transport emissions, for example) with only a partial life-cycle for other sectors. Even though this was acknowledged by the authors of the later FAO report, the flawed figures of the 2006 report are still quoted by the makers of *Cowspiracy*.[9]

Danny Chivers, author and lead external carbon analyst for Christian Aid and ActionAid, has dismissed *Cowspiracy*'s figures:

> The 51 percent number comes from a single non-peer-reviewed report by two researchers—a report littered with statistical errors. This study counts the climate impact of methane from animals as being more than three times more powerful as methane from other sources, adds in an inappropriate chunk of extra land use emissions and incorrectly includes all the carbon dioxide that livestock breathe out.[10]

But acknowledging the limitations of the *Cowspiracy* figure is not to downplay the significance of livestock, or agriculture in general, in terms of climate change. In the UK, for instance, government figures show that agriculture is responsible for 9 percent of total GHG emissions, which includes 79 percent of total nitrous oxide emissions, 48 percent of methane emissions and 1 percent of carbon dioxide emissions.[11] Methane is a significant greenhouse gas with a warming impact 23 times greater than carbon dioxide. It originates from a number of sources, such as the decomposition of organic material, but is particularly important in livestock farming because animals such as cattle, sheep, goats, pigs and buffalo produce large quantities as part of their digestion. Methane is also emitted when animal manure is stored to be used as fertiliser. Nitrous oxide is emitted mostly through the use of synthetic fertilisers.

In March 2014, the FAO produced figures showing that in 2011 global agricultural emissions were the highest in history, 5,335 megatonnes of CO_2 equivalent (about 9 percent higher than the average for the preceding decade), and are projected to increase by 30 percent by 2050.[12] The Intergovernmental Panel on Climate Change (IPCC) estimates that global emissions from agriculture,

---

9 The FAO's acknowledgement of "methodological refinements and improved data" is in Gerber and others, 2013, p15. See Paarlberg, 2013, p132 for more on the limits of the 2006 FAO report. The "flawed" figures are still quoted at www.cowspiracy.com/facts/ for example.

10 Chivers, 2016.

11 DEFRA, 2015b, pp16-19. Total UK emissions from agriculture in 2013 were 53.7 million tonnes of CO_2 equivalent, a decrease of 19 percent since 1990. The decrease has a variety of causes, including a reduction in the amount of livestock and "substantial" reductions in the use of nitrogen fertilisers. Annual figures for the UK can be found in DEFRA, 2015a, p12.

12 Tubiello and others, 2014, p20 and p23. "CO_2 equivalent" means the amount of CO_2 that would have the same warming effect.

forestry and other land use are around 24 percent of the world's total.[13] A 2012 study argues that food systems as a whole contribute between 19 and 29 percent of GHG emissions, of which 80 to 86 percent is from agriculture.[14]

Agriculture is a large contributor to climate change for three main reasons. Firstly, an increasing part of agriculture is the growing of crops to produce feed for animals and biofuels. Secondly, agriculture is a significant cause of deforestation (71 percent of tropical deforestation between 2000 and 2012 was linked to clearances for cultivation[15]), and finally the whole of modern, industrialised agriculture is reliant on the use of fossil fuels.

The growing of crops is the conversion of nutrients from the soil and carbon dioxide in the atmosphere into plants that can be eaten. Some plants cannot be directly eaten by humans but can be consumed by animals, turning them into meat or milk, or giving them energy to pull a plough or transport materials. Since ancient times farmers have known that applying extra nutrients to soil can improve crop yields. Historically animal manure has been used to do this, but from the 19th century onwards, as scientific understanding of chemical processes grew, the application of other fertilisers became common. At first this included sources of nutrients such as ground up bones or bird guano. But, as the industrial revolution developed, artificial fertilisers became the most common way of replenishing the soil. Today the manufacture of fertiliser requires enormous energy inputs from fossil fuels. In the developed world oil is also essential to the harvesting, ploughing and transport of crops and animals, and the food that they are processed into. Another significant use of fossil fuels is in the manufacture of pesticides that are used to kill weeds and insects.

The rising demand for meat and other products of the meat industry, such as milk, eggs or cheese, means that livestock farming has become enormous. The global population (2013) of chickens is calculated at 21 billion birds, while there are estimated to be 1.4 billion cattle, 1.1 billion sheep and 977 million pigs.[16]

Emissions from cattle farming are the single biggest emissions of livestock farming. Most of this comes from beef production (41 percent of total livestock emissions) with 20 percent coming from milk production. In some developing areas of the world, emissions from livestock used for transport or draught-power remain high—accounting for a quarter of emissions in South Asia and sub-Saharan Africa.[17] Environmentalists who argue that stopping climate change

---

13 IPCC, 2014, p816.

14 Vermeulen, Campbell and Ingram, 2012.

15 Jones, 2014.

16 FAO figures from http://faostat3.fao.org/home/E

17 Gerber and others, 2013, p23.

requires reducing numbers of cattle and buffalo rarely suggest an alternative to those communities who rely on animals for farming and transport.

The sheer scale of emissions from livestock farming is worth examining. Take the example of the South American beef industry. According to the FAO, this is responsible for 31 percent of the global beef sector. This contributes about 1 billion tonnes of CO_2 equivalent to GHG emissions. There are two main sources of emissions. Firstly, enteric fermentation, the digestive process by which micro-organisms in an animal's stomach break down food so it can be absorbed into the bloodstream, produces methane (which, for the South American beef industry, is responsible for 30 percent of emissions). Secondly, the use of manure as fertiliser and land-use change, such as deforestation to expand grazing areas, contribute to emissions by 23 percent and 40 percent respectively.[18]

Even under the existing system there is potential for significant reductions in emissions. But these will often require technological improvements or changes to agricultural practices, so may be rejected by companies that are unwilling to reduce profits or farmers who lack the capital to introduce them. But they do demonstrate the way a food system that is driven by need, not by profit, could reduce emissions. For instance, the FAO notes that emissions from the livestock sector could be reduced by 18 percent by generalising from the best practices of those with the lowest emissions and by utilising existing technologies, but this is dependent on "conducive policies and market signals" existing to encourage the adoption of these best practices.[19] The FAO also notes that reducing deforestation, reducing the expansion of agricultural areas and improving how and where animals are grazed could also lead to the further sequestration of greenhouse gases in soil (some 409 million tonnes of CO_2 equivalent per year). Other practices, such as the sowing of legumes (plants such as peas, clover and beans) on grassland, can significantly improve the ability of the soil to absorb carbon.[20]

Concern about emissions from agriculture is not simply their impact on the environment; emissions also reflect inefficiencies in the agricultural process itself. For example, animal feed is often the most expensive part of livestock farming, and methane emissions represent a waste of the energy input in the form of feed. Therefore reducing emissions can also reduce farming costs through energy reduction in the food system.[21]

Emissions from livestock agriculture vary dramatically from region to region, often reflecting different types of farming, or land use in the particular region.

18 Gerber and others, 2013, pp68-69.
19 Gerber and others, 2013, p46.
20 Gerber and others, 2013, pp50-51.
21 Gerber and others, 2013, p40.

For instance, globally, land use change is responsible for 15 percent of the beef industry's emissions, but for chicken production it is 21 percent. This is because land use change originates in deforestation for beef, but for chickens it is related to the production of their soybean feed. This creates a further difficulty in estimating industry emissions, because soybeans are traded internationally so their emissions are attributed in different locations worldwide, but deforestation emissions are considered locally.[22] There is also enormous variety between countries reflecting different industrial practices.[23] But broadly speaking, agriculture in the most affluent areas of the globe has high emissions when measured against the land area. But the emissions per unit of agricultural production are low.[24]

Production methods can also affect the level of emissions per unit of production. There is a strong negative correlation between the amount of milk produced by cows and emission intensity. In other words, as yield increases, the amount of emissions per unit of production decreases. There are three reasons for this, with implications for reducing total emissions from farming. The first is that as total yields grow, emissions are spread over a larger amount of production. Secondly, improvements in productivity (such as the use of different feeds, mechanised milking machines or drugs to improve production) are often related to improved technologies and practices that can also reduce emissions. Finally, improvements to herd management, as well as animal health and husbandry, "increase the proportion of resources utilised for productive purposes rather than simply being used to maintain the animals".[25]

The use of technology can help reduce both total emissions and the amount of emissions per unit of production at least in some areas of livestock agriculture, such as milk production. Because the amount of methane cows produce varies naturally, current research suggests that selective breeding could mean future animals may be less polluting than currently, even without using extra technologies.[26]

OECD countries have only 20 percent of the global dairy cows, but produce 73 percent of the world's milk. Average emissions for OECD milk production are thus much lower than the world in general. The FAO's case study of this sector suggests that "feasible improvements in manure management, energy use, feed quality and animal performance" could lead to reductions of between 14 and 17 percent of GHGs (which is between 4 and 5 percent of the emissions from the global milk sector). The exact way of doing this would depend on regional factors—in Western

22 Gerber and others, 2013, p41.

23 Gerber and others, 2013, p42.

24 Gerber and others, 2013, p53.

25 Gerber and others, 2013, p42.

26 Ince, 2014. I am indebted to John Parrington for pointing this out to me.

Europe better energy use is the most significant factor, while in North America "wider use of anaerobic digesters" to break down animal waste is suggested.[27]

But with agriculture, as with other sectors such as energy generation or transport, we have to be wary of simply seeing either technology or particular production methods as necessarily leading to lower emissions. Take chicken farming. There are three types of chicken production: backyard and industrial layers, that produce meat and eggs, and industrial broilers, that produce only meat. Industrial broiler and egg farming has the lowest emission intensity for similar reasons to that of milk production in cows. Chickens running free in a backyard have high emission intensity per egg as the animals grow more slowly and produce fewer eggs, their feed tends to be of lower quality, and the ratio of unproductive to productive animals is higher than in industrial production. So industrial poultry production produces less energy emissions per unit than backyard farming.

However, we must be careful not to lose sight of the wider context. Although industrial poultry farming results in fewer emissions, there are other negatives. Chickens are kept in terrible conditions and live short, often painful lives, with a high usage of antibiotics and other drugs to encourage rapid growth. The use of drugs to produce cheap meat may well have health impacts for consumers. Mass poultry farming is also unhealthy for those who work in the industry—a US Bureau of Labor Statistics report showed that the poultry industry is one of those with the highest levels of occupational illness.[28] US poultry farming is dominated by a few massive corporations, that contract out the growing of chickens to smaller farms (while the animals themselves remain the property of the corporation). This leads to farmers being trapped in an unequal relationship, at the beck and call of the businesses solely motivated by profits.[29]

But when we consider the emissions from pig farming, the "difference in emission intensities between the various production systems is not substantial". While the majority of total emissions from the pig sector still come from industrial farming, emissions are similar when considered against backyard production. The reason for this is mostly linked to the lower quality of food given to backyard animals (often waste from other sources), which means lower emissions.[30] So it is not automatic that switching to industrialised farming, or to highly technological practices will reduce emissions.

I will return to strategies to reduce emissions later. But for now it's worth noting two conclusions. First, there is a large potential to reduce emissions from

27 Gerber and others, 2013, pp76-78.

28 Lymbery, 2014, p193.

29 For more on the industrial chicken, see Lymbery, 2014, pp187-196.

30 Gerber and others, 2013, pp35-36.

agriculture and particularly livestock farming. The use of improved technology and other practices can, in certain circumstances, have a significant impact on the amount of emissions. I have already noted the FAO conclusion that emissions could be reduced by between 18 and 30 percent if producers in particular regions were all able to take up the practices used by the 10 to 25 percent of producers who have the lowest emissions.

Secondly, emissions reductions can be achieved in both the developed and developing world, but the methods may vary. High emissions from industrialised farming might be better achieved through "on-farm efficiency, such as better manure management and energy saving devices" but elsewhere better land management, herd management and changes to feeding practices are needed.[31] There is no one size fits all solution to reducing emissions from agriculture, rather a wide variety of answers.

How climate change effects agriculture

Finally, it's worth highlighting how climate change will impact on agriculture. It used to be commonly thought that global warming would be beneficial to farmers, as higher carbon dioxide levels would act as a fertiliser and improve crop yields. While this is true (yields of some crops, such as wheat, can rise by 30 percent if CO_2 doubles), any improvement also depends on other factors such as nutrient levels, water availability and average temperatures.

Fish and shellfish are highly vulnerable to temperature changes, and increasing acidification of the oceans will further impact on already low stocks. This in turn can have a further negative impact on agriculture as something like a third of the world's fish catch ends up as animal feed. The practice of feeding farm animals and fish on other fish and krill from the oceans is also significantly damaging to the ocean's ecosystems.

Extreme weather events, such as droughts and floods, are likely to become more intense and frequent as the world warms. Since agriculture is often concentrated in particular regions, this can lead to major risks to crop production. For instance, a third of all wheat, corn and rice that is traded internationally originates in the United States. In 2012 America experienced its worst drought since 1950 with 60 percent of US farms experiencing moderate to extreme drought in August. As a result, corn production was down to 2006 levels and export prices rose by 33 percent in the summer.[32]

The melting of glaciers also threatens agriculture. In the Himalayas some 15,000 glaciers feed about half the Brahmaputra, Ganges and Indus rivers' annual

31 Gerber and others, 2013, p44.

32 Adonizio, Kook and Royales, 2012, p2.

flow. As those glaciers melt there will be an initial surge in water levels, but a warming world ultimately threatens a billion people who rely on the rivers' water. In South America, Andean glaciers supply water and hydroelectric energy to nearly 80 million people. In 2010 Henry Pollack wrote that "one quarter of Earth's population will within another few decades begin to be affected significantly by lesser snowfall and glacial ice loss".[33]

Climate change will hit agriculture and food in other ways. A US report, published in April 2016, highlights some of these. It suggests that some illnesses such as salmonella and e. coli will become more common in warmer weather and notes that higher carbon dioxide levels will reduce protein levels in food. The frightening conclusion is that extreme weather could interrupt food supply chains, will intensify pesticide use in reaction to changing insect populations and will lower concentrations of essential minerals such as iron and zinc in food.[34]

The wider environmental impact of agriculture

Historically agriculture has been the most significant way that humans have altered their environment. The emergence of agriculture around 10,000 years ago can be linked to a wide variety of environmental and ecological changes. These have included deforestation, changes to water courses for irrigation and the selective breeding of plants and animals for domestication. Under capitalism, like earlier human societies, we continue to alter the environment and agriculture forms a significant part of this process. But the nature of production under capitalism has meant the transformation of nature has been taken to a new level. John Bellamy Foster, Brett Clark and Richard York have described how Karl Marx developed an understanding of the way that capitalism created a "metabolic rift" in the "exchange between humanity and nature":

> The context was the robbing of the soil of the countryside of nutrients and the sending of these nutrients to the cities in the form of food and fibre, where they ended up contributing to pollution. This rupture in the soil nutrient cycle undermined the regenerative capacities of the ecosystem. Marx argued that it was necessary to "restore" the soil metabolism to ensure environmental sustainability for the generations to come.[35]

This rift has its origins in a system of production that treats the natural world only as part of the productive process itself, a source of raw materials or energy, or a dump for the waste of that productive process. While no agricultural production

33 Pollack, 2010, pp200-202.

34 USGCRP, 2016.

35 Foster, Clark and York, 2010, p46.

can fail to have an impact upon nature, the industrialised farming that currently dominates produces, in Marx's words, "an irreparable rift in the interdependent process of social metabolism".[36]

The almond industry presents a stark example of this. Some 80 percent of the world's almonds come from highly intensive farms in Central Valley, California. Around 60 million almond trees are planted in orchards covering 240,000 hectares of land. The area has so little rain it is classified as "semi-desert". In addition to almonds there are giant dairies and huge fields of fruit, nuts and vegetables. In *Farmageddon*, Philip Lymbery describes this as:

> a deeply disturbing place where not a blade of grass, no tree or hedgerow grows, except in private gardens and the ruthlessly delineated fields. The phenomenal output of fruit and veg is possible only thanks to a cocktail of chemicals and the plundering of the crystal-clear rivers that run down from the Sierra Nevada mountains...farmers have been able to pull off a multi-billion-dollar conjuring trick, extracting harvests from soil that is so depleted of natural matter it might as well be brown polystyrene.[37]

Industrialised agriculture like this means there are no longer enough bees to pollinate the crops, so every year 3,000 lorries carry 40 billion bees across the United States to California where they pollinate the almond trees at a cost of $250 million a year.[38]

Honeybees, central to the production of food, are themselves victims of industrial farming. Colony collapse disorder has been linked to pesticides called neonicotinoids, but other factors are closely linked to industrial farming. For instance, in Central Valley hedges and unploughed field margins where bees might have lived have been removed to create giant orchards. More problematically, these mono-cropped areas rely on the heavy use of artificial fertilisers. Historically farmers allowed soils to replenish themselves through crop rotation—leaving a field fallow, or sowing a crop such as clover, which also encourages bees. But large-scale, monocropped industrial farming simultaneously reduces food sources and poisons and destroys the places where bees live.[39]

One Indian ecologist, Dr Parthiba Basu, argues that declining forests and increased pesticide use are key factors in the collapse of bee populations:

> I had hoped that pollinator loss would not be nearly as serious in developing countries as it is in the West, but that does not seem to be the case. It is very sad.

36 Marx, 1992, p949.
37 Lymbery, 2014, p13.
38 Lymbery, 2014, pp63-64.
39 Lymbery, 2014, p68.

> It is going to take a lot of effort to turn this around, but unfortunately the developing world is going down the opposite route right now, embracing Western-style intensification. That means more mono-cropping and chemical fertiliser and pesticide use, and more loss of the wilderness habitats on which bees depend.[40]

But using industrially bred bees in vast quantities is not a fail-safe solution. In 2014 between 15 and 25 percent of beehives brought to California for almond pollination were severely damaged, leading to the death of millions of bees. It seems likely that the cause was the use of new "adjuvants", chemicals used to improve the efficiency of pesticides but which make hitherto safe pesticides lethal to bees.[41] So the almond industry has created and become dependent on a bee industry, but the farming practices used also threaten the viability of the bee industry itself. There can be no better example of the "metabolic rift" in modern agriculture.[42]

Karl Marx might have been writing about the almond and bee industries when he commentated about capitalist farming:

> agriculture no longer finds the natural conditions of its own production within itself, naturally, arisen, spontaneous, and ready to hand, but these exist as an independent industry separate from it—and, with this separateness the whole complex set of interconnections in which this industry exists is drawn into the sphere of the conditions of agricultural production.[43]

The almond industry also highlights another important environmental aspect of farming—the question of water. Growing crops and animals requires vast quantities of water. Some 3,400 litres of water are needed to grow a kilogram of rice, 3,900 for a kilogram of chicken and between 15,000 and 100,000 litres for a kilogram of beef.[44] A single almond requires slightly over 4 litres of water.[45]

A hectare of "high-yield" rice needs about 11 million litres to produce 7 tons of rice. Soybeans require about 5.8 million litres to get three tons per hectare. Wheat uses "only" about 2.4 million litres for 2.7 tons per hectare. Vandana Shiva has pointed out that these high-yield seeds should really be known as "high-response" varieties as they require such increased inputs in the form of chemicals and water.[46] Growing crops using irrigation as opposed to rainwater

---

40 Lymbery, 2014, p70.
41 Philpott, 2014a.
42 I am indebted to Adam Rose for this point.
43 Quoted in Foster and Clark, 2016.
44 McMahon, 2013, p89.
45 Philpott, 2014b.
46 Shiva, 2014, p222.

alone requires three times more energy to grow the same amount of grain, adding to the GHG emissions.[47]

Agriculture is helping to rapidly deplete freshwater reserves, particularly underground aquifers. Some wells are replenished naturally, but others, known as fossil aquifers, hold water that has been there for thousands of years and is not replenished. In the United States the Ogallala aquifer provides about 30 percent of irrigation water used by the country's farmers, and it may dry up within 25 years.[48] The deeper or more inaccessible the water, the more energy must be expended in pumping it to the surface, which means more fossil fuels being burnt, increasing emissions. The World Bank estimates that 175 million people in India and 130 million in China depend on grain produced by over-pumping.[49]

Agriculture also causes pollution of rivers, lakes and the sea. One cause of this is the pollution from animal manure. Britain's animals annually produce 80 million tons of manure. In Britain an "average-sized dairy herd of a hundred cows can produce as much effluent as a town of 5,000 people. Across the country there are a total of 1.8 million dairy cows, not to mention many millions of pigs, chickens and other farm animals".[50] In the past manure from cows was spread back on the fields as fertiliser, but intensive dairy farming (or factory farming of chickens and pigs) produces such vast quantities of manure that it cannot possibly be spread on the soil. Some is stored in vast pools, and leakages can pollute groundwater and emit gases into the air.[51] Lymbery quotes Kevin Hamilton, a respiratory therapist in the previously described Central Valley on the impact of pollution from high-intensity farming:

> We're talking about heart disease, birth defects, and stunted lung development among children who spent a lot of time outside playing sport. We're talking about high blood pressure and increased risk of stroke. We have the second highest level of childhood asthma in the whole of the US.[52]

Some mega-dairies in the region have tens of thousands of cows.[53] The waste from these, plus the chemicals and pesticides used, is creating a health crisis.

---

47 Magdoff and Tokar, 2010, p243.

48 McMahon, 2013, p66.

49 McMahon, 2013, p66.

50 Lymbery, 2014, p172.

51 Agriculture run-off in the UK is one of the major reasons why the UK is not expected to meet the Water Framework Directive well beyond the deadline of 2021.

52 Lymbery, 2014, p23.

53 China also has enormous cow factories. In July 2015 one was being built to house 100,000 cattle to supply milk and cheese to Russian markets. Go to www.fwi.co.uk/livestock/china-building-100000-cow-dairy-unit-to-supply-russian-market.htm

Hamilton continues: "You have to use a phenomenal amount of chemicals to push multiple crops out of the soil we have here... These pesticides are capable of penetrating the human body to genome level—meaning they can affect the very building blocks of the body".[54]

Leakages and rainfall can wash the manure into streams and rivers, and the amassed nutrients can lead to "dead zones" in water. Agriculture run-off from "excessive" fertiliser use on farms in the Mississippi watershed has caused a 6,000 square mile dead zone in the Gulf of Mexico no longer able to support life.[55]

In developed countries such as Britain and the US farmers' organisations have been able to organise to prevent government action to reduce such pollution. In the US, "Congress does not regulate excess nitrogen runoff from farms and does not tax farm fertiliser use." Instead it pays farmers to temporarily leave land unused to reduce pollution. In other words, the government is paying the polluters, rather than punishing them for polluting. In one case, when Al Gore planned to tax sugar growers in Florida to fund a clean-up of the Everglades, a sugar baron simply telephoned then president Bill Clinton to cancel the tax plan.[56]

The human impact of pesticide use is not just limited to those living near to highly industrialised farms. In the developing world larger proportions of populations are engaged in agriculture, threatening more people. Plantation crops such as tea, cotton, coffee and vegetables are pesticide intensive and expose large areas and large numbers of people to the chemicals. The World Health Organisation estimates that 20,000 workers die from exposure to pesticides every year, most of them in the developing world.[57]

Pesticide use brings both benefits and potential problems. The "Green Revolution" of the 1970s saw crop yields dramatically increase as new strains of crops were developed. Alongside this, the use of pesticides increased, closely associated with higher government subsidies. Sometimes over-use of pesticides was associated with wider environmental destruction (as well as costs to human health). In Indonesia, for instance, in the early 1980s, massive government subsidies for fertilisers and pesticides led to excessive use on rice fields. As well as killing pests, over-use of pesticides also destroyed species that were essential to insect control (such as spiders). When "bad insects" such as planthoppers evolved pesticide resistance, the government had to intervene to ban 75 different insecticides allowing the recovery of insects to control the pests.[58]

---

54 Lymbery, 2014, p24.

55 Paarlberg, 2013, pp117-118.

56 Paarlberg, 2013, pp127-128.

57 Hashmi and Khan, 2011, p161.

58 Paarlberg, 2013, pp72-73.

One response to this has been for some farmers and consumers to turn to organic crops to reduce the use of artificial pesticides. Organic farming is an attempt to make agriculture more sustainable, biologically diverse and healthy by reducing the use of artificial chemicals. For example methods such as crop rotation, manure and cover-crops are used to replenish the soil, rather than relying on artificial fertilisers.

This is an understandable reaction to industrialised farming, but again we should be wary of neglecting the very real benefits of technological improvements to agriculture as represented by the Green Revolution. For instance, in 1964 India produced 12 million tons of wheat on 14 million hectares; 30 years later production was 57 million tons from 24 million hectares. Calculations show that without the benefits of the Green Revolution, an additional 36 million hectares of farming land would have been needed.[59] Organic farming does not on its own prevent health dangers. In 2006 three people died and hundreds became ill as a result of e. coli infections from spinach grown on a Californian organic farm, nine died from salmonella linked to organic peanut plants in Texas and Georgia and in 2011 53 people died from e. coli after eating bean sprouts grown on a German organic farm.[60] Such examples suggest that the problem is not simply pesticides and the solution simply organic farming, but a whole range of processes in agriculture that can lead to health issues.

Because organic farming is less dependent on fossil fuels (used in the manufacture of artificial chemicals and pesticides), it can lead to significant reductions in overall greenhouse gas emissions. A 2006 report, for instance, concluded that if 10 percent of all US maize were grown organically, it could save 4.6 million barrels of oil. This can also be true of the meat industry. The Soil Association in the UK has calculated that organic milk uses 38 percent less energy than non-organic; for beef the figures are 35 percent less, lamb 25 percent less.[61] But again we must be wary of seeing these figures out of context. A 2012 Oxford University report concluded that "organic systems were often better for the environment per unit of land, but conventional systems were often better per unit of production". This report also contradicted the Soil Association figures quoted above, suggesting that "organic milk, cereals, and pork production generated higher greenhouse gas emissions per unit of output than the conventional alternative".[62]

---

59 Paarlberg, 2013, p73.

60 Paarlberg, 2013, p173.

61 Figures from, Lymbery, 2014, pp238-239.

62 Paarlberg, 2013, p175. The Oxford University study is summarised at www.ox.ac.uk/news/2012-09-04-organic-farms-not-necessarily-better-environment

The key conclusion is that organic farming methods have much to offer from an environmental point of view. But benefits are not automatic, and depend on volume and scale, as well as the use of technology in a way that is designed to reduce environmental impacts. Colin Tudge, a British campaigner for "enlightened farming", argues that "organic farming need not be the absolute requirement... But it should be the default position: what farmers do unless there is a very good biological reason to do something else".[63]

One final environmental and health impact of farming is particularly associated with the meat industry. This is the use of antibiotics to treat animals and improve their growth and productivity: "80 percent of antibiotic use in America is on farms, 70 percent...to boost growth or prevent disease rather than to treat it".[64] Antibiotic use is particularly associated with factory farming, where the close confinement of animals provides the potential for disease to spread easily.

But heavy use of antibiotics is breeding resilience in the bacteria it is intended to destroy, which then enter the food chain or can spread to humans through manure, etc. Over half of Dutch pig farmers and 40 percent of Dutch pigs, for instance, carry a strain of pig-MRSA, and tests suggest it is present in 35 percent of raw meat in the Netherlands. In Britain in 2011, 15 cases of a new strain of MRSA were found in milk from British dairies. Factory farming and over-use of antibiotics are helping to create super-strains of diseases. One study of salmonella in British chickens found that smaller flocks and non-caged birds were less likely to carry the disease.[65] In 2010:

> Over 18 percent of caged flocks tested positive for salmonella enteritidis, the most common strain causing food poisoning, compared with less than 3 percent of non-caged flocks. The largest flocks of 30,000 birds or more were seven times more likely to carry salmonella than the smallest flocks of 3,000 hens or less.[66]

Viral diseases such as bird flu and swine flu are closely associated with intensified farming for chickens and pigs, which provide perfect conditions for the evolution of new strains of these bugs.

There is no doubt that industrialised agriculture is a threat to the environment and to human health.[67] What has caused this to happen?

63 Tudge, 2011, p68.
64 Lymbery, 2014, p139.
65 Lymbery, 2014, pp144-145.
66 Lymbery, 2014, p145.
67 While this article focuses on agriculture, these conclusions are also true of the fishing industry. See Lymbery, 2014, chapter 5, and Ensor, 2016.

Agriculture under capitalism

Agriculture is closely associated with the rise of capitalism. Marx saw "the expropriation of the agricultural producer...from the soil"[68] as being key to the primitive accumulation that formed the basis for the development of capitalist society. This process created the basis for capitalist production, but also transformed the nature of agriculture and fuelled the growth of urban industry:

> The spoliation of the church's property, the fraudulent alienation of the State domains, the robbery of the common lands, the usurpation of feudal and clan property, and its transformation into modern private property under circumstances of reckless terrorism, were just so many idyllic methods of primitive accumulation. They conquered the field for capitalistic agriculture, made the soil part and parcel of capital, and created for the town industries the necessary supply of a "free" and outlawed proletariat.[69]

Agriculture under capitalism is, like every other branch of production, shaped by the need for the capitalists to accumulate wealth for the sake of further accumulation. Space precludes a detailed overview of modern agriculture, but the key point is that the agriculture of the developed world, supported by massive government subsidises and dominated by a small number of corporations, comes at the expense of the more traditional, small-scale and subsistence farming that has historically characterised most of the world.[70]

This domination can be summed up by Cargill Inc. Founded in 1865 and based in Minnesota, Cargill is now one of the world's largest private corporations, with 2015 sales of $120.4 billion and earnings of $1.58 billion. It employs over 150,000 people in 70 countries, trading everything from cotton to animal feed, meat, cocoa and salt. The company says that "Cargill Beef is one of North America's largest beef processors, harvesting more than eight million cattle and producing nearly eight billion pounds of boxed beef and by-products each year". The company owns its own fleet of 500 ships to help distribute its products, including 120 "capesize" vessels, the largest dry goods ships in service.[71]

Corporations like Cargill have enormous influence in the world food system. In 2005 four companies controlled processing of 80 percent of US beef, three of them, together with another fourth company, controlled 60 percent of US pork, and 50 percent of chicken production comes from another four companies.

---

68 Marx, 1990, p876. See Saito, 2014, for an important study of how Marx developed his understanding of capitalist agriculture in the context of contemporary scientific debates.

69 Marx, 1990, p895.

70 I've explored this in detail in chapter 10 of Empson, 2014.

71 All information on Cargill Inc. from www.cargill.com (accessed March 2016).

Silvia Ribeiro and Hope Shand explain the negative role of big business in agriculture:

> Corporate concentration in agriculture has allowed a handful of powerful corporations to seize the agricultural research agenda, influence national and international trade and agricultural policy and engineer the acceptance of new technologies as the "science-based" solution to maximising food production. Although frequently promoted in the name of addressing the needs of the world's poor and hungry, the benefits of these technologies typically [accrue] to those who develop and control them.[72]

Because they are driven by maximisation of profits, companies like Cargill put their profits before the interests of the environment or people. Cargill, for instance, has been the focus of a campaign against destructive production of palm oil, which, according to the Rainforest Action Network, meant the company had a "role in orangutan extinction, rainforest destruction, child labour and human rights abuses".[73] Palm oil is widely used in food production, but increasingly is used as an ingredient in biofuels. Biofuels are promoted as an alternative to fossil fuels, but there are significant environmental problems associated with them and question marks over their ability to reduce emissions compared to existing fossil fuels.

Cargill has an estimated $1 billion investment in the biofuels sector.[74] But while acknowledging the dangers to food security and the environment, the company is concerned that its ability to make profits from the biofuel industry is not hampered by regulation:

> Cargill believes biofuels can play an important role in meeting global energy and environmental needs, bringing capital investment to agriculture and boosting economic development in farm communities. However, the production of biofuels from food crops should be balanced against the need to provide food for a growing global population. We support dialogue among governments, farmers, cattle, pork and poultry producers, food manufacturers and the public to consider ways to balance the need for renewable energy with the importance of maintaining a secure food and feed supply. We favor market-driven policies, not inflexible mandates, subsidies and tariffs.[75]

Despite serious questions over their environmental credentials, biofuels are big business. In the run up to the passing of the 2014 Farm Act in the United

---

72 Quoted in Bello, 2009, pp110-111.
73 Rainforest Action Network, 2014.
74 Bello, 2009, p109.
75 Go to www.cargill.com/news/issues/climateenergynaturalresources/biofuel-policy/index.jsp

States, major energy companies lobbied to ensure that subsidies for the fuel were protected. The amounts spent on lobbying can be astronomical. A report by the US Taxpayers for Common Sense, "Political Footprint of the Corn Ethanol Lobby", says that between 2007 and 2014 Cargill spent over $11 million on lobbying. Another major international food corporation, Archer Daniels Midland (ADM), spent over $12 million and the American Farm Bureau and State Organisations almost $49 million.[76]

The biofuel industry has a significant impact on food security and the environment. Yet the potential profits mean that corporations are prepared to fight to ensure they can continue to grow the crops. Paul McMahon explains the problem:

> US biofuels policies have been strongly criticised for driving up the price of food, while delivering few environmental benefits...[these] policies have nothing to do with the environment, nor with feeding the poor. To a minor extent they are driven by a desire for energy security... But the primary objective of the biofuels policy is to provide financial support to American farmers. It is the latest in the long line of attempts to find uses for the country's grain surpluses.[77]

There is a close link between the interests of agribusiness and those of national governments. The 2008 food crisis demonstrated that many countries were ill-prepared for price rises. In response a number of countries have begun to protect their interests by securing food elsewhere. Sometimes this has meant countries or corporations purchasing land for agriculture (or biofuels) in Africa and South America. These "land-grabs" have become shorthand for the way that peasant producers, local farming practices and the rights of indigenous peoples are brushed aside in the search for food security and profits.

Corporations often use the question of food security to justify their actions. In 2009, for instance, the Japanese trading house Mitsui was looking for "agricultural investments" in Central America, Asia and Eastern Europe. It offered "inputs and machinery to farmers in exchange for the right to buy harvests", explaining that this was "not only good business; it would also satisfy the Japanese government's desire to strengthen national food security".[78]

It was through meetings of the G8 and G20 that the major countries tried to shape a response to the 2008 food crisis. While globally the International Monetary Fund (IMF) and World Bank, as well as the World Trade Organisation, have shaped a neoliberal approach towards the development of the world

76 Go to www.taxpayer.net/library/article/updated-political-footprint-of-the-corn-ethanol-lobby

77 McMahon, 2013, p58.

78 McMahon, 2013, p171.

economy, in terms of food and agriculture there are three key United Nations organisations. These are the International Fund for Agricultural Development, the World Food Programme (designed to manage food assistance to areas struck by drought, etc) and the Food and Agricultural Organisation (FAO). Finally, the Consultative Group in International Agricultural Research (CGIAR) is a body linked to the World Bank that tries to "extend the legacy of the original green revolution of the 1960s and 1970s by using science to develop improved seeds and more productive and sustainable farming...in the developing world".[79]

All these bodies serve to ensure that neoliberal policies continue to sink deeper into world food and agriculture. What this means in practice can be seen from the World Bank and IMF structural adjustment programmes (SAPs) of the 1980s and 1990s. These systematically reduced the role of the state in agriculture in the developing world and promoted the production of food for trade. As US agriculture secretary John Block explained in 1986, "the idea that developing countries should feed themselves is an anachronism from a bygone era. They could better ensure their food security by relying on US agricultural products, which are available in most cases at a lower cost".[80]

But even the World Bank had to admit that the result of the SAPs was a disaster for agriculture. In its 2008 *World Development Report* it acknowledged:

> Structural adjustment in the 1980s dismantled the elaborate system of public agencies that provided farmers with access to land, credit, insurance, inputs and cooperative organisations. The expectation was that removing the state would free the market for private actors to take over these functions... Incomplete markets and institutional gaps impose huge costs in forgone growth and welfare losses for smallholders, threatening their competitiveness and, in many cases, their survival.[81]

World Bank policies decimated African smallholder and peasant farming in the interests of corporate agri-business. The consequences were appalling, with the rural population displaced, driven into unemployment or underemployment or forced to seek work in the cities.

As neoliberal policies enforce a switch to larger-scale farming at the expense of local, small-scale agriculture, they also have negative consequences for the environment. Even the UK government admitted in 2011 that:

> Many systems of food production are unsustainable. Without change, the global food system will continue to degrade the environment and compromise the

79 Paarlberg, 2013, pp210-211.

80 Quoted in Bello, 2009, p76.

81 Quoted in Bello, 2009, p81.

> world's capacity to produce food in the future, as well as contributing to climate change and the destruction of biodiversity... Nothing less is required than a redesign of the whole food system to bring sustainability to the fore.[82]

Is meat eating the problem?

Reducing emissions from agriculture will not be tackled by individuals switching to a non-meat based diet. The environmental damage from farming is a result of the nature of the industry under capitalism, with production determined by the need to make profits. Arguing for a switch to a meat-free diet is a dangerous strategy for the environmental movement because it places the blame on individuals as consumers, not the system as a whole.

As one scientist commented while reviewing *Cowspiracy*:

> Movies like *Cowspiracy* aren't believable, not only because of how they twist the science, but also because of what they ask us to believe: that the fossil fuel industry...aren't the main cause of global warming; that the transition to clean energy isn't what matters most for our future and our grandchildren's; and that thousands of scientists have covered up the truth about the most important environmental issue of our time.[83]

The much derided "Western diet" that we are told is unhealthy and destructive for the environment is not a consequence of consumer choice, but is a result of corporate interests. Beef production on the US grasslands became closely associated with the production of grain. So profitable was the growing of grain for cattle feed, that from the late 1950s there was a drive to encourage more beef consumption. As Elaine Graham-Leigh has pointed out: "beef eating was so profitable that it was in companies' interests to ensure that US consumption remained high. Consumers may have felt they were making a free choice to eat hamburgers, but there was in fact a concerted effort to encourage them to do so".[84]

The choices that individuals make about food are very personal, but they are also shaped by the world that they live in. Processed food might be worse for the environment and your health, but for the parent returning home from a long shift it's a quick way to feed their children. Time is one factor, but so is the cost of food with junk food being cheaper per calorie than other options.[85]

This is not to say we should not criticise the meat industry for its impact on

---

82 Quoted in McMahon, 2013, p69.

83 Boucher, 2016.

84 Graham-Leigh, 2014, p56.

85 Graham-Leigh, 2014, p172.

the environment or our health. Questions of obesity and malnutrition are questions of class, as much as those of production. Elaine Graham-Leigh writes:

> An argument which says that the production of large amounts of nutrient-poor, energy-dense food in the West is problematic for food consumption worldwide and for the climate (and has a tendency to make some individuals become fatter than they would otherwise be) is a world away from one which says that regardless of the interests vested in that pattern of food production and consumption, the responsibility lies only with those people who become fat because of it.[86]

The struggle for a sustainable agriculture will simultaneously be a struggle for healthier diets, with a corresponding decrease in meat consumption for some, but an increase for others. Doing this sustainably will mean challenging the priorities of a food system which, because it is driven by profit not the need to feed people, can waste a third of food produced for human consumption, equivalent to more than half the world's annual cereal crops.[87] It means changing the energy intensive factory farming that currently dominates in the developed world which means that a tonne of maize grown in the US uses 160 litres of oil compared to less than 5 litres in Mexico.[88] It will also require an end to factory farming and the over-production of meat, which uses vast areas of land to grow livestock food, with an enormous impact on the environment, and promotes an unhealthy diet. Currently the cereals used to feed factory farmed animals could feed 3 billion people.[89]

Production under capitalism is not determined by need, or simply by consumer demand, but what is profitable; and the food industry is particularly adept at creating demand for its products. Fighting for sustainability in food and agriculture will not come by lecturing individuals demanding they stop buying meat products, but through a root and branch transformation of the food system itself.

The alternative

As we have seen, greenhouse gas emissions from agriculture could be significantly reduced even within the existing system. But whether or not farmers and agribusiness will find it worthwhile to invest in technology or change established practices to reduce environmental impacts will depend on incentives and their

86 Graham-Leigh, 2014, p17.

87 See the FAO's "Key Facts on Food Loss and Waste you Should Know!"—www.fao.org/save-food/resources/keyfindings/en/

88 Magdoff and Tokar, 2010, p65.

89 Lymbery, 2014, p253.

ability to maintain profits. As the FAO points out in regard to livestock farming, though it applies equally to other sectors of agriculture: "In the absence of financial incentives (eg mitigation subsidies) or regulations to limit emissions, most producers are unlikely to invest in mitigation practices unless they increase profits or provide other production benefits such as risk reduction".[90]

Creating a truly sustainable agriculture capable of feeding a growing world population through the 21st century will mean challenging the priorities of the world food system, the interests of agricultural big business and international bodies such as the World Bank. This will require political and economic struggles by the world's working class and peasantry.

One solution offered by some commentators is "biodiverse ecological farming". This means rejecting industrialised agriculture and encouraging small-scale farming. One of the leading proponents of this approach, Vandana Shiva, notes that "under globalisation, the farmer is losing her/his social, cultural and economic identity as a producer. A farmer is now a 'consumer' of costly seeds and costly chemicals sold by powerful global corporations through powerful landlords and moneylenders locally".[91]

Agriculture, as practised by millions of smallholders and peasant farmers in the developing world, can be more sustainable, and more efficient at feeding populations healthily and well. However, a longer-term vision for sustainable farming cannot simply be a return to smallholding farming on a global scale. This is not to dismiss peasant agriculture. Small farms are usually portrayed as being unproductive, but the opposite is true and they tend to have other benefits—a lower impact on the environment, lower use of fossil fuels, the promotion and protection of biodiversity, and greater resilience to storms and hurricanes.[92] Because smallholders avoid monoculture farming, they also produce more food per area than highly focused industrialised farming. However, this relies on the back-breaking work of peasant families. The working population in agriculture is about 1.3 billion people worldwide. A third of these rely on animal power and a further third use only manual tools. Thus some 400 million peasants feed a further 1 billion using only manual tools, without fertiliser, tractors, pesticides or livestock feed. This requires long hours of hard manual labour.[93]

As the German Marxist Karl Kautsky noted in his classic 1889 study *The Agrarian Question*, it would take "a very obdurate admirer of small-scale land ownership to see the advantages derived from forcing small cultivators down to the

90 Gerber and others, 2013, p60.

91 Quoted in Bello, 2009, pp35-36.

92 Altieri, 2009.

93 Mazoyer and Roudart, 2006, p13.

level of beasts of burden, into a life occupied by nothing other than work—apart from time set aside for sleeping and eating".[94]

There are, however, growing social movements among small and peasant farmers for greater control of land and their livelihoods. One recent comparative study of social movements in South and Central America concludes:

> For thousands of landless people in Brazil and for thousands of indigenous peasants in Chiapas, joining the MST [The Brazilian Landless Movement] or the EZLN [the Mexican Zapatista Army of National Liberation] is a profoundly life-changing experience. Casting their lot with the MST or the EZLN is a political experience that has allowed them to gain or protect their access to land and provide for their families. It is an experience that politicises them and generates a sense of individual and collective agency that throughout their lives they often felt they did not have.[95]

But these social movements are not enough to transform the global food system and its domination by big agribusiness. Doing this will require the development of wider alliances that can directly challenge the capitalist agriculture system.

As Miguel A Altieri has pointed out:

> Rural social movements understand that dismantling the industrial agri-food complex and restoring local food systems must be accompanied by the construction of agro-ecological alternatives that suit the needs of small-scale producers and the low-income non-farming population, and that oppose corporate control over production and consumption... Moving toward a more socially just, economically viable, and environmentally sound agriculture will be the result of the coordinated action of emerging social movements in the rural sector in alliance with civil society organisations that are committed to supporting the goals of these farmers' movements.[96]

Small farmers are locked into a wider global network of commodities, with capital tending to invest upstream and downstream in the supply of pesticides, genetically modified crops and equipment or in the distribution of food. In fact, the persistence of small-scale farmers and the peasantry is itself in part a result of the needs of a larger agricultural capitalism which needs their labour at specific times of the year, but requires them to subsist on their own smallholdings in between.[97] For millions of peasants there is no way out of this trap without fundamental changes to the economic system. In the developed world most farmers are

94 Kautsky, 1988, p111.
95 Vergara-Camus, 2014, p301.
96 Altieri, 2009, p112.
97 See Boltvinik, 2012.

no longer the smallholding producers they are traditionally seen as, but contractors servicing the bigger corporations and dependent on the whims of the supermarkets.[98] Breaking this cycle of poverty and hard labour means the transformation of agriculture, not the romanticisation of a particular form of peasant agriculture.

Conclusion

In his studies of the works of the German chemist Justus von Liebig, Karl Marx developed a critique of the unsustainable nature of agriculture under capitalism, closely linked to his concept of the metabolic rift. Marx argued that there could be a rational agriculture, but it would mean the transformation of production and land ownership. Under capitalism, "instead of a conscious and rational treatment of the land as permanent communal property, as the inalienable condition for the existence and reproduction of the chain of human generations, we have the exploitation and the squandering of the powers of the earth".[99]

In 1964 Tony Cliff wrote a self-described "revisionist" account: "Marxism and the Collectivisation of Agriculture". Cliff argued that the immediate impact of a socialist revolution would probably be to "give the private farm a new lease of life under the socialist regime". But the transformation of production would gradually undermine this:

> The socialist regime, by raising living standards all round, assuring security of employment, and comprehensive pensions for old age and sickness, will deflate the value of economic "independence" represented in the private ownership of the farm... Thus the organisation of agriculture in co-operative farms is bound to be an extremely slow process, impeded by some factors that are brought into play by the new socialist regime, not gaining much stimulation from the assumed decline of small farming under the technical superiority of the large ones. The process of the transition of agriculture from individual to collectivist methods will thus be the result of the abundance of wealth and culture in highly developed societies. Individual farming will not be overthrown, but sublimated.[100]

It is only agriculture like this, rooted in the collective ownership of the land and the means of production, that will be able to produce enough healthy food to feed the world in a sustainable way in the long term.

98 Thanks to Ian Rappel for this point.

99 Marx, 1992, pp948-949. It should be noted that here Marx criticises both "small-scale" and "large-scale" agriculture for this failing, but argues that they fail for different reasons. Small-scale farming is at fault because of "a lack of the resources and science needed to apply the social productive powers of labour", but in the case of large-scale agriculture it is because of the "exploitation of such means for the most rapid enrichment of farmer and proprietor".

100 Cliff, 1964.

References

Adonizio, Will, Nancy Kook and Sharon Royales, 2012, "Impact of the Drought on Corn Exports: Paying the Price", *Beyond the Numbers* (US Bureau of Labor Statistics), volume 1, number 17, www.bls.gov/opub/btn/volume-1/pdf/impact-of-the-drought-on-corn-exports-paying-the-price.pdf

Altieri, Miguel A, 2009, "Agroecology, Small Farms and Food Sovereignty", *Monthly Review*, volume 61, issue 3, www.monthlyreview.org/2009/07/01/agroecology-small-farms-and-food-sovereignty/

Bello, Walden, 2009, *The Food Wars* (Verso).

Boltvinik, Julio, 2012, "Poverty and the Persistence of the Peasantry", background paper, Poverty and Peasant Persistence in the Contemporary World seminar (March), www.crop.org/viewfile.aspx?id=261

Boucher, Doug, 2016, "There's a Vast Cowspiracy about Climate Change", Union of Concerned Scientists, http://blog.ucsusa.org/doug-boucher/cowspiracy-movie-review

Chivers, Danny, 2016, "Cowspiracy: Stampeding in the Wrong Direction?", New Internationalist Blog, http://tinyurl.com/gm665so

Cliff, Tony, 1964, "Marxism and the Collectivisation of Agriculture", *International Socialism 19* (first series, winter 1964-5), www.marxists.org/archive/cliff/works/1964/xx/

DEFRA, 2015a, "2013 UK Greenhouse Gas Emissions, Final Figures" (February), www.gov.uk/government/uploads/system/uploads/attachment_data/file/407432/20150203_2013_Final_Emissions_statistics.pdf

DEFRA, 2015b, "Agricultural Statistics and Climate Change, 6th edition" (July), www.gov.uk/government/uploads/system/uploads/attachment_data/file/476879/agriclimate-6edition-13nov15.pdf

Empson, Martin, 2014, *Land and Labour: Marxism, Ecology and Human History* (Bookmarks).

Ensor, Sarah, 2016, "Two Books That Swim Against the Tide", *International Socialism 150* (spring), http://isj.org.uk/two-books-that-swim-against-the-tide/

Foster, John Bellamy, Brett Clark and Richard York, 2010, *The Ecological Rift: Capitalism's War on the Earth* (Monthly Review Press).

Foster, John Bellamy, and Brett Clark, 2016, "Marx's Ecology and the Left", *Monthly Review* (June), http://monthlyreview.org/2016/06/01/marxs-ecology-and-the-left/

Gerber, Pierre, Henning Steinfeld, Benjamin Henderson, Anne Mottet, Carolyn Opio, Jeroen Dijkman, Alessandra Falcucci and Giuseppe Tempio, 2013, "Tackling Climate Change Through Livestock: A Global Assessment of Emissions and Mitigation Opportunities", FAO, www.fao.org/3/i3437e.pdf

Goodland, Robert, and Jeff Anhang, 2009, "Livestock and Climate Change", *World Watch Magazine*, volume 22, number 6 (November-December), www.worldwatch.org/node/6294

Graham-Leigh, Elaine, 2014, *A Diet of Austerity: Class, Food and Climate Change* (Zero Books).

Hashmi, Imran, and Dilshad A Khan, 2011, "Adverse Health Effects of Pesticides Exposure in Agricultural and Industrial Workers of Developing Country", in Margarita Stoytcheva (ed), *Pesticides: The Impacts of Pesticide Exposure*, http://tinyurl.com/zjt94sw

Ince, Martin, 2014, "The Case for Low Methane-emitting Cattle" (10 January), http://tinyurl.com/z7b3a7j

IPCC, 2014, *Climate Change 2014: Mitigation of Climate Change, Fifth Assessment Report* (Cambridge University Press), www.ipcc.ch/report/ar5/wg3/

Jones, Sam, 2014, "Tropical Forests Illegally Destroyed for Commercial Agriculture", *Guardian* (11 September), http://tinyurl.com/lthlluv

Kautsky, Karl, 1988, *The Agrarian Question*,

volume 1 (Zwan Publications).
Klein, Naomi, 2015, *This Changes Everything: Capitalism vs the Climate* (Penguin).
Lymbery, Philip, 2014, *Farmageddon: The True Cost of Cheap Meat* (Bloomsbury).
Magdoff, Fred, and Brian Tokar, 2010, *Agriculture and Food in Crisis: Conflict, Resistance, and Renewal* (Monthly Review Press).
Marx, Karl, 1990, *Capital*, Volume 1 (Penguin).
Marx, Karl, 1992, *Capital*, Volume 3 (Penguin).
Mazoyer, Marcel, and Laurence Roudart, 2006, *A History of World Agriculture: From the Neolithic Age to the Current Crisis* (Monthly Review Press).
McMahon, Paul, 2013, *Feeding Frenzy: The New Politics of Food* (Profile).
Paarlberg, Robert, 2013, *Food Politics: What Everyone Needs to Know* (Oxford University Press).
Pollack, Henry, 2010, *A World Without Ice* (Penguin).
Philpott, Tom, 2014a, "Are Your Delicious, Healthy Almonds Killing Bees?" *Mother Jones* (29 April), www.motherjones.com/tom-philpott/2014/04/california-almond-farms-blamed-honeybee-die
Philpott, Tom, 2014b, "Your Almond Habit is Sucking California Dry", *Mother Jones* (14 July), www.motherjones.com/tom-philpott/2014/07/your-almond-habit-sucking-califoirnia-dry
Rainforest Action Network (RAN), 2014, "Pressure is Working, Cargill is on the Move" (29 July), www.ran.org/pressure_is_working_cargill_is_on_the_move
Saito, Kohei, 2014, "The Emergence of Marx's Critique of Modern Agriculture: Ecological Insights from his Excerpt Notebooks", *Monthly Review* (October) http://monthlyreview.org/2014/10/01/the-emergence-of-marxs-critique-of-modern-agriculture/
Shiva, Vandana, 2014, *The Vandana Shiva Reader* (Kentucky University Press).
Steinfeld, Henning, Pierre Gerber, Tom Wassenaar, Vincent Castel, Mauricio Rosales, Cees de Haan, 2006, "Livestock's Long Shadow: Environmental Issues and Options", UN Food and Agriculture Organisation (November), www.fao.org/docrep/010/a0701e/a0701e00.HTM
Tubiello, F N, M Salvatore, R D Cóndor Golec, A Ferrara, S Rossi, R Biancalani, S Federici, 2014, "Agriculture, Forestry and Other Land Use Emissions by Sources and Removals by Sinks", UN Food and Agriculture Organisation (March), www.fao.org/docrep/019/i3671e/i3671e.pdf
Tudge, Colin, 2011, *Good Food for Everyone Forever: A People's Takeover of the World's Food Supply* (Pari Publishing).
USGCRP, 2016, *The Impacts of Climate Change on Human Health in the United States: A Scientific Assessment* (US Global Change Research Program).
Vergara-Camus, Leandro, 2014, *Land and Freedom: The MST, the Zapatistas and Peasant Alternatives to Neoliberalism* (Zed Books).
Vermeulen, Sonja J, Bruce M Campbell and John S I Ingram, 2012, "Climate Change and Food Systems", *Annual Review of Environment and Resources*, volume 37.

Real capitalism: turbulent and antagonistic, but not imperfect

Michael Roberts

A review of *Capitalism: Competition, Conflict, Crises*
Anwar Shaikh
Oxford University Press (2016), £35.99

Anwar Shaikh is one of the world's leading economists who draws on Karl Marx and the classical economists ("political economy", if you like). He has taught at New York's New School for Social Research for more than 30 years, and authored three books and six dozen articles.[1] This is his most ambitious work. As Shaikh says, it is an attempt to derive economic theory from the real world and then apply it to real problems. He applies the categories and theory of classical economics to all the major economic issues, including those that are supposed to be the province of mainstream economics, like supply and demand, relative prices in goods and services, interest rates, financial asset prices and technological change.

A classical approach

Shaikh says that his approach "is very different from both orthodox economics and the dominant heterodox tradition".[2] It is the classical approach as opposed to the

1 Go to www.newschool.edu/nssr/faculty/?id=4e54-6b79-4d77-3d3d

2 Shaikh, 2016, p4.

neoclassical one. In other words, he rejects the approach that starts from "perfect firms, perfect individuals, perfect knowledge, perfectly selfish behaviour, rational expectations, etc" and then "various imperfections are introduced into the story to justify individual observed patterns" although there "cannot be a general theory of imperfections". Instead Shaikh starts with actual human behaviour instead of the so-called "economic man", and with the concept of "real competition" rather than "perfect competition". This is emphasised in Chapters 3, 7 and 8 in particular.

However, unlike the recent effort of Ben Fine and Ourania Dimakou in their two-volume *Microeconomics* and *Macroeconomics*, Shaikh does not conduct a critique of mainstream orthodox economics as such.[3] Rather he aims to present a completely alternative economic approach, which he calls "classical", following the tradition of the first political economists of industrial capitalism, Adam Smith, David Ricardo and Karl Marx.

The book is a product of 15 years work, so it has taken longer to gestate than Marx took from 1855 to 1867 to deliver volume one of *Capital*. But it covers a lot. All theory is compared to actual data in every chapter, as well as to neoclassical and Keynesian/post-Keynesian arguments. Shaikh develops a theory of "real competition" and applies it to explain empirical relative prices, profit margins and profit rates, interest rates, bond and stock prices, exchange rates and trade balances. Demand and supply are both shown to depend on profitability and interact in a way that is neither Say's Law nor Keynesian, but based on the classical theory of value. A classical theory of inflation is developed and applied to various countries. A theory of crises is developed and integrated into macrodynamics.

That's a heap of things. But readers can follow in detail Shaikh's arguments through a series of 21 video lectures that cover each chapter of the book.[4] These can be quite technical in part, but are worth the effort of concentration. See Lecture 15 in particular for Shaikh's overall summary of capitalism. There are also short interviews with Shaikh on the main message of his book, all nicely compiled by Shaikh on his website.[5]

There are two basic pivots to his "classical" approach. Firstly, the profit motive, not making things or carrying out services, is seen as the driving force of capitalism: "Capital is a particular social form of wealth driven by the profit motive. With this incentive comes a corresponding drive for expansion, for the conversion of capital into more capital, of profit into more profit".[6]

3 Fine, 2016; Fine and Dimakou, 2016. See also Roberts, 2016a, and my forthcoming review of both books in *International Socialist Review*, fall 2016.

4 Go to www.hgsss.org/anwar-m-shaikh-capitalism-competition-conflict-and-crises/

5 Go to http://realecon.org/

6 Shaikh, 2016, p259.

Secondly, the capitalist economy should not be viewed as a "perfect" market economy with accompanying "imperfections", but as individual capitals in competition to gain profit and market share. Monopoly should not be counterposed to competition, as neoclassical, orthodox, and even some Marxist economists do. Real competition is a struggle to lower costs per unit of output in order to gain more profit and market share. In the real world, there are capitals with varying degrees of monopoly power competing and continually changing as monopoly power is lost with new entrants to the market and new technology that cuts costs. Real competition is an unending struggle for monopoly power (dominant market share) that never succeeds in total or forever: "each individual capital operates under this imperative...this is *real competition*, antagonistic by nature and turbulent in operation. It is as different from so-called perfect competition as war is from ballet".[7]

A theory of value: classical or Marxist?

Shaikh's work, with his analysis of crises under capitalism and his avowed support for Marx's theory of value, has usually been considered as part of the Marxist tradition. But it is no accident that Shaikh does not want to be called a Marxist economist or for his *Capitalism* to be seen as a modern Marxist critique following Marx's own similarly titled work (although Marx never used the word "capitalism", only "capital"). Instead Shaikh subsumes Marxist theory into classical theory and attempts to bridge the gap between Marxist economic analysis and that of the major classical economist of modern capitalism, David Ricardo,[8] along with the theories of Piero Sraffa, the 20th century "neo-Ricardian".

Sraffa's aim was similar to Shaikh's: to draw on and reconcile Ricardo's theoretical constructs with those of Marx. But the reality was that Sraffa dropped a theory of value (what things are worth and priced at) that was based on the labour time involved in producing them and instead went backwards into measuring things (and services?) by the physical amount of commodities and inputs that go into a new product. Thus Sraffa's key work is not for nothing called *The Production of Commodities by Means of Commodities*.[9]

Sraffa breaks entirely with Marx's theory of value and as a result is really unable to explain the nature of capitalist production as a process of exploitation for profit initiated by the input of money capital to employ labour to produce commodities that make more money. For Marx, the capitalist production process is M–C–P–C'–M' (where "M" stands for money, "C" for commodity, and "P" for

7 Shaikh, 2016, p259.

8 Ricardo, 2004.

9 Sraffa, 1960.

production, where labour is put to work). Thus money makes more money (value) but only because of labour expended to create more value. Sraffa's process is C–C'. For Sraffa, the role of labour disappears—it is just another "commodity".

Marx greatly valued the work of Smith and Ricardo for their objective recognition that only labour creates value. But he was highly critical of their failure to see that through systemically. Smith was illogical. With one hand, he recognised that labour created value, but when he came to calculate value in a national economy, he reckoned that value should be added up from wages for labour, profits from capital and rents from land. And the underlying source of value was subsumed, while the accumulated capital used up in fixed assets and raw materials was ignored.

Marx exposed Ricardo's failure to explain how prices for individual commodities differed from the labour time going into them. The answer of Sraffa and the neo-Ricardians was to drop the labour theory of value; Marx's solution was to show that values of commodities are transformed into prices of production by the equalisation of profit rates across the economy through competition among individual capitals. Thus total value in an economy would equal total prices, but individual values would diverge from individual prices, depending on the size and composition of the capital invested and the average rate of profit.

Shaikh knows this and is very vocal in his theoretical and empirical analysis in the book to show that Marx's solution was right and provides the best understanding of the movement of prices in the capitalist economy. But he also adopts a version of the Sraffian production process that cannot be reconciled with Marx and, more important, which fails to provide a logical explanation of capitalist production.

Fred Moseley, in his excellent new book, *Money and Totality*, provides an analysis of Marx's logic in *Capital* and his method of transforming value embedded in commodities into prices in the market.[10] Moseley takes up the contradiction in Shaikh's position. In earlier works Shaikh argued that, by a multi-step "iterative" process (that he reckoned Marx also used), total value can eventually equal total prices, although total surplus value in an economy will not equal total profit (contrary to Marx) unless we add in profit held by capitalist households outside the production process. So Shaikh starts with Sraffa's approach of profit as "surplus product" and tries to deliver the Marxist transformation of values into prices—unsuccessfully in Moseley's view.

It is interesting to find that in Shaikh's *Capitalism*, the "iterative solution" has been replaced by one based on another classical economist, James Steuart,[11] and

10 Moseley, 2015. See also Roberts, 2016b.

11 Shaikh, 2016, pp221-224. Steuart was also discussed by Marx in part one of *Theories of Surplus Value*—Marx, 1863.

on another revisionist "new interpretation" proposed by Marxist economists Gerard Duménil and Duncan Foley,[12] which in Moseley's view (and that of Andrew Kliman[13]) also fails to interpret Marx correctly. Shaikh, unnecessarily in my view, adopts Steuart's "crucial insight" that there are "two sources of aggregate profit, profit on production and profit on transfer". This is clearly contradictory to Marx's own transformation of values into profit, where there is only one source of profit: surplus value in production.

This all sounds complicated—does it matter that Shaikh attempts to reconcile Marx's theory of value with that of Steuart and the neo-Ricardian Sraffa? Well, yes and no. The prodigious empirical work by Shaikh in many chapters of *Capitalism* appears to follow Marxist categories and delivers compelling support for the Marxist economic analysis of capitalism over the mainstream approach. For example, Shaikh delivers deep empirical evidence to back up his theory of real competition leading to an equalisation of profit rates across sectors, as Marx argued, over cycles of "fat and lean years".[14] This leads to a critique not only of mainstream theory à la Paul Samuelson[15] that profit rates will rise with new technology, but also of the neo-Ricardian theory of Nobuo Okishio[16] and of Sraffa.[17]

On the other hand, if Marx's value theory is superseded by classical theory or "corrected" by neo-Ricardians, it opens the door to a rejection of exploitation for profit as the underlying driver of capitalism (which Shaikh holds to, but Smith, Ricardo and Sraffa did not), and undermines Marx's theory of crisis, based on his law of the tendency of the rate of profit to fall. Indeed, Marx's law is never spelt out in the 759 pages of *Capitalism*. And the term, the "organic composition of capital", is never used in explaining how profitability moves under capitalism. So we get an interesting, if ambiguous, suggestion that the empirically falling rate of profit can be explained "in neoclassical terms, as a falling average productivity of capital", in Marxist terms as due to rising "money ratio of constant capital to living labour" and in Sraffian terms as a reduction in the maximum rate of profit (surplus product).[18] But which is the right explanation?

Empirical backing

Moreover, Shaikh attempts to verify empirically the Ricardian argument that prices of individual commodities equal their values in labour time by showing

12 Foley, 1982; Moseley, 2015.

13 Kliman, 2006.

14 Shaikh, 2016, pp301-313.

15 Samuelson, 1957.

16 Okishio, 1961.

17 Shaikh, 2016, p320, note 36.

18 Shaikh, 2016, p251.

Figure 1: The US rate of profit: Shaikh and Roberts.

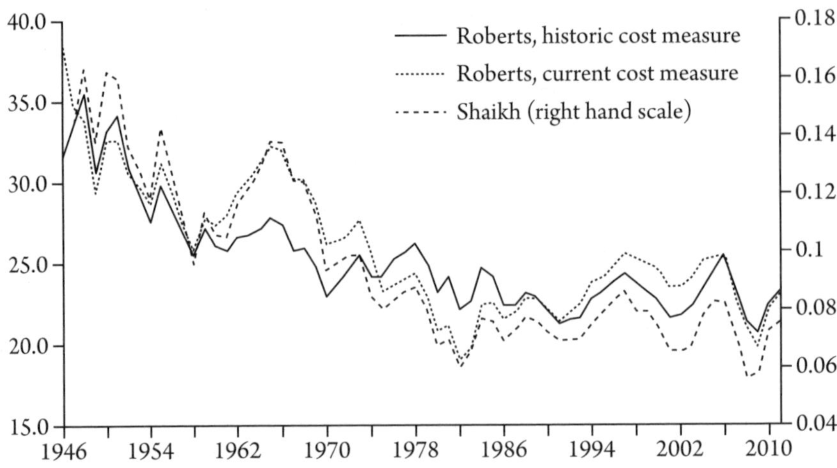

Source: Author's calculations.

that empirically they nearly do; they are only 7 percent out.[19] This is an interesting observation that has been attacked by others.[20] Trying to reconcile the Sraffian transformation of prices with Marx's values to prices leads to an attempt empirically to say that total profits are "nearly" equal to total value (by just 1.6 percent).[21] Thus, according to Shaikh, "the real difference between Marx's and Sraffa's prices is [just—MR] one of the degree of sensitivity".[22]

Nevertheless, Shaikh is keen to measure the profitability of capital à la Marx because he recognises that it is essential in understanding booms and slumps (and longer waves) under capitalism. So he measures profit and capital (in the United States) with care and precision.[23] He makes some important adjustments to the official (US Department of Commerce) data by adding in interest to corporate profit and widening the definition of capital to include inventories and adjusting more accurately for depreciation. The result is that Shaikh confirms what many others before (including him) have shown—the profitability of corporate capital in the US has been in secular decline since the end of the Second

19 Shaikh, 2016, pp413-416.
20 See Kliman, 2006.
21 Shaikh, 2016, p433.
22 Shaikh, 2016, p437, note 18.
23 Shaikh, 2016, pp243-256.

World War with only a moderate stabilisation or recovery from the early 1980s in the so-called neoliberal era.[24]

In best modern practice, like Thomas Piketty with his book with a similar title (but an entirely different objective and method), *Capital in the Twenty-First Century*, Shaikh provides all the data used and worked up in the book online for others to follow and/or replicate.[25] I ran Shaikh's data for the US rate of profit against my own calculations (which use different assumptions, which is why the actual rate of profit differs)—see figure 1. Shaikh uses current cost measures of fixed capital contrary to the view of Kliman (and myself) who use historic costs.[26] But either way the story is much the same; there is a secular decline in US post-war profitability, but with a limited recovery from the 1980s. So perhaps you could argue that the obscure debate over value theory becomes less important when pitched against real data and results.

Exposing the neoclassical and the heterodox

Shaikh takes up every aspect of the capitalist process and in doing so provides Marxist (sorry, classical) answers to the confusions and failures of mainstream economics. For example, his critique of Ricardo's theory of comparative advantage as a justification for "free trade" benefiting all despite the obvious evidence to the contrary is terrific. In the US the big losers from the current wave of globalisation have been the working class, as Branko Milanovic of the City University of New York details in his new book, *Global Inequality*.[27] Jobs will go as more efficient economies take trade share from the less efficient and with open markets (no tariffs and special restriction or quotas).

But the idea that "free trade" is beneficial to all countries and to all classes is a sacred tenet of mainstream economics. In Chapter 11 Shaikh analyses in detail the fallacious proposition that if each country concentrated on producing goods or services where it has a "comparative advantage" over others (and therefore lower "comparative costs"), then all would benefit. Trading between countries would balance and wages and employment would be maximised. Shaikh shows that this is not only demonstrably untrue (countries run huge trade deficits and surpluses for long periods, have recurring currency crises, and workers lose jobs to competition from abroad without getting new ones from more competitive sectors). Shaikh also explains why it is not comparative advantage or costs that drive trade, but the absolute costs. If Chinese labour costs are much lower than American

24 See Roberts, 2015a.

25 Go to http://realecon.org/data

26 See Roberts, 2011, and Basu, 2012.

27 Milanovic, 2016; see also Milanovic's website at http://glineq.blogspot.co.uk/

companies' labour costs in any market, then China will gain market share, even if America has some so-called "comparative advantage". What really decides is the productivity level and growth in an economy and the cost of labour:"free trade will lead to persistent trade surpluses for countries whose capitals have lower costs and persistent trade deficits for those whose capitals have higher costs".[28]

Although Shaikh's *Capitalism* is not a critique of heterodox economic theory, at various places he delivers powerful blows not just to neoclassical theory but also to those heterodox and Marxist analyses that start by accepting the neoclassical view of "perfect competition" as "adequate to some earlier stage of capitalism" and "the necessary point of departure" for an "ever-accreting list of real world deviations" and then seek to amend it.

In particular, Shaikh's criticisms of post-Keynesian economics, currently the dominant view of leftists in the labour movement internationally, and of the *Monthly Review* school of "monopoly capitalism", are persuasive.[29] He notes that the MR school considers competition as equivalent to "perfect competition", thus ruling out capitalism as competitive and leaving us with monopoly capitalism. It's as though there "was an imaginary golden age of perfect competition that at some time somehow metamorphosed itself into the monopolistic age, whereas it is quite clear that perfect competition has at no time been any more of a reality than it is at present".[30]

As Shaikh retorts, the model of the MR school "is not true".[31] "The vision of competition to which the Marxian monopoly capitalism school pledges its allegiance was never valid, not then and not now...and this fact seems to have escaped them entirely". In the imaginary mode of perfect competition, prices are set for firms; and under the equally imaginary polar opposite, firms are price setters.[32] But this is contrary to a Marxist view of real competition "where firms always set prices" and there is a "turbulent equalisation of long-run rates of return of the price leaders".[33] Thus "disorder is its order".[34]

Similarly, post Keynesian economics seems to depend at the outset on the imaginary model of "perfect competition". Prices are costs plus a mark-up and that mark-up depends on the degree of monopolisation.[35] Thus post-Keynesian authors argue that price-setting is a symptom of monopoly power. Shaikh

28 Shaikh, 2016, p514.
29 Shaikh, 2016, p355.
30 Schumpeter, 1947, p40.
31 Shaikh, 2016, p356.
32 Shaikh, 2016, p363.
33 Shaikh, 2016, p363.
34 Marx, 1847.
35 Shaikh, 2016, p360.

counterposes that with real competition whereby firms "always set prices".[36] So capitalism has not changed its spots; the enemy is not monopoly power as such but capitalism, which is still the same leopard.

Shaikh argues that the failure of heterodox theory to start with real competition but merely try to counterpose perfect competition with monopoly also leads to wrong macroeconomic policy: "what neoclassical economics promises through the workings of the invisible hand of the market, Keynesian and post-Keynesian economics promise through the visible hand of the state".[37]

On the macroeconomic front, Shaikh consummately dismisses the post-Keynesian argument that it is the change in the *share* of wages and profits that matters for crises and not the *production* of profit. And he dismisses the post-Keynesian view that investment depends on the "expectations" of entrepreneurs or on the expectation of future profits rather than profitability when investment was undertaken or even in some preceding period: "the present is not independent of the past. Just as the future is not independent of the present".[38] Indeed, Shaikh reckons that profitability is "the appropriate foundation for Keynes's theory"—an argument that is a stretch, in my view.[39]

Shaikh shows sympathy with George Soros's theory of "reflexivity", which assumes that the expectation of profit can affect the actual profit as investment takes place assuming a certain return, only for that expectation to be brought "crashing down to earth" so that the expected rate of profit "fluctuates in a turbulent manner around the mutually constructed center of gravity".[40]

Shaikh also delivers his verdict on Thomas Piketty's rival book on capitalism: "Piketty's measure of the rate of profit is logically inconsistent." He excludes capital gains in his profit measure but adds in residential property in his fixed capital. This makes his rate of profit too low and "highly susceptible to fluctuations in the market value of assets".[41] This is similar to the critique presented by me and others that Piketty's so-called stable rate of return is really a return on financial assets and not on productive ones.[42]

Profitability and cycles

For me, Shaikh's book takes off when he deals with the nature of the current economic stage through which capitalism is passing. Shaikh reckons that, on

36 Shaikh, 2016, p363.
37 Shaikh, 2016, p235.
38 Shaikh, 2016, p594-595.
39 Shaikh, 2016, p745, and Roberts, 2013a.
40 Shaikh, 2016, p608.
41 Shaikh, 2016, p759.
42 Roberts, 2015b.

the surface, the last crisis—the Great Recession—might look like a crisis of excessive financialisation. But this fails to identify the real cause of the crisis. Keynesians and post-Keynesians argue that the cause of the current crisis is rising inequality and falling wages, so there is a need to maintain a stable wage share and to use fiscal and monetary policy to maintain full employment. But Shaikh argues that such policies would not work because, at least in the US, the post-Keynesians have got the causes of the crisis wrong. The real cause is the movement in profitability—the dominant factor under capitalism.

The crisis was preceded by a long fall in the rate of profit. The neoliberal attack on labour from the 1980s suppressed wage growth and reduced the wage share in order to stabilise the rate of profit. And the enormous fall in the interest rate in the 1980s that fuelled credit expansion and massive debt finance also served to raise the net (or enterprise) rate of profit. So Keynesian fiscal policy by itself may pump up employment, but it will not restore growth. For growth it is necessary to raise the net rate of profit—and interest rates are already at record lows (and even negative).

Shaikh emphasises that it is profit under capitalism that drives growth. There are cyclical fluctuations in profitability which are expressed in business and fixed capital cycles inherent in capitalist production. The history of market systems reveals recurrent patterns of booms and busts over centuries, emanating precisely from the developed world—crises are normal in capitalism. The key crises under capitalism are "depressions", such as that of the 1840s, the "Long Depression" of 1873-1893, the "Great Depression" of the 1930s, the "Stagflation Crises" of the 1970s and the Great Global Crisis now.

Shaikh revives the concept of long waves in capitalist production, something first identified by the Russian economist Nikolai Kondratieff and which Shaikh first cited in a paper in 1992.[43] In that paper, according to Shaikh, Kondratieff's main point is that business cycles are recurrent and "organically inherent" in the capitalist system. They are also inherently nonlinear and turbulent: "the process of real dynamics is of a piece. But it is not linear: it does not take the form of a simple, rising line. To the contrary, its movement is irregular, with spurts and fluctuations."

Kondratieff believed that depressions were linked to long waves: "during the period of downward waves of the long cycle, years of depression predominate; while during the period of rising waves of a long cycle, it is years of upswing that predominate". In a paper that Shaikh presented in 2014, he brought up to date his analysis of this, which is also developed in *Capitalism*.[44]

---

43 Shaikh, 1992.

44 Shaikh, 2014; Shaikh, 2016, pp724-745.

Table 1: Kondratieff cycles and profit cycles

	Profit cycles	
K-cycle 1 (58 years) 1786-1815: peak 1815-1844: trough	1785-1802	spring: up
	1802-1815	summer: down
	1815-1830	autumn: up
	1830-1844	winter: down
K-cycle 2 (48 years) 1844-1871: peak 1871-1892: trough	1844-1849	spring: up
	1849-1859	summer: down
	1859-1871	autumn: up
	1871-1892	winter: down
K-cycle 3 (54 years) 1892-1920: peak 1920-1946: trough	1892-1899	spring: up
	1899-1918	summer: down
	1918-1929	autumn: up
	1929-1946	winter: down
K-cycle 4 (72 years) 1946-1982: peak 1982-2018? trough	1946-1965	spring: up
	1965-1982	summer: down
	1982-1997	autumn: up
	1997-2018?	winter: down

Source: Roberts, 2016c.

Shaikh reckons Kondratieff's long waves have continued to operate, and that this is especially clear when measured by the gold dollar price, the key value measure in modern capitalism. He reckons that prices of commodities became a poor indicator of Kondratieff cycles in the post-war period of the 20th century and now looks to the gold price. Shaikh presents a graph of these waves as measured by the gold price of commodities.[45]

In my analysis, first outlined in my book *The Great Recession*, I found that the movement of interest rates also provides a very good proxy indicator of Kondratieff waves because it follows the movement in production prices. Kondratieff waves can also be synchronised with profit waves or cycles as in table 1.[46]

So Shaikh's position is similar to my own on the causes of capitalist crises, the nature and existence of depressions, and the role of Kondratieff and profit cycles.[47] It is no accident that both of us made reasonably early (and independent)

45 Shaikh, 2016, p727, figure 16.1.

46 Roberts, 2009.

47 Roberts, 2013b.

predictions of the Great Recession of 2008-9. Shaikh made his as early as 2003; I did so in 2005, when I said:

> There has not been such a coincidence of cycles since 1991. And this time (unlike 1991), it will be accompanied by the downwave in profitability within the downwave in Kondratieff prices cycle. It is all at the bottom of the hill in 2009-2010! That suggests we can expect a very severe economic slump of a degree not seen since 1980-82 or more.[48]

From *Capital* to *Capitalism*

Shaikh summarises his main theme "which is that theory is important to an understanding of the economy".[49] He says he has taken a "different path" from modern mainstream neoclassical economics and heterodox alternatives like post-Keynesianism. They start from perfect competition as the model and then arrive at reality by "throwing a bucketful of grits" in the machinery of that model. Shaikh says he starts from a theory of "real competition" and uses it to ground theories of aggregate demand and persistent unemployment with profitability playing the dominant role. He has backed up his analysis with the "relevant empirical evidence" to focus on the real patterns of this "turbulent and dynamic system" that is capitalism. This approach is to be commended even if Shaikh's own theory may have some shaky areas.

Capitalism is a book for economists and brave activists who want to get a bigger grip on the underlying processes of capitalism. It is a monster of a book (even more than Piketty's), it is not easy to read (even Marx's *Capital* is easier, in my view) and it can be very technical. The book covers a lot of ground on economic theory and empirical analysis, perhaps sometimes with a little too much repetition (and there are some editing and data errors—understandable in such a large book and with such detail). But those readers who stick to the task will be rewarded with new insights into the capitalist process and insightful critiques of mainstream and heterodox arguments. If you cannot "wade" through the whole book, at least read the opening introduction to whet your appetite and the comprehensive summary and conclusions.[50]

Next year will be the 200th anniversary of David Ricardo's main work of political economy, which laid the theoretical foundations for the classical tradition that Shaikh adheres to in *Capitalism*. But it will also be 150 years since Karl Marx published volume one of his *Capital: A Critique of Political Economy*. Last

48 Roberts, 2009.

49 Shaikh, 2016, p745.

50 Shaikh, 2016, pp3-56 and pp746-759.

year we had the opus from Thomas Piketty that became a bestseller and replaced Stephen Hawking's *A Brief History of Time* as the most bought but least read book ever.[51] This year Anwar Shaikh's *Capitalism* will get less media praise, but it will be read much more than Piketty's, even if Marx's *Capital* still remains the most prescient analysis of the capitalist mode of production.

51 Roland, 2014.

References

Basu, 2012, "Replacement versus Historical Cost Profit Rates: What is the Difference? When Does it Matter?" (4 January), https://thenextrecession.files.wordpress.com/2012/11/basu-on-rc-versus-hc.pdf

Fine, Ben, 2016, *Microeconomics: A Critical Companion* (Pluto Press).

Fine, Ben, and Ourania Dimakou, 2016, *Macroeconomics: A Critical Companion* (Pluto Press).

Foley, Duncan, 1982, "The Value of Money the Value of Labor Power and the Marxian Transformation Problem", *Review of Radical Political Economics*, volume 14, number 2.

Kliman, Andrew, 2006, *Reclaiming Marx's "Capital": A Refutation of the Myth of Inconsistency* (Lexington Books).

Marx, Karl, 1847, "Wage Labour and Capital", in Robert C Tucker (ed), *The Marx-Engels Reader* (W W Norton).

Marx, Karl, 1863, *Theories of Surplus Value* (Progress Publishers), www.marxists.org/archive/marx/works/1863/theories-surplus-value/

Milanovic, Branko, 2016, *Global Inequality: A New Approach for the Age of Globalization* (Harvard University Press).

Moseley, Fred, 2015, *Money and Totality: A Macro-Monetary Interpretation of Marx's Logic in Capital and the End of the "Transformation Problem"* (Brill).

Okishio, Nobuo, 1961, "Technical Change and the Rate of Profit, *Kobe University Economic Review*, number 7.

Ricardo, David, 2004 [1817], *The Principles of Political Economy and Taxation* (Dover Publications).

Roberts, Michael, 2009, *The Great Recession: Profit Cycles, Economic Crisis—A Marxist View* (Lulu Enterprises).

Roberts, Michael, 2011, "Measuring the Rate of Profit; Profit Cycles and the Next Recession", paper presented to the 13th conference of the Association for Heterodox Economics" (July), http://gesd.free.fr/mrobprof.pdf

Roberts, Michael, 2013a, "The Contributions of Keynes and Marx to Understanding the Crisis and Finding Solutions", speech at the Anti-Capitalist Initiative Summer School (August), https://thenextrecession.files.wordpress.com/2013/08/contributions-of-keynes-and-marx.pdf

Roberts, Michael, 2013b, "Cycles in Capitalism", paper presented to the 15th conference of the Association for Heterodox Economics (July), https://thenextrecession.files.wordpress.com/2013/07/cycles-in-capitalism.pdf

Roberts, Michael, 2015a, "The US Rate of Profit Revisited" (20 December), https://thenextrecession.wordpress.com/2015/12/20/the-us-rate-of-profit-revisited/

Roberts, Michael, 2015b, "Unpicking Piketty", Paper to SASE Conference (July), https://thenextrecession.files.wordpress.com/2015/06/unpicking-piketty-sase.pdf

Roberts, Michael, 2016a, "Modelling the Mainstream by Fine and Rodrik"

(10 June), https://thenextrecession.wordpress.com/2016/06/10/modelling-the-mainstream-by-fine-and-rodrik/

Roberts, Michael, 2016b, "Fred Moseley and Marx's Macro-monetary Theory" (29 April), https://thenextrecession.wordpress.com/2016/04/29/fred-moseley-and-marxs-macro-monetary-theory/

Roberts, Michael, 2016c, "Capitalism and Anwar Shaikh" (4 April), https://thenextrecession.wordpress.com/2016/04/04/capitalism-and-anwar-shaikh/

Roland, Denise, 2014, "Has Anyone Finished Thomas Piketty's Capital in the 21st Century?", *Telegraph* (7 July), www.telegraph.co.uk/finance/economics/10951407/Has-anyone-finished-Thomas-Pikettys-Capital-in-the-21st-Century.html

Samuelson, Paul A, 1957, "Wages and Interest: A Modern Dissection of Marxian Economic Models", *The American Economic Review*, volume 47, number 6.

Schumpeter, Joseph, 1947, *Capitalism, Socialism and Democracy* (Harper and Brothers).

Shaikh, Anwar, 1992, "The Falling Rate of Profit as the Cause of Long-waves: Theory and Empirical Evidence", in Alfred, Klienknecht, Ernest Mandel and Immanuel Wallerstein (eds), *New Findings in Long-wave Research* (Palgrave Macmillan), https://thenextrecession.files.wordpress.com/2016/04/shaikh92w.pdf

Shaikh, Anwar, 2014, "Profitability, Long Waves and the Recurrence of General Crises", paper presented at the International Initiative for Promoting Political Economy Conference (September), https://thenextrecession.files.wordpress.com/2016/04/profitability-long-waves-crises-2.pdf

Shaikh, Anwar, 2016, *Capitalism: Competition, Conflict, Crises* (Oxford University Press).

Sraffa, Piero, 1960, *Production of Commodities by Means of Commodities: Prelude to a Critique of Economic Theory* (Cambridge University Press).

Hungary 1956: a socialist revolution

G M Tamás

We tend to forget the importance of the experience of people participating in historical events. The mainstream political literature presents 1945 in Eastern Europe as a Russian occupation that gradually forced a rootless system on a reluctant and recalcitrant population who obeyed out of fear. But almost nobody seems to have taken the pain to explain why even conservative or monarchist contemporaries called 1945 not only "liberation" but "revolution". The new system—at the beginning pluralist and democratic—found in Hungary tens of thousands of surviving volunteers of the Red Army in 1919 and hundreds of thousands of participants of the 1919 revolution and of the Council Republic, hundreds of thousands of trade unionists trained by the slightly rigid and old-fashioned Marxism taught by social democracy.[1]

What is being currently emphasised is the fact that the formerly illegal Communist Party had only a few hundred members. This is small wonder if you consider that membership entailed heavy prison sentences; two of the main leaders of the party spent 16 years in jail each. But the Communist milieu—and the independent hard left harboured by the social democrats and by the more radical trade unions such as the metal workers and the typesetters—of sympathisers,

1 The Hungarian Council Republic was set up in March 1919 and overthrown by a Romanian invading army in August.

from unskilled labourers to avant-garde artists, was enormous. These groups were immediately joined by millions of peasants mobilised by land reform. The voters of the agrarian parties were not anti-Communist, anything but.

1945 meant the end of the old ruling classes and political elites, the end of the landed aristocracy, of the immensely rich and rather unpopular Catholic Church with its feudal customs and giant estates, of the old officer corps and of the state bureacracy staffed by the gentry, an end to the feared gendarmerie which had terrorised the countryside without regard for legality or humanity, and an end to racial laws and to ethnic and gender discrimination.

Spontaneous communist experiments started by Council Republic veterans (not to speak of the former prisoners of war who took the Bolshevik side in the Russian civil war in 1918-20) were suppressed by the party and the Soviet military authorities. But it was plain that socialist and Communist workers and peasants wanted socialism, not some half-baked people's democracy. They wanted an immediate *Commune* order (this was the popular name of the Council Republic, spelt "*Kommün*"), total socialisation of all means of production, consumer equality, free state education for all, abortion and divorce on demand, a citizens' army and police and a council system in workplaces and localities. We know what the Stalinists did with all this. They were always fighting the left—and people tend to forget that in the 1940s social democracy was *to the left* of the Communist Party; this is why it was so mercilessly persecuted.

Nevertheless, by 1950, the anti-feudal and anti-theocratic measures were in place and redistribution favoured the urban proletariat. Tyranny, police state, censorship, brutal conformism, fanaticism and poverty, yes, but also a clear social bias to the advantage of the lower strata. There was also a cultural revolution of sorts. Free education, cheap books, a modern publishing industry for the first time, cheap—frequently free—theatre, concert and cinema tickets, free museums, kindergartens, very modest social housing, together with the terrible shortages, with an ill-fed and ill-clothed nation, looking awful in the faded black and white photographs of the period, crazy industrialisation and the rest. It was made abundantly clear that physical work was at the pinnacle of the social and moral value scale—for the first time in world history. (It was no longer "spirit" embodied by the church, or "blue-blooded" caste excellence represented by royalty, the aristocracy and nobility, or the bourgeois superiority of wealth.)

These socialist thoughts and practices were not questioned basically by the unrest that went with the unravelling of the Stalinist regime after the dictator's death in 1953. The brief course of reforms then, led by prime minister Imre Nagy (a veteran Communist who returned in 1945 from exile in Moscow), aimed at the re-establishment or establishment of "true socialism" including plenty of food, proper heating, full shops, less work and no innocents in jail. And especially, an end to the propagandistic mendacity that got on the nerves of the working people—"truth" was one of the most important demands.

Following the Twentieth Congress of the Communist Party of the Soviet Union in February 1956 Nikita Krushchev's so-called secret speech about Stalin's crimes was read to millions of party members in closed meetings across Russia and beyond, and disseminated by the BBC Hungarian programme, The Voice of America and Radio Free Europe and by the Yugoslav state radio's Hungarian-language broadcasts. After this and the resignation of Stalinist leader Mátyás Rákosi and reappointment of the reformer Imre Nagy as prime minister (he was fired in 1955), the most important event was the rehabilitation and the solemn reburial of László Rajk, a former secretary of the Central Committee. Rajk was the executed defendant in the main show trial in 1949. He was reburied on 6 October 1956 in a dramatic, torch-lit mass meeting of hundreds of thousands of people in Budapest. 6 October is a significant day in Hungary: 13 generals of the Hungarian rebel army were executed by the Habsburg counter-revolution on the same day in 1849 (and, separately, Count Batthyány, one of the prime ministers of the revolution in 1848, was also shot in Pest).

In this way, the re-establishment of truth, the identification of true socialism with justice, a total rejection of Stalinism and a solemn oath next to Rajk's catafalque, "Never again", went hand in hand to constitute the ideology of the 1956 Hungarian Revolution.

The revolution of bad conscience

Again we must keep in mind that the anti-Stalinist rebellion was started and sustained by the generation of 1945, by those who wanted social equality, that is the end of the semi-feudal *ancien régime*, and who wished for the political supremacy of the working class, socialisation of the means of production, state ownership of the banks, public transport, housing, egalitarian redistribution, workers' co-management in the entreprises, a multi-party system for the anti-fascist forces, friendship with the formerly hostile Eastern European nations, anti-imperialist solidarity, internationalism, freedom of expression, wage equality for women, free education and retraining for adults and so on. These demands were denied by the Stalinist one-party state and they were immediately resurrected as the repression was alleviated.

In party cells, trade unions, student associations and intellectual circles a feverish wave of debates and discussions took the place of the deathly silence of the dictatorship. One of the most conspicuous features of these months was the repentance and self-criticism of Communist intellectuals who rejected the slavish, uncritical, fanatical and quasi-religious fervour of the Stalinist period and their own complicity in the reprisals and the inhuman savagery of Stalinist state capitalism. The "Never again!" of 6 October was prepared for by this extraordinary re-examination of the revolutionary conscience, the recapture of the pathos of freedom characteristic of both revolutionary moments, 1945 and 1956. Famous poems, essays, confessions, pamphlets—still remembered today—inflamed the imagination of society. Responsibility assumed by the self-critical Communist intellectuals was extended to the party leaders, and innocent leftists just freed from the Stalinist prisons reappeared as the ghosts of liberation, demanding not revenge but justice.

The wavering party leadership hesitated between being seduced to join either the movement or its violent suppression. All the grand ideas of socialist revolution reappeared. There was a permanent mobilisation of rational debate—reminiscent of the *Nuit debout* conversations in Paris this year, but on a much larger scale—that promised an authentic renewal of socialism. It was perfectly clear that nobody desirous of being heard would advocate capitalist or reactionary restoration; the masses would not hear of it. There was a passionate interest in parallel phenomena in Poland, a great curiosity concerning Yugoslav experimentations with workers' self-management and Third World ideas of democratic socialism.

But most of all this was a moral uprising, a rejection of Stalinism, of *nomenklatura* privileges, of militarism and xenophobic isolation from the rest of the world. What has later been dubbed "nationalism" by outside observers was nothing more than the principle of equality between socialist nations—which meant, of course, the repudiation of Russian control—in other words, internationalism. But the essence was the strong disgust for official lies, a powerful desire for honesty, sincerity and responsibility, for revolutionary purity.

This moral rejuvenation of socialism has also meant forgiveness for those who were innocent dupes of Stalinist propaganda—and indeed, many intellectuals and activists, guilty of shameful acts of obeisance in the 1950s, had become subsequently heroes and martyrs of the anti-Stalinist revolution.

Social discontent and moral revulsion characterised this first episode of 1956. It developed into a fully fledged revolutionary movement only after the attempts to repress it.

The socialist democratic revolution

On 23 October 1956 a huge demonstration took place in Budapest. The special forces fired on the crowd, as a result the government fell, Imre Nagy returned, a multi-party system was declared and the Soviet troops withdrew. The centre of power was in the hands of the proletariat, of the swiftly formed workers' councils. But the focus was on political liberty, pluralism, freedom of expression and on a new constitutional republic.

It was made clear, once again, that the nationalised and socialised enterprises and institutions would remain in the hands of the people, but ruled by the people, not by the apparat. No significant force demanded joining the Western alliances. Privatisations and the introduction of a market economy were deliberately and decisively rejected. At the same time, people demanded the departure of the Russian troops and true national independence. The spectre of counter-revolution appeared, too, in acts of summary justice and a few cases of lynching of party officials and of special forces. This, however, was greeted with indignation and revulsion by the majority.

The Communist Party dispersed and, although at the helm of the state, the surviving organisation understood that it had no chance of winning the coming elections. A separate social democratic party was again becoming stronger, and it might have become the leading force in society, given the opportunity. The newly formed Politburo and the Nagy government—with members such as the celebrated Marxist philosopher Georg Lukács—advocated a pluralist socialist democracy, based on the collective ownership of the means of production and on democratic planning, subject to the free decision of the nation in multi-party elections and workplace democracy.

There seemed no risk of a move to Western-style free market capitalism. Nevertheless, the rest of the Soviet bloc had decided that the Hungarian Revolution was not to be tolerated. A Russian military attack was launched on 4 November, and the Hungarian revolutionary government quit the Warsaw Pact and declared Hungary's neutrality. The country was occupied and the revolutionary leadership arrested and deported. Formally, a Quisling government headed by János Kádár (who, until that moment, was a loyal member of the Nagy government and was no different from the rest of the democratic Communist leadership) was supposed to take over, but the real power belonged to the KGB and to the Russian military.

The Hungarian people's resistance was unanimous; the Kádár clique was totally isolated; there was no trace of treason. Hundreds of thousands fled through the Austrian frontier. The foci of armed struggle were very difficult to subdue. The Hungarian army, trained and armed by the Soviet Union—many officers were heroes of the clandestine anti-fascist resistance during the war—all refused to participate in the occupation and the repression. The special forces were disbanded, and the police were passive or hostile to the Russians. The semi-legal press kept to the popular line of neutrality, independence and socialist democracy. It was the Soviet Union that was accused of betraying socialism, as indeed it had. The quiet heroism and the patience of the population were extraordinary.

And the most wonderful chapter of the revolution was only to come with the beginning of the general strike.

The revolution of the workers' councils

Workers' councils were formed in all factories, entreprises and state institutions before 4 November. Then they shared their influence with the "reform Communist" government, with the newly formed or reborn democratic parties and with the trade unions. As these latter were all banned by the Russian military authorities and the local puppet government, the councils found themselves to be the only remaining legitimate political institution in Hungary. Their weapon—and a formidable one—was the general strike which was observed in spite of the curfew and of the state of siege, as millions of Hungarian workers and other employees simply did not turn up at work.

In all revolutionary moments, from the Paris Commune to the October Revolution, Munich and Budapest in 1919, Barcelona, Canton and Shanghai, the proletarian state form has always been and remains the form of non-representative, direct democracy at the workplace. Solidarność, the Polish resistance that is supposed to have put an end to Soviet-style state "socialism", was no trade union as it was not organised according to crafts and professions, but as a territorial network of workers' councils and factory cells, akin to the original communist party idea. Even if Solidarność was ideologically and rhetorically conservative, its formal principle—direct workplace democracy—was fundamentally proletarian and communist.

I recall talking to Sándor Rácz, the chairman of the Greater Budapest Workers' Council, one of the leaders of the resistance, in 1992. He was by then a deeply reactionary public figure and a brave and honest Hungarian patriot. I asked him whether he thought his present role was consonant with his past. He said, laughing, "No, in 1956 I was a Communist; I became a Catholic and a nationalist only in prison". He was 23 years old during the revolution, a convinced far-left figure and a cunning, clever negotiator who managed to stay the outbreak of state violence for months. For a long time the Hungarian proletariat has kept the idea of social ownership and of free socialism alive, against the strongest military power on earth—and against the indifference and connivance of the "liberal" West.

And this is what they call an anti-communist revolution, a vindication of an authoritarian past, a nationalist uprising and even, according to the far-right historian David Irving, an anti-Jewish rebellion, while many of the hanged revolutionaries were Jewish communists. After the defeat of the general strike the Kádár regime executed only the leftists—the conservatives who joined the people's cause were already being given literary prizes and medals in 1957, when the firing squads were still busy pacifying Hungary. They knew exactly who the real enemies were. They were people like you, dear reader.

The British Empire and the First World War: the colonial experience

Talat Ahmed

The First World War is still widely perceived to be a white man's war based on the Western front. Popular images of brave young white men dying for king and country dominate museum exhibits. But some 4 million non-white men were mobilised into the European and American armies during the war, in both combatant and non-combatant roles.[1]

The colonies were critical to the war effort as a source of both labour and materials. Empires could not prosecute a successful war without colonial troops. Paradoxically, the call to arms to defend empire coexisted with the inferior status of non-white people within the imperial hierarchy. War reinforced racism and the imperial division of the world but it also challenged the colonial set up and produced resistance to its rule.

Nearly 1.5 million Indian soldiers fought for the British Empire in the First World War, both in Asia and in Europe. And at the other end of the Empire over 16,000 men from the West Indies also served. The British West Indies Regiment (BWIR) was created in 1915 to serve overseas by grouping together volunteers from the Caribbean; 15,600 men in the regiment's 12 battalions served with the Allied forces, with two thirds of the volunteers coming from Jamaica and the

1 Thanks to Alex Callinicos, Christian Høgsbjerg, John Newsinger, Tony Phillips, Camilla Royle and Ian Taylor for their very helpful and critical comments on this article in draft.

rest from Trinidad and Tobago, Barbados, the Bahamas, British Honduras (now Belize), Grenada, British Guiana (now Guyana), the Leeward Islands, St Lucia and St Vincent. As well as serving in France, the BWIR played a vital role in active combat against the Turkish army in Palestine, Jordan, Mesopotamia and Egypt and also served in northern Italy.[2]

This article will focus primarily on the experiences of Caribbean and Indian soldiers within the British Empire to demonstrate how oppressed peoples were mobilised to defend the empires of their oppressors, but other belligerent countries also made use of colonial troops. France had 90,000 indigenous troops already under arms when the war started. Between 1914 and 1918 they recruited nearly 500,000 colonial troops, including 166,000 West Africans, 46,000 Madagascans, 50,000 Indochinese, 140,000 Algerians, 47,000 Tunisians and 24,300 Moroccans. Most of these French colonial troops served in Europe, though the majority of Africans across the colonies served as labourers or carriers in Africa. In total over 2 million Africans were involved in the conflict as soldiers or labourers; 10 percent of them died, and among the labourers serving in Africa, the death rates may have been as high as 20 percent.[3] Additionally, nearly 140,000 Chinese contract labourers were hired by the British and French governments, forming a substantial part of the migrant labour force working in France during the war. Over 20,000 black South Africans served in the South African Native Labour Contingent formed in September 1916, and more were attached to the Cape Auxiliary Horse Transport Companies in France.[4]

With the entry of the United States into the war, nearly 400,000 African American troops were inducted into the US forces, of whom 200,000 served in Europe. By comparison Britain's white dominions in total furnished just over 1.4 million with 640,000 Canadians, 401,000 Australians, 136,000 white South Africans and 220,000 from New Zealand.[5]

Germany also made use of its colonies to provide troops for the war. Some 2,500 Africans were enlisted from East Africa and 1,650 from German Cameroon in West Africa.[6] The colonial forces for German Southwest Africa consisted of volunteers from the imperial army and navy, including some Austrians and white Afrikaners from South Africa, but essentially comprised members of German regiments. For Germany, the war was in large part waged to revise the imperial division of the world in 1914, but for Britain and France

2 Sherry, 2014, p101.
3 Strachan, 2004, p3.
4 Levine, 1998, p104.
5 Pati, 1996, p39.
6 Farwell, 1989, p109.

it was to defend the existing order and the deployment of colonial forces reflected this.

Non-combatant labour: capitalist exploitation

In September 1914, only a month after the outbreak of war, two divisions of infantry and cavalry of the Indian Army journeyed across a continent to the Western front. Even at this early stage allied forces had already suffered huge casualties, making reinforcements an urgent necessity to plug holes in the British defensive line. European rulers initially thought it would be a quick war—"over by Christmas"—but it soon became evident this was to be a long haul and so preparations were made for total war. To that end the entire resources of empires were put at the disposal of the war effort turning it into a global conflict.

The capitalist war machinery went into overdrive to ensure every aspect of the colonial economy—materials and labour power—was subordinated to the needs of war. The West Indian colonies contributed nearly £2 million from tax revenue and voluntary donations, which provided war supplies such as planes and British Red Cross ambulances. West Indian produce such as sugar, rum, cocoa and rice continued to be sent to Britain. Trinidadian oil production increased three-fold to meet wartime demand and Sea Island cotton was used in aircraft production.[7] Similarly India contributed an initial £100 million to the war effort and provided a further £20 million to £30 million in annual contributions.[8] Indians at home endured higher taxes, material shortages and rising prices to pay for this, which would all be exacerbated by the failure of the monsoon in 1918-19. These donations were made in spite of severe hardships caused by major increases in the cost of living throughout the colonies.

In Europe and Africa accommodation and fortifications had to be built; thousands of miles of trenches had to be dug; roads, railways and canals had to be built and maintained; telephone lines and cabling had to be installed; and ships, trains and trucks had to be loaded and unloaded at the docks, railheads and distribution centres. Military equipment had to be maintained and horses had to be fed and looked after. In addition to these essential tasks, the generals and senior officers were cosseted behind the frontlines with 65,000 men and women servants allocated to wait on them. All this ancillary work required huge amounts of labour and increasingly the generals could not afford to use combat forces on such work. Initially it was undertaken by labourers and tradesmen sent

7 Go to http://westindiacommittee.org/caribbeansgreatwar/map/africa/topics/richard-smith-memories-of-british-west-indian-service-in-the-first-world-war

8 Vadgama, 1984, p92.

from Britain and grouped into Labour Companies of the Army Service Corps. Latterly this work was also carried out by women workers, organised in the Women's Auxiliary Corps.

Despite all these measures, the chronic shortage of labour persisted and workers from all parts of the British Empire (informal as well as formal), notably China, Egypt and the West Indies, were brought to work on the Western front, mainly in France. It is estimated that as many as 100,000 labourers came from the colonies. Indians were recruited for military work services, work on the railways and inland water transport, in the Ordinance Labour Corps and in other positions such as telegraphists, cooks, carpenters, shoemakers, tailors and washermen. BWIR troops were engaged in numerous support roles on the Western front, including digging trenches, building roads and gun emplacements, acting as stretcher bearers, loading ships and trains and working in ammunition dumps. This work was often carried out within range of German artillery and snipers. In July 1917, 13 men from the BWIR were killed by shellfire and aerial bombardment. Several battalions of the BWIR were deployed to Egypt and Palestine. Here too they were mostly used in support functions, such as guarding prisoners and holding reserve posts and outposts. Black and Indian troops were seen as suited to menial tasks.

Recruitment policy

The War Office, headed by Lord Kitchener, was initially opposed to the use of any black soldiers alongside whites. Kitchener's poster plea "Your country needs you" meant white men only. True to his racist outlook, Kitchener believed black faces would be too conspicuous on the battlefield and that the German army would laugh at the mighty British Empire relying on black soldiers. But there were also deep concerns that black soldiers might actually outperform their white counterparts in military prowess and valour and that this would lead to demands for greater self-governance after the war, particularly if they had rifles in their hands. However, the Colonial Office and the monarch himself, George V, decided otherwise. Keen to show a united empire in wartime, they were also concerned that excluding black troops would undermine British authority in the colonies. Hence the BWIR, as a separate black unit within the British army, came into being. It was to be commanded by white officers and no Caribbean soldier could rise above the rank of sergeant. Similarly, Indian regiments were all commanded by a white officer class and it was very rare for an Indian to rise above the rank of a *subedar*—a rank below British commissioned officers and above non-commissioned officers.

Some joined quite enthusiastically as a means of demonstrating patriotism to the mother country. In 1914 George Blackman joined the British West Indies Regiment, telling the recruiting officer he was 18 when he was actually 17. "Lord

Kitchener said with the black race, he could whip the world," Blackman recalls. "We sang songs: 'Run Kaiser William, run for your life, boy'".[9] "We wanted to go. The island government told us the king said all Englishmen must go to join the war. The country called all of us".[10]

Many West Indians were keen to fulfil pledges of loyalty by volunteering for military service. The enthusiasm to play a military role is clearly expressed by this Barbadian: "We have put up sugar and money...but that won't win our battles. It's lives we desire to give...it is only fair to give these colonies the opportunity of showing the true spirit of patriotism that they have always evinced in the past".[11] Similarly, hundreds of thousands of Indians flocked to volunteer for service. One wrote home to his brother from the Western front: "We shall never get another chance to exalt the name of race, country, ancestors, parents, village and brothers, and to prove our loyalty to the government... We go singing as we march, and care nothing that we are going to die".[12]

One Indian soldier in France urges another soldier in the Punjab to get more recruits: "This is not time for slackness. Consider the way in which the whole country is exerting itself and doing its duty".[13] Another was enthusiastic about France and England, particularly about the possibility of travel: "What am I to say to you about England? May God grant victories to our King. If I were to set about writing down the praises of Marseilles, my hand would be wearied with writing. Further, I went to Paris for seven days. What is Paris? It is heaven!"[14]

The identification with the British cause and empire patriotism at times even withstood the death of friends, as this letter testifies: "He was buried in a Muslim cemetery near London with great honour and dignity. The exalted government has showered every blessing on us here, which I shall remember all my life, and which will bind me in complete loyalty".[15]

Others, however, were motivated by more mundane concerns such as obtaining regular food and wages in economies characterised by casual and low-paid employment. Most Caribbean recruits were plantation workers and artisans. Of the first 4,000 men enlisted into the BWIR, 1,033 were labourers, 657 were

9 Quoted in Rogers, 2002.

10 Rogers, 2002.

11 *West India Committee Circular*, 17 November 1914, p502.

12 Letter number 226, Signaller Kartar Singh to Kunar Khan, Ludhiana District, Punjab 22 January 1916, in Omissi, 1999, p141.

13 Letter number 263, Peshawar Singh (Sikh) to Sirdar Mahindar Singh (19th Lancers, Sialkot District, Punjab), 9 March, 1916, in Omissi, 1999, p161.

14 Letter number 260, Mahomed Firoz Din (Punjabi Muslim) to Firoz Khan (19th Lancers, Sialkot, Punjab), 7 March 1916, in Omissi, 1999, p160.

15 Letter number 215, Muhammad Hussein Khan (Punjabi Muslim) to Lumberdar Said Hafiz Khair Muhammad (Jullundur, Punjab, India), 10 January 1916, in Omissi, 1999, p136.

cultivators, 356 carpenters, 245 bakers, 42 police constables and 40 teachers.[16] In 1914 unemployment was high in the Caribbean, particularly for urban youth, with many West Indians working for as little as nine pence a day. One young Jamaican man, Eugent Clarke, who volunteered aged 21 stated: "It wasn't easy to find work in Jamaica, and the pay was nothing. It was mainly cultivation. Only one or two factories were in the island. The people couldn't get work".[17]

There were clearly economic factors propelling some to join the volunteer force. Though conscription was introduced into Britain, it was not a feature of colonial recruitment in the First World War and thousands of men in the Caribbean and India came forward "willingly" to sign up.

Patriotism was nurtured by the approach of liberal nationalists who believed loyalty to the empire would lead to equal treatment as citizens of empire and consequently to greater forms of self-governance. While some declared it a white man's war and refused to sign up, leaders such as the Jamaican Marcus Garvey said young men from the islands should fight in order to prove their loyalty and to be treated as equals. The Universal Negro Improvement Association (UNIA), founded by Garvey in Jamaica on the eve of the war, telegrammed a resolution to the Colonial Office in London "express[ing] our loyalty and devotion to His Majesty the King, and empire...pray[ing] for the success of British arms on the battlefields of Europe and Africa, and at sea".[18]

Similarly, Mohandas Gandhi called on Indians to fight on the Allied side. "We are, above all, British citizens of the Great British Empire," he told them. Gandhi, who had been in London when war broke out, circulated a letter to Indians in the UK that declared, "we, the undersigned have, after mature deliberation decided for the sake of the motherland and the empire to place our services unconditionally, during this crisis, at the disposal of the authorities".[19]

In an open letter to the Indian public the former Liberal MP and Indian nationalist, Dadabhai Naoroji, wrote: "Fighting as the British people are...in a righteous cause to the good and glory of human dignity and civilisation, and moreover, being the beneficent instrument of our own progress and civilisation, our duty is clear—to do everyone our best to support the British fight with our life and property".[20]

In April 1918 the British Viceroy Lord Chelmsford convened the Indian War Conference (also known as the manpower conference) in Delhi. Its purpose was to set in motion the recruitment of half a million Indians, starting in June

16 Quoted in Bourne, 2014, p66.
17 Quoted in Bourne, 2014, p63.
18 Letter to Right Honourable Lewis Harcourt, MP, Secretary of State for the Colonies, 16 September 1914, quoted in Hill, 2011, p76.
19 *Indian Opinion*, 16 September 1914.
20 *The Times*, 5 September 1914, p9.

that year. Gandhi responded by supporting the resolution "with a full sense of responsibility".[21] And he assured the Viceroy that "I love the English nation, and I wish to evoke in every Indian the loyalty of the Englishman".[22] In a speech in Patna, Gandhi made clear his view that India should provide men for the war and not make this contingent on self-rule as "any calamity that overtakes the empire is one that overtakes India as well".[23] These views reflected the middle class basis of elite nationalism which was wedded to constitutional reforms and aimed more at finding accommodation with imperial rule than in fighting for genuine national liberation.[24] Under colonialism indigenous elites comprised wealthy landowners; industrial magnates such as G D Birla, financier of many of Gandhi's projects, and the Tata family; as well as aristocrats from the princely states. Their liberal nationalism opposed foreign rule and sought change in the imperial set up. But their approach was moderate, favouring lobbying and petitioning in legislative councils for representation. This social layer, often Western educated, hankered after recognition and a space for themselves within the colonial government rather than mass agitation. Consequently, their class base mitigated against militant nationalism from below that emphasised mass direct action against imperialism.

However, the limitations of liberal nationalism did not prevent ordinary Indians and West Indians from joining the war effort. For many this was a chance not only to prove loyalty but also to demonstrate their own sense of personal worth and courage.

Reality in the ranks and at the front

The ideology of colonial recruitment was expressed by a *Manchester Courier* propaganda piece of September 1915 under the banner "Unity and Honour of the Empire": "Nothing has surprised the enemy more than the solidarity of the British Empire. Every part of King George's dominions is helping the Mother Country, and the spirit and devotion shown by our fellow-subjects overseas in upholding the unity and honour of the empire has met with general admiration".[25] And it continued to boast: "It is hoped, and there is no doubt, they will receive a particularly hospitable welcome".[26] However, the stark reality of war coupled with institutional racism would sorely test the loyalty of even the most pro-British black recruit.

As George Blackman recalls, conditions were appalling: "It was cold. And everywhere there were white lice. We had to shave the hair there because the lice grow

21 Gandhi, 1918-19, p5.
22 Gandhi, 1918-19, p8. Letter to Viceroy, 29 April 1918.
23 Gandhi, 1918-19, p37.
24 See Ahmed, 2009.
25 *Manchester Courier*, 25 September 1915.
26 *Manchester Courier*, 25 September 1915.

there. All our socks were full of white lice".[27] The colonial soldiers' initial journey to England was perilous, with hundreds suffering from severe illnesses and hardship. In March 1916 a ship transporting BWIR men from Jamaica, the *SS Verdala,* was diverted into a blizzard near Halifax, Canada, to avoid any lurking German warships. The soldiers' winter uniforms were left locked up while they froze in thin summer clothes. As a result of inadequate equipment, over 600 men suffered from exposure and frostbite, 106 required amputations and at least five died.

A sense of their lived experiences can be gleaned from letters sent home. All correspondence was heavily censored by the British, ever watchful for signs of rebellion and seditious literature being exchanged. This was overseen by the India Base Post Office set up in Rouen and then Boulogne in December 1914. It was staffed by members of the Indian Civil Service whose job was to read letters and send short reports to the Secretary of State for India, India Office, War Office, Foreign Office, Buckingham Palace and the Commanders of Indian Divisions. Indian soldiers, like all troops, were aware of this elaborate layer of checking and censorship and for every letter praising king and mother country there were those that spoke of wartime realities:

> I went into the trenches on 7 August and returned on 28 August. Some of our men were wounded. I am not permitted to give any fuller details. The battle is raging violently, and various new ways of fighting have been introduced. The ground is honeycombed, as a field with rat holes. No one can advance beyond the trenches. If he does so, he is blown away. Mines are ready charged with explosives. Shells and machine guns and bombs are mostly employed. No one considers rifles nowadays, and serviceable rifle ammunition is lying about as plentifully as pebbles. At the trenches, thousands of mounds of iron, representing exploded shells, lie on the ground. At some places corpses are found of men killed in 1914, with uniform and accoutrements still on. Large flies, which have become poisonous through feasting on dead bodies, infest the trenches, and huge fat rats run about there. By the blessing of God the climate of this country is cold, and for that reason corpses do not decompose quickly. It rains frequently and that causes much inconvenience. At the present time we are suffering, as the horses are tethered outside and the rain has converted the ground into slush. Sometimes we have to march in the rain and then the cold is intense. However after two years' experience, we have grown used to all these troubles and think lightly of them. I have lots to write about, but I have no leisure, nor have I permission to do so. Even this I have had to write very prudently, otherwise it would be withheld.[28]

---

27 Rogers, 2002.

28 Letter number 394, Daya Ram (Jat) to Kalu Ram (Ambala City, Punjab, 2nd Lancers, Urdu), 6 September 1916, France, in Omissi, 1999, p231.

One soldier, though part of the censorship machine, begs friends not to enlist: "If you have any relatives, my advice is don't let them enlist. It is unnecessary to write any more. I write so much to you as I am *Pay Havildar* [commander] and read the letters to the double company commander. Otherwise there is a strict order against writing on this subject".[29]

Another letter offers advice on how to circumvent the censorship regime:

> It is a great pity that you never write any real account of the war in France. No doubt your officers read the letters. But cannot you devise any way of dodging them? I will tell you what to do. When you write a letter, on one page write in invisible ink made out of lemon juice and I will read everything. If you cannot get this, take some lime which has not been wetted and grind it up and mix it with water and write and I shall be able to read it all.[30]

Others sent coded messages to their family urging them not to enlist. One man wrote to his brother: "Think over what I say and you will understand what I mean when I say, 'stay in the village'".[31] Upon a friend from his unit being injured, a Pathan civilian in India wrote to him imploring him to exaggerate the extent of his back injury so that he would be sent home: "wherever you go, do not straighten your back. Then, please God, something good will come of it... I wish to impress this upon you as strongly as I can...do not straighten your back. Your position is a very good one".[32]

In sharp contrast to notions of duty, honour and fighting for king and country, colonial troops faced a whole range of inequalities in military equipment, mobility and privileges that separated them from their white counterparts. Non-white colonials were routinely segregated and closely watched. Black South Africans stationed in France were housed in closed compounds, prohibited from entering the houses of Europeans, expressly forbidden to speak to white women and were allowed alcohol for one hour a day but only with a white non-commissioned officer present.[33] Indians in France fared no better. They were subject to curfews and other restrictions.

When Indian soldiers were wounded and brought to hospitals on the south coast, concerns over white nurses tending to "native" soldiers led to "absolutely

---

29 Letter number 67 Havildar Abdul Rahman (Punjabi Muslim to Naik Rajwali Khan (31st Punjabis, Fort Sandeman, Zhob Distict, Baluchistan), 20th May 1915, in Omissi, 1999, p61.

30 Letter number 408 Farrier Major Khan to Wali Mahomed Khan (Punjab Muslim, 18th Lancers, France), Jhelum, Punjab (Urdu), 19 September 1916, in Omissi, 1999, p239.

31 Letter number 22, A Wounded Sikh to his Brother, 14 February 1915, in Omissi, 1999, p37.

32 Letter number 103, Khan Muhammad (40th Pathans) to Sher Jang (40th Pathans, a hospital, France), 26 July, 1915, in Omissi, 1999, p81.

33 Levine, 1998, p107.

inflexible rules" keeping them within hospital precincts.[34] Even in rare occasions of recreation segregation ruled. In London, Cook's Tours organised trips for small groups of Hindu and, separately, Muslim soldiers. The supervised tours allowed tourist combatants an hour's shopping at a department store and a ride on the Underground as well as escorted visits to royal and other tourist sights in the capital.[35] No such supervision, restrictions or rules governed the soldiers from the white dominions in any theatre of war.

Some Caribbean soldiers were involved in actual combat in France. Photographs from the time show black soldiers armed with British Lee Enfield rifles, and there are reports of West Indies Regiment soldiers fighting off counter-attacks. One account tells how a group fought off a German assault armed only with knives they had brought from home. Interviewed in 2002 at the age of 105, Blackman still remembered trench fights he fought in, alongside white soldiers: "They called us darkies... But when the battle starts, it didn't make a difference. We were all the same. When you're there, you don't care about anything. Every man there is under the rifle." He recalled one attack with particular clarity: "The Tommies said, 'Darkie, let them have it.' I made the order: 'Bayonets, fix,' and then 'B company, fire.' You know what it is to go and fight somebody hand to hand? You need plenty nerves. They come at you with the bayonet. He pushes at me, I push at he. You push that bayonet in there and hit with the butt of the gun—if he is dead he is dead, if he live he live.".[36]

The horror of trench warfare certainly hit home. Young Eugent Clark, like many colonial soldiers, served in Ypres:

> The war was raging in Europe. The Germans never ceased fire. Night and day, bombs. We had to live under the earth in dugouts. The Somme was bad, man. You stuck in the mud. We had a rough time in that country. The wind would cut you. How we cold. We had to have double socks. Every soldier had to wear double or the cold would have killed us.[37]

And similarly death brought the sheer brutality of war to intimate levels:

> I was in the trench when they started to shell. Shells coming, man. What happened with my friend, Eustace Phillips. So, he was on the hilltop and he was just going into the Bivouac [shelter] when he and the shell met together. Dead! And those things always make you feel you shouldn't have been in the army. I didn't get to see

34 India Office Records: IOR/L/MIL/17/5/2016, Colonel Sir Bruce Seton, "A Report on Kitchener Indian Hospital, Brighton", 1916.

35 Visram, 1986, p128.

36 Rogers, 2002.

37 Quoted in Bourne, 2014, p69.

> his funeral because when you're in the front line you don't have no funerals. They just make a hole and sometimes four or five of you go in the hole, you know.[38]

Detachments of the second battalion of the BWIR were deployed against German forces in the Tanganyika campaign and the first, second and fifth battalions remained as part of the Egyptian Expeditionary Force (EEF) until the end of the war. In July 1917, during the Palestine campaign, the machine gun section of the BWIR was involved in several raids on Turkish trenches at Umbrella Hill in Gaza. Some Indians fought in Gallipoli 1915-16 and over 1,300 died.

The following description by a British officer of two Indians being captured by Germans, leaving their mules behind by a haystack, highlights both the tremendous courage of colonial soldiers and paternal admiration by their officers: "After a time, their captors being fully occupied with their own affair the two Indians managed to slip away. They did not make straight for our lines. Not a bit of it. They sought and found the haystack, recovered their mules, reloaded them with the ammunition-boxes and strolled in".[39]

The same officer also describes one of the first Indian men to be given the Military Cross that was killed in action as "white a man as ever lived".[40] General Edmund Allenby reported to the Jamaican governor that he had "great pleasure in informing you of the excellent conduct of the Machine Gun Section... All ranks behaved with great gallantry under heavy rifle fire and shell fire, and contributed in no small measure to the success of the operations".[41] Military combat exposed deep contradictions at the heart of the imperial army: they could simultaneously take great pride in and admire colonial troops for their valour while being wedded to racist notions of empire.

Racism and "martial races"

British imperial rule depended on co-opting sections of the colonised societies, using a policy of divide and rule to bestow privilege and favour in return for loyal service. This was intertwined with racism and theories of racial categorisation to justify oppression which, when it came to deploying young men of the colonies to fight on behalf of empire, led to the theory of "martial races"—those born to fight. In this endeavour the British made full use of colonial constructions that incorporated notions of honour and duty that were ascribed to subjects. In India British officers took the Persian/Urdu term *izzat*, loosely translated as "honour" and incorporating feelings of self-respect, personal dignity, familial duty and

38 Quoted in Bourne, 2014, p69.
39 Alexander, 1917, p71.
40 Alexander, 1917, p61.
41 Cipriani, 1940, p20.

community obligations, to pathologise Indian behaviour. In the military context the concept of *izzat* proved to be a powerful motivator.

The Great Indian Uprising of 1857, referred to by Britain as the Indian Mutiny, had a decisive impact on the development of British imperial concepts of "martial races". Racial categorisation had been a key feature of colonial conquest and early Victorian paternalism had hardened into "unashamed racism" that viewed all colonial subjects as inherently inferior.[42] This was reflected in army recruitment patterns as preference was given to certain types of Indian for army service, notably Nepalese, Punjabis and people from North-west Frontier and Baluchistan in what is now Pakistan. These areas were held to be relatively quiet during the 1857 rising and therefore a more reliable source of loyal stock. Conversely, Bengal, the northern province of Awadh and Delhi, as sites of resistance, were deemed untrustworthy. Under the East India Company,[43] initial Indian recruitment came from mercenaries and low-caste volunteers but the elite Bengal Army eventually became composed largely of high caste Hindus and landowning Muslims. These two elite groups were seen as traitors during the uprising; consequently the recruitment of sepoys (soldiers) began to favour low caste, peasant, uneducated groups, those deemed as "relatively backward minorities whose then privileged position would depend on the continuation of British rule".[44] Hence, Nepalese Gurkhas, Pathans, peasant Sikh and Muslim Punjabis and Baluchis were deemed brave warriors with the requisite "manly" qualities required for soldiering and loyalty. Educated, urban Bengalis were contemptuously dismissed as idle, spineless and effeminate.

Some have argued that the concept of martial races was "less a theory than a catch-all phrase" used to justify different roles for Indian troops.[45] Intellectual laziness certainly epitomised British officers in India and elsewhere in empire but the martial race doctrine did have theoretical underpinnings rooted in colonial "sciences" that pitted white Europeans at the top and black and brown skinned peoples at the bottom. The latter groups were further divided into a set of characteristics based on models of social Darwinism and crude biological racism, thus providing a suitable and comforting justification for

42 Greenhut, 1984, p16.

43 The East India Company (EIC) was a British joint stock company established in 1600 under a Royal Charter, making it the oldest of several European East India companies. Its shareholders were aristocrats and wealthy merchants with the British state exercising indirect control. The EIC aggressively pursued trade across the East Indies and Indian Ocean. It came to pre-eminence in India from 1707, where it ruled large areas and took control of administrative areas, known as presidencies, backed up by its own private army. Its effective rule in India lasted from the 1757 Battle of Plassey in Bengal to 1858, when its rule was deposed following the 1857 Indian Uprising.

44 Greenhut, 1984, p15.

45 Cohen, 1971, p45.

empire. Colonial officials produced several documented accounts espousing a highly structured doctrine of martial races that directly corresponded to their experiences of Indian resistance. Commenting on Gandhi, Lieutenant-General Sir George MacMunn argued:

> The gentle yet merciless race of hereditary moneylenders, from which Lala Ghandi springs, only kept within bounds by an occasional flaying and roasting, have never been able or even tried to protect their own hoards. Not for them, nor for the classes whence come the political lawyer, was the troopship that led the martial men of India westwards, to fight in the war of freedom.[46]

This was in sharp contrast to his admiration of those classified as martial:

> The Jat Sikhs mighty and curled of beard, kin perhaps to the men of Kent, the Jutes from Jutland, with them Moslem and Hindu Rajput, the fierce hillmen from the frontiers, the Tartar from Nepal that we know as Gurkha, recking little else than that the Badshah or Padishah, the great White King, had summoned them and that his white officers would lead them and his white troops fight by their side.[47]

Similarly, a British Indian army officer wrote that Sikhs and Gurkhas were the only people he had encountered who "really liked fighting"[48] and that Sikhs had distinguishing marks such as uncut hair and steel bracelets to remind them of their martial heritage.[49] Another officer wrote that he had "soldiered with Rajputs, Pathans, Sikhs, Gurkhas, Punjabi Mahomedans, Madras Sappers and Miners, Dogras, Garhwalis and other races. Each had its characteristics, and these must be recognised by any one entrusted with the command of Indian troops".[50]

Each had their own specific qualities. So the Dogras are "quiet, steady, clean soldiers"; the Pathans "have quicker wits than the other races" and Sikhs are "fine manly soldier[s]", but should not be spoiled or pampered.[51] Military historians are not noted for their critical gaze on army matters but Jeffrey Greenhut is spot on when he asserts that the concept of martial races had an "elegant symmetry" in that it posited intelligent, educated Indians as cowards, while those "defined as brave were uneducated and backward", thus leaving the combined qualities of intelligence and courage with the British officer class.[52] Thus the practice of

46 MacMunn, 1933, p3.
47 MacMunn, 1933, p4.
48 Yeats-Brown, 1945, p31.
49 Yeats-Brown, 1945, p30.
50 Willcox, 1920, p7.
51 Willcox, 1920, pp56-57.
52 Greenhut, 1984, p16.

racism was backed up by imperial intellectual gloss that was fundamental to the ideological foundation of the Indian army.[53]

Paternalistic racism pervaded every aspect of army life. One officer stated Indians "are of course splendid fighters, but are very lost without their officers".[54] James Willcocks, commander of the Indian Corps in France, summed up the officer corps' attitude to Indian soldiers thus: "No one has greater admiration for the Indian soldier, and officer when he lives up to it, than I have. He's generally brave, nearly always loyal—but he is seldom *if ever* fit to replace the British officer".[55] In this way martial theory neatly dovetailed every racist stereotype to buffer colonial armies. And these notions persist into the present, with the Gurkhas remaining a highly recognised section of the British army, celebrated for their fighting prowess but until recently ignored and rejected by the state when it came to paying pensions.[56]

Racist theories were similarly important to the French Empire. General Charles Mangin, a keen advocate of West African military recruitment, wrote *La Force Noire* in 1910 in which he put forward a racial and military justification for the use of African soldiers. Mangin had long held the view that the "black force" was comprised of "natural warriors", "primitives, for whom life counts so little and whose young blood flows so ardently, as if avid to be shed".[57] His chief concern was the creation of a large reserve of African troops to counter France's demographic imbalance in the face of Germany.

Like those of his British counterparts, Mangin's arguments were based on biological determinism that ranked Africans in order of physical size, "military strength" and apparent loyalty. So West Africans from Senegal, Ivory Coast and central Africa were prized as loyal subordinates who had demonstrated previous valour and support for the French in Africa. For Mangin these "select" African peoples "have precisely those qualities that are demanded in the long struggles in modern war: rusticity, endurance, tenacity, the instinct for combat, the absence of nervousness, and an incomparable power of shock".[58]

As early as 1909 French military theoreticians supported Mangin's proposals asserting that in the coming war "the 'black' troops will have no rivals when it is a matter of delivering the final shock". Traits such as savage impetuosity in attacks with the bayonet, cold-blooded and fatalistic temperament were taken as inherited qualities of the "black race".[59] However, Mangin had his critics within the

53 Greenhut, 1983, p70.
54 Quoted in Greenhut, 1983, p61.
55 Quoted in Greenhut, 1983, p66.
56 Press Association, 2011.
57 Mangin, 1910, p258.
58 Mangin, 1910, p343.
59 Quoted in Lunn, 1999, p525

French military command too. General Charles Moinier was suspicious of black soldiers. He had his own racial hierarchy stipulating that Africans were "simply not capable of adapting themselves with the same facility [as Europeans and North Africans] to the necessities of modern warfare".[60] Moinier was stationed in Madagascar and other generals based in North Africa were more pre-disposed towards Arab soldiers than those from sub-Saharan Africa.

Just as racism informed their preferred choice of colonial soldier, it also guided their reservations about others particularly in relation to latent fears about the very presence of non-white men in Europe with their close physical proximity to white civilians. Fraternisation with white women, in particular, was a key component of wartime anxiety. Colonial fantasies of uncontrolled black male desire and wartime nymphomania became an obsession. Inter-racial relationships had long exercised the minds of American generals in terms of black Americans stationed in Europe. Now similar fears afflicted British politicians and the high army command. Sex, or even the prospect of it, was troublesome. Lieutenant-Colonel Evelyn Howell, the first Indian mail censor and later foreign secretary to the government of India, argued that, were Indians allowed "to conceive a wrong idea of the 'izzat' [honour] of English women...[it] would be most detrimental to the prestige and spirit of European rule in India".[61]

Indian troops enjoyed slightly more freedom in France than in Britain. For most soldiers, of any nationality, this was their first time away from home, surrounded by new and unusual sights, smells and sounds. With death ever-present any chance of human intimacy with civilians afforded some possibility of normal life. And colonial troops were desirous of this as much as any other soldier. One Indian soldier wrote: "In England there are very beautiful women. But they do not even give us one".[62] So even the human touch was circumscribed by a combination of material paucity and racial subordination.

In his fictional account of Indians sent to France, *Across the Black Waters*, Mulk Raj Anand refers to the "unwritten law that no sepoy was to be seen on familiar terms with the women in this country". The English "did not like...the brown-skinned Indians to look at white women".[63] This point is illustrated well in his novel when he describes the reactions of sepoys on their first visit to a French brothel:

> They were eager to taste this new sensation, but even as they waxed enthusiastic they were restrained by the humility of their position as sepoys who had never

60 Quoted in Lunn, 1999, p525.

61 India Office Records: IOR, L/MIL/5/825, 18 June 1915, pp60-61.

62 India Office Records: IOR, L/MIL/5/825, part VII, 28 October 1915, p1,183.

63 Anand, 1940, pp105 and 264.

> dared to look at a white woman with the eyes of desire. And the sense of the poverty of their pockets threatened to put all these pleasures beyond their reach.[64]

In 1917 a race riot, foreshadowing the larger riots of 1919, broke out when white youths in London's working class East End, "incensed" by "the infatuation of the white girls for the black men", attacked the houses of the latter.[65] The Home Office inspector of constabulary spoke of the "irresistible fascination" of women for Chinese men;[66] while in Sheffield, newspapers reported in shocked tones that Salvation Army workers were horrified by young women "consorting with and listening to the persuasions of coloured men".[67] These were indeed considered dangerous liaisons!

Resistance

The tensions in wartime would eventually spill over into active resistance. This took two forms: anti-colonial rebellions of civilians and resistance in the ranks. The former included the Chilembwe Uprising of January 1915 in Nyasaland (modern day Malawi) and the Easter Rising of 1916 in Dublin.[68] But in some respects the more significant and of immediate concern for the British was talk of mutiny. In 1917 Chinese and Egyptian dock workers drafted into the port of Boulogne by the British came out on strike alongside British and Commonwealth Army mutineers at Étaples. Field Marshall Haig ordered reprisals in which 27 of these strikers were shot dead.[69] There are two other highly significant mutinies involving soldiers who had seen battle.

The Singapore Mutiny of February 1915

The 5th Light Infantry Regiment of the Indian Army had been sent from Madras to Singapore in October 1914 to replace the Yorkshire Light Infantry, which itself was bound for the Western front. This unit was, unusually, an entirely Muslim unit, made up of Rajputs and Pathans, two groups, termed "martial races". One month after its arrival in Singapore it was announced that the regiment would be sent to Hong Kong. The same month Turkey, responding to the prompting

64 Anand, 1940, p63.

65 *The Times*, 3 July 1917, p5.

66 Chinese contract labourers had been brought over as part of the Chinese Labour Corps working in the south of England, London and Liverpool—O'Neill, 2014.

67 Home Office Archive: HO45/10724/251861, memorandum of Leonard Dunning, H M Inspector of Constabulary, 19 October 1914; *Sheffield Weekly Independent*, 4 August 1917, p2.

68 The Chilembwe revolt was centred on the black middle class and encouraged by grievances against the colonial system, including forced labour, discrimination and the new demands on the indigenous population caused by the outbreak of war.

69 Fuller, 2014, p23.

of its ally Germany, declared war on Britain and its allies. The Ottoman Sultan, Mehmed V, was the Muslim Caliph. So the Germans, aware that nearly half of the world's 270 million Muslims lived under British, French or Russian rule, calculated that if they could foment rebellion among the allies' Muslim subjects, this huge fifth column could be potentially devastating.

As the day of embarkation approached, a rumour took hold among the Indian infantry that their actual destination was not Hong Kong but Turkey, where they would be thrown into battle against Turkish Muslims. At 3.30pm on 15 February 1915 some 800 soldiers broke out of their barracks and killed several British officers before moving on to other areas of the city.

Responding to British pleas for help, French, Russian and Japanese warships docked in Singapore on 17 February. Some 75 Japanese sailors, 22 Russians and 190 French marines landed and alongside Singaporean police, British sailors and Malay States Volunteer Rifles, they began to round up mutineers who had taken refuge in the jungle to the north of Singapore. That evening 432 mutineers had been captured and the remaining subversives were finally rounded up by 20 February.[70] By the time the revolt was quashed, the mutineers had killed 39 Europeans—both soldiers and civilians. Three days later an inquiry, initially held in camera, identified three Indian officers as key conspirators but more than 200 sepoys were tried by court martial with 47 executed, 73 given terms of imprisonment ranging from seven to 20 years and 64 transported for life. The public executions by firing squad took place at Outram Prison, and were witnessed by an estimated 15,000 people "packed on the slopes of Sepoy Lines looking down on the scene".[71] These very public reprisals were designed to send a warning to the entire population.

The remnants of the 5th Light Infantry, numbering 588 sepoys plus seven British and Indian officers, left Singapore on 3 July 1915 for Africa and by 1922 it was disbanded. The British believed that soldiers had been incited to riot and mutiny by outside agents of either religious agitators or nationalists such as the Gadar Party.[72] Although the mutiny was quashed, it took almost a week for the British to restore order. To enhance Singapore's internal security, the British passed the Reserve Force and Civil Guard Ordinance in August 1915, requiring compulsory military service from all male subjects between 15 and 55 years of age

70 Harper and Miller, 1984, pp172-179.

71 See "Execution of Twenty-Two Renegades", *Straits Times*, 26 March 1915.

72 The Ghadar Party was an organisation founded by Punjabi Indians in the US and Canada with the aim of securing India's independence from British rule. Imperial interests dictated that colonial troops were servile, unthinking military fodder and their "natural" state was unswerving loyalty to Pax Britannica. Consequently for the British, mutiny could only be a result of external agitation. The lack of indigenous agency in these accounts has quite rightly been challenged—See Singh, 2014, pp184-186.

who were not already in the armed forces, volunteers or police.[73] It also proved that they could no longer depend on Indian soldiers to garrison the colony, thus demonstrating not only that they were caught off-guard but also how this episode shook the very foundations of British rule in Singapore. Subsequently all Indian nationals in Singapore were required to register, thereby alienating a previously acquiescent community, as well as showing the limits of empire.[74]

Taranto: Armistice Day

The port of Taranto was a logistical centre for the British army on the south eastern tip of Italy. On Armistice day, 11 November 1918, nine BWIR battalions that had served in France and Italy were concentrated at the port to prepare for demobilisation. Three further BWIR battalions that had served in Egypt and Mesopotamia joined them. There were severe labour shortages at Taranto and the allies used colonial troops to furnish their infrastructure needs. Demoted to labour units this meant the West Indian troops had to carry out the arduous work of loading and unloading ships, as well as the demeaning task of building and cleaning toilets used by white soldiers and Italian labourers. To add insult to injury, white soldiers were awarded a pay rise of six pence a day while the black soldiers were not as the War Office designated them mere "natives". On top of this they had to endure separate and inferior hospital access and segregated recreational facilities. All cinemas and YMCA huts open to British troops were off limits to West Indians. Some black soldiers wrote a letter of complaint to the governor of Barbados stating that this racist policy was "not only an insult to us who have volunteered to fight for the empire, but also an insult to the whole West Indies".[75]

For the BWIR troops this was the final indignity. On 6 December 1918 the men of the 9th Battalion revolted and attacked their officers. On the same day a group of about 180 black sergeants forwarded a petition to the secretary of state for the colonies demanding a 50 percent pay increase on a par with the rest of the British army and argued for officers' commissions to be open to non-white men. During the mutiny, which lasted about four days, a black NCO shot and killed one of the mutineers in self-defence and there was also a bombing. Disaffection spread quickly among other soldiers and on 9 December the "increasingly truculent" 10th Battalion refused to work and a "generally insubordinate spirit prevailed".[76] A senior commander, Lieutenant Colonel Willis, who had ordered

73 Ban, 2001, pp56-58.
74 Sareen, 1995, p822.
75 Quoted in Elkins, 1970, p100.
76 Public Record Office, CO 318/347.

some BWIR men to clean the latrines of the Italian Labour Corps, was also subsequently assaulted.

Both the 9th and 10th Battalions were disbanded and the men distributed to the other battalions, which were all subsequently disarmed. On the fourth day a battalion of the Worcestershire Regiment, including machine gunners, was dispatched to restore order and the "ringleaders" were rounded up with 60 West Indian soldiers later tried for mutiny and 49 of them convicted. One was executed by firing squad, another imprisoned for 20 years and others received sentences ranging from three to five years.

Although the mutiny at Taranto was crushed, bitterness persisted. On 17 December 1918 about 60 NCOs held a meeting to discuss the question of black rights, self-determination and closer union in the West Indies. An organisation called the Caribbean League was formed at the gathering to further these objectives. Another meeting on 20 December, under the chairmanship of one Sergeant Baxter, argued that "the black man should have freedom and govern himself in the West Indies" and that "force must be used, and if necessary blood shed to obtain that object".[77] The majority of those present loudly applauded his sentiments. These words, coming so shortly after the Russian Revolution, struck fear into the imperial establishment. Even the more modest aim of the promotion "of all matters conducive to the general welfare of the islands constituting the British West Indies and the British Territories adjacent thereto", was one that British Imperialism and the West Indian plantocracy would find impossible to meet in the post-war economic crisis.[78]

The aftermath of war

More than 74,000 Indian and 1,250 British West Indian troops died in the war. Tens of thousands more were wounded and maimed. The Commonwealth war graves at Seaford in Sussex have 19 headstones displaying the crest of the BWIR and the Menin gate at Ypres, Belgium bears a stone inscribed with the names of Abbas Khan, Ahmed Khan and Aiman Singh Gurung. These are testimony to their sacrifice.

But those who survived would be severely disappointed if they hoped victory would bring respect, equality and freedom from colonial rule. Just as racism was functionally necessary to the stability of imperial rule and war, it was critical to its aftermath. Post-war Britain was characterised by economic hardship with workers, particularly seamen, competing with each other for scarce jobs. As demobilised black troops joined settled Caribbean, Arab, Chinese and Somali

77 Major Maxwell Smith, Commanding Officer of 8th BWIR Battalion to Major General H F Thuillier, Commanding Troops, Taranto, 27 December 1918, Public Records Office, CO 318/350.

78 Quoted in Smith, 2008, p229.

communities in port cities, a wave of racist agitation resulted in riots targeting them. Some trade union leaders actively discouraged the employment of black workers and armed groups of racist thugs whipped up a frenzy of violence against black people as "outsiders stealing our jobs". Peter Fryer's excellent book *Staying Power* chronicles the series of riots in South Shields, Liverpool, South Wales and London's East End. For Fryer: "the end of the First World War ushered in the most troublous and stormy age of profound social crisis" in Britain.[79] It was against this backdrop that black troops were not allowed to take part in a London Peace March on 19 July 1919 to celebrate the end of the war.

Wartime racial anxieties spilled over into peacetime with a grotesque racist propaganda campaign following the deployment of African troops in the Rhineland. In 1919 between 25,000 and 40,000 French colonial troops from Algeria, Madagascar, Morocco, Senegal and Tunisia were stationed on the Rhine. Controversy erupted in Germany with sensationalist headlines accusing African troops of rape and molestation of white women. The German press denounced the use of "primitive black troops to watch over a white nation" and lurid cartoons carried hysterical imagery of "black sexual debauchery threatening German womanhood and white racial purity".[80] The campaign, orchestrated by German nationalists opposed to the French occupation, quickly achieved international notoriety as it was championed by radical voices in Britain, the US and Canada.

The most pernicious example of this was Edmund Dene Morel's 1920 article "Black Scourge in Europe: Sexual Horror Let Loose by France on the Rhine", in which he described how France "is thrusting her black savages...into the heart of Germany" where "primitive African barbarians", carriers of syphilis, have become a "terror and a horror".[81] This was made even more deplorable by the fact that Morel was an opponent of colonialism who had campaigned for African rights in the Belgian Congo. He was also a pacifist and member of the Independent Labour Party who went on to become a Labour MP in 1922. It was the *Daily Herald*, then a leading daily left paper, that published Morel's piece. It was later published as a pamphlet, entitled *The Horror on the Rhine*, in which Morel wrote that black troops "must be satisfied upon the bodies of white women".[82] The pamphlet was so popular that eight editions of it appeared and a free copy was distributed to delegates at the Trades Union Congress in 1920. Morel uncritically accepted reports that German women had been assaulted and raped. Of course, there was no evidence for this at all but it did not stop a whole range of liberals, radicals and

79 Fryer, 1984, p312.
80 Wigger, 2010, pp34-35.
81 Morel, 1920, quoted in Reinders, 1968, p1.
82 Quoted in Fryer, 1984, p317.

women's groups from joining the chorus, supposedly in the name of feminism and defending German womanhood. Throughout the spring and summer of 1920 the *Labour Leader* opened its columns to Morel and other writers discussing the black troops issue. *Foreign Affairs* devoted a special supplement in July 1920 to the subject and even the circular of the Northumberland Miners' Association spread Morel's word to its readers.[83] The liberal *Commonweal* referred to "hordes of Senegalese savages" and the "lust of black soldiery", while *The Nation* talked of black men as "savages" and "black terrorists".[84]

In spite of their anti-imperialism, certain sections of the British left reflected racist attitudes of the imperial powers. Fortunately, a minority of Marxist anti-imperialists stood against this tide and the young Jamaican socialist, poet and novelist Claude McKay responded to Morel's tirade in a letter published in *The Workers' Dreadnought*, edited by Sylvia Pankhurst.[85] McKay demanded: "Why all this obscene, maniacal outburst about the sex vitality of black men in a proletarian paper?" And he continued, "I, a full-blooded Negro, can control my sexual proclivities when I care to, and I am endowed with my full share of the primitive passion... Besides, I know hundreds of negroes of the Americas and Africa who can do likewise".[86] He was disgusted by the racist hysteria that seemingly gripped sections of Britain's left.

Post-war demands for freedom were met with savage repression throughout the empire, but nowhere more than in India where British forces, led by the odious General Dyer, massacred peaceful protesters in Amritsar in April 1919, killing 379. At the same time victory led Britain and France to extend their imperial possessions. They seized former German colonies in Africa and divided up the defeated Ottoman Empire in the Middle East according to the Sykes-Picot Agreement, which took its name from its negotiators, Sir Mark Sykes of Britain and Georges Picot of France.[87] At a meeting in Downing Street, Sykes pointed to a map and told the prime minister: "I should like to draw a line from the 'e' in Acre to the last 'k' in Kirkuk".[88] And so the modern day Middle East, replete with entrenched sectarian divisions, was created by the hasty drawing of straight lines on a map in crude chinagraph pencil. The post-war carve-up was designed to suit the imperial victors in their strategic and political goals. They set up the

---

83 Reinders, 1968, p11.

84 Quoted in Fryer, 1984, pp317-318.

85 McKay, 1920.

86 Quoted in Donlon, 2016.

87 Both were quintessential "empire men", aristocrats seasoned in colonial administration, and believers in the notion that the people of the region would be better off under the benevolence of European empires.

88 Acre is a coastal town in northern Israel and Kirkuk is in northern Iraq.

League of Nations to provide a figleaf of legitimacy to their cherry-picking that Lenin rightly described as "a thieves' kitchen". Another 1.8 million square miles of territory and 13 million people were added to the British Empire.

But the war irrevocably changed attitudes of the veterans to imperial authority. The shift in the Anglo-imperial world from empire patriotism to greater assertion and confidence in demanding equal rights and freedom was brought home in a memo by a senior Colonial Office official from 1919 that sharply revealed colonial anxieties: "the black man has come to think and feel of himself as good as the white".[89] In addition, nationalist stirrings had been awakened and sharpened. These could not be neatly packed away. At the end of the war Britain faced a war for independence in its closest colony—Ireland—and colonial revolts in India, China, Egypt, Mesopotamia and in the Caribbean, where discontent among demobbed West Indian soldiers fused with the anger of workers protesting against the economic hardships caused by the war.

When disgruntled BWIR soldiers began arriving back in the West Indies, they quickly joined a wave of strikes resulting from a severe economic crisis produced by the war and the influence of black nationalist ideology espoused by Pan-Africanist leader Marcus Garvey, who by now had altered his stance towards British rule in the Caribbean. Disenchanted soldiers and angry workers unleashed a series of protest actions and riots in a number of territories including Jamaica, Grenada and especially in British Honduras, where demobilised soldiers attacked the businesses and homes of the ruling commercial elites. Similarly disturbances hit Port of Spain, Trinidad, with militant strike action in December 1919.[90] Protests following the Amritsar massacre proved to be a turning point in forcing the British government to concede constitutional reforms, which would propel Gandhi and other nationalist leaders to be bolder and more assertive in fighting for independence.

The Russian Revolution of 1917, which hastened the end of the war and broke up the Tsarist empire, showed colonial rule could be broken and imperialism overthrown by mass movements led by organised workers. The Irish rose in revolt and won the liberation of most of the island. Anti-colonial movements developed across the British and French Empires, with Britain facing fierce resistance in Iraq, for example. But tragically these movements would come to fruition only after the empires and their peoples had been convulsed by a second world war.

---

89 Gilbert Grindle, Assistant Under-Secretary at the Colonial Office in London, quoted in Bourne, 2014, p71.

90 Elkins, 1970, p103.

References

Ahmed, Talat, 2009, "Gandhi: The Man Behind the Myths", *International Socialism 123* (summer), http://isj.org.uk/gandhi-the-man-behind-the-myths/

Alexander, Heber M, 1917, *On Two Fronts: Being the Adventures of an Indian Mule Corps in France and Gallipoli* (Heinemann).

Anand, Mulk Raj, 1940, *Across the Black Waters* (Jonathan Cape).

Ban, Kah Choon, 2001, *Absent History: The Untold Story of Special Branch Operations in Singapore 1915–1942* (SNP Media Asia).

Bourne, Stephen, 2014, *Black Poppies: Britain's Black Community and the Great War* (The History Press).

Cipriani, Arthur A, 1940, *Twenty-five Years After: The British West Indies Regiment in the Great War 1914-1918* (Trinidad Publishing Co).

Cohen, Stephen P, 1971, *The India Army and its Contribution to the Development of a Nation* (University of California Press).

Donlon, Anne, 2016, "'A Black Man Replies': Claude McKay's Challenge to the British Left", *Lateral: Journal of the Cultural Studies Association*, volume 5, issue 1, http://csalateral.org/wp/issue/5-1/claude-mckay-british-left-donlon/

Elkins, W F, 1970, "A Source of Black Nationalism in the Caribbean: the Revolt of the BWIR at Taranto, Italy", *Science and Society*, volume 33, number 2.

Farwell, Byron, 1989, *The Great War in Africa: 1914-1918* (Norton & Company Ltd).

Fryer, Peter, 1984, *Staying Power: Black People in Britain Since 1504* (Pluto Press).

Fuller, Chris, 2014, "Fighting the War on the Home Front", *Socialist Review* (February), http://socialistreview.org.uk/388/fighting-war-home-front

Gandhi, Mohandas Karamchand, 1918-19, *Collected Works of Mahatma Gandhi*, volume 17 (Ministry of Information and Broadcasting, India), www.gandhiserve.org/cwmg/VOL017.PDF

Greenhut, Jeffrey, 1983, "The Imperial Reserve: The Indian Corps on the Western Front, 1914-1915", *The Journal of Imperial and Commonwealth History*, volume 12, issue 1.

Greenhut, Jeffrey, 1984, "Sahib and Sepoy: An Inquiry into the Relationship between the British Officers and Native Soldiers of the British Indian Army", *Military Affairs*, volume 48, number 1.

Harper, R W E, and Harry Miller, 1984, *Singapore Mutiny* (Oxford University Press).

Hill, Robert (ed), 2011, *The Marcus Garvey and Universal Negro Improvement Association Papers* (Duke University Press).

Levine, Philippa, 1998, "Battle Colors: Race, Sex, and Colonial Soldiery in World War I", *Journal of Women's History*, volume 9, number 4.

Lunn, Joe, 1999, "'Les Races Guerrières': Racial Preconceptions in the French Military about West African Soldiers during the First World War", *Journal of Contemporary History*, volume 34, issue 4.

MacMunn, George, 1933, *The Martial Races of India* (Sampson Low, Marston and Co).

Mangin, Charles, 1910, *La Force Noire* (Hachette).

McKay, Claude, 1920, "A Black Man Replies," *The Workers' Dreadnought* (24 April).

Morel, Edmund Dene, 1920, "Black Scourge in Europe: Sexual Horror Let Loose by France on the Rhine", *Daily Herald* (10 April).

Omissi, David E, 1999 (ed), *Indian Voices of the Great War: Soldiers' Letters, 1914-1919* (Palgrave).

O'Neill, Mark, 2014, The *Chinese Labour Corps* (Penguin).

Pati, Budheswar, 1996, *India and the First World War* (Atlantic).

Press Association, 2011, "Gurkhas take Pensions Fight to European Court of Human Rights", *Guardian* (20 June), www.theguardian.com/world/2011/jun/20/gurkhas-pension-fight-european-court

Reinders, Robert C, 1968, "Racialism on the Left: E D Morel and the 'Black Horror on the Rhine'", *International Review of Social History*, volume 13, issue 1.

Rogers, Simon, 2002, "'There Were No Parades

For Us'", *Guardian* (6 November), www.theguardian.com/uk/2002/nov/06/britishidentity.military

Sareen, Tilak Raj, 1995, *Secret Documents on Singapore Mutiny 1915* (Mounto Publishing House).

Sherry, Dave, 2014, *Empire and Revolution: A Socialist History of the First World War* (Bookmarks).

Singh, Gajendra, 2014, *The Testimonies of Indian Soldiers and the Two World Wars: Between Self and Sepoy* (Bloomsbury).

Smith, Richard, 2008, "West Indians at War", *Caribbean Studies*, volume 36, number 1.

Strachan, Hew, 2004, *The First World War in Africa* (Oxford University Press).

Vadgama, Kusoom, 1984, *India in Britain: The Indian Contribution To The British Way Of Life* (Robert Royce).

Visram, Rozina, 1986, *Ayahs, Lascars, and Princes: Indians in Britain 1700-1947* (Pluto Press).

Wigger, Iris, 2010, "'Black Shame': The Campaign Against 'Racial Degeneration' and Female Degradation in Interwar Europe", *Race and Class*, volume 51, number 3.

Willcox, James, 1920, *With the Indians in France* (Constable and Company).

Yeats-Brown, Francis, 1945, *Martial India* (Eyre and Spottiswoode).

Into the digital void?

Martin Upchurch

Technical advances in new information and communication technologies (ICT) have led to debates on the left about the impact of digitalisation on the world of work. Alongside digitalisation and advances in interactive web-based communication, we have also witnessed new advances in robotics, 3D printing, artificial intelligence (AI) and self-tracking technology such as Fitbit or smartphone apps.

In combined form they represent a kind of intensified or "deep" automation that has implications not only for the world of work but for our understanding of capital accumulation strategies. Advances in communication and digital technology are alleged by many orthodox and heterodox economists alike to have a fundamental and positive effect on raising productivity by liberating knowledge-based labour from the rigours of the production process and, by implication, from Karl Marx's labour theory of value. It is suggested that we are entering a new era of "cognitive" or "communicative" capitalism in which "the object of accumulation consists mainly of knowledge, which becomes the basic source of value, as well as the principal location of the process of valorisation"—that is, the extraction of surplus value.[1]

On these views, the "digital economy", as Richard Barbrook postulates, has become a mixture of computer-based networks serviced by "digital artisans"

1 Moulier Boutang, 2012, p57. See also, Dean, 2005.

often producing and distributing information and knowledge for free as part of a "gift economy" that will pave the way in the future for a new form of anarcho-communism. It is a new era where the accumulation of knowledge usurps the accumulation of capital as the driver of the system. Such a world, Barbrook argues, allows many workers to "escape from the petty controls of the shop floor and the office".[2] Rather than being dependent on a single employer, office space may also be shared in new co-working spaces, where digital artisans, developers, designers and translators hire spaces to conduct work activities that are marketed across the ether.[3]

Alongside the rise of digital labour we have also recently seen the growth of robotics and associated debates on artificial intelligence. The prospect of a world where machines (computers, robots, AI and algorithms) do all the work has been termed a state of "singularity" by commentators from as early as the 1950s. They envisage not only humanless factories and paperless offices but also driverless cars, and homes with robots fulfilling housework and other domestic chores. Healthcare services, it is claimed, might also dispense with doctors as smartphone apps and robots diagnose and treat the sick.[4] "Singularity", as a realistic future, has since been popularised by the futurologist Raymond Kurzweil.[5] In this world our intelligence, it is argued, would become "non-biological" and creativity would be unbounded by human limitations. Machines would dominate production through processes of self-improvement, rewriting their own software to outstrip the functional capabilities of the human brain. Such prospects for machine over man/woman are clearly cataclysmic. So what is reality and what is science fiction?

In this article these debates, old and new, are reviewed, and a Marxist interpretation is presented. The relationship between technology, innovation and capital accumulation is rehearsed, before focusing on computerisation and digitalisation as distinct forms of innovation. Marxist theory, particularly the concepts of socially necessary labour time and abstract labour, helps illuminate the real role of ICT at work. Computers and related technologies are not neutral agents of change; they are rather used by capital as part and parcel of exploitative labour practices and capital accumulation.

Technology and capitalism

Technical innovation can act to reduce unit labour costs by increasing labour productivity to such an extent that it more than offsets the cost of introducing

2 Barbrook, 1998.
3 For a review of unions and co-working see http://tinyurl.com/zb85naw
4 Kirkup, 2016.
5 Kurzweil, 2005.

the technology in the short term (although as we shall see later the longer-term implications may be different). The drive to reduce unit labour costs and increase worker productivity is central to the competition inherent in the capitalist dynamic, and hence technical innovation is crucial to the survival of individual capitals. Certain technologies have more impact on the world of work than others, sometimes producing a great leap forward in production processes. For example, James Hargreave's spinning jenny, invented in England in 1764, transformed the process of weaving. Steam power allowed railway expansion and the cheaper exploitation of natural resources, and beam engines produced a transformation in textile production. A key example of non-digitised technical innovation in the modern industrial age is the automation of the production line made possible by electronically-controlled (rather than manually controlled) machines. We can point to other technical innovations that spurred processes of urbanisation, such as underground sanitation and water supply, and to other communication technologies such as the telegraph, the telephone and the jet engine that condensed both time and space.

Technology and labour

A consequence of all technical innovation, both old and new, is a degree of labour-shedding as machine replaces individual worker, leading to a parallel rise in the organic composition of capital measured by the ratio between constant capital (itself a product of past or "dead" labour) and variable capital (the "living" labour of workers in the production process). This steady rise of the organic composition of capital was considered by Marx as the key factor in explaining capitalism's tendency towards crisis. This is because it is living labour, the activity of workers at work, that creates new value. Dead labour, embodied in machinery and previously extracted raw materials, creates no new value; it merely passes on its value to the end product in the process of becoming utilised by living labour. As the ratio changes in favour of fixed capital investment in machines, and capital-bias takes effect, the relative share of labour in any one production process is reduced and hence the rate of return on capital investment (or rate of profit) falls correspondingly. So while individual capitals are always forced to adopt technical innovations in order to compete, they are at the same time potentially sowing the seeds of stagnation and decline, by over-reliance on fixed at the expense of variable capital. In order to overcome this tendency, countervailing factors would have to be applied by capital, which might involve attempting to get "more for less" from individual workers.

Hence technical innovation within the capitalist labour process is inevitably a cause of tension, with the promise of strategies of resistance from affected workers. Marx, in considering this tension, related the formation and reformation of human society generally to the "change and development of the material means of production, of the forces of production" and thus "the mode of production of material life conditions the social, political and intellectual life process in general".[6] Indeed, resistance by the workers in the dying trades and occupations has often defined both industrial relations and the societal conditions of the age. Most importantly we can observe that the composition of the working population continually shifts and changes as a result of technical innovations. In *The Making of the English Working Class*, E P Thompson elegantly describes such a process of change when he records resistance to the onset of the factory system in cotton based trades. The breaking of the new machines by displaced stockingers and croppers in the late 18th century was "very much more than a particular group of skilled workers defending their own livelihood… Luddism can be seen as a violent eruption of feeling against unrestrained industrial capitalism, harking back to an obsolescent paternalistic code, and sanctioned by traditions of the working community".[7]

Other more recent examples of resistance include the unofficial stoppages by dockers in the 1970s against the technology of containerisation which threw them out of work (the strikes led to the jailing of the Pentonville dockers and the eventual fall of the 1971 Industrial Relations Act).[8] Prior to containerisation ships spent almost half their time in dock, and the sacks and pallets that contained the goods were taken off ship by crane and hooked ashore by individual dockers. Containerisation allowed for mass transit via overhead platforms, onshore storage of goods and direct loading to lorries. It also required deep water ports to accommodate larger ships and make use of economies of scale. As a result of these changes many small ports closed and work shifted seawards away from river inlets to deeper water. The number of dockers in the port districts of East London, for example, fell by 150,000 in a ten-year period between 1966 and 1976.[9]

A more vivid example of the immediate impact of the introduction of new technology came in the "old" media in the 1980s as hot metal compositing and typesetting were replaced by computer-based digital input. The year-long major confrontation between print workers and Rupert Murdoch's News International at Wapping, East London, had been preceded by a union-busting operation led by proprietor Eddy Shah at his *Stockport Messenger* group of newspapers in 1983. Shah successfully used the new anti-union laws to break the union closed shop

6 Marx, 1977.
7 Thompson, 1982, pp599-601.
8 Darlington, 2016.
9 El-Sahli and Upward, 2015, p2.

at his plants and later went on to found a new newspaper, *Today,* produced by computer input.

The Wapping dispute in 1986 was led by Rupert Murdoch against the traditional print unions (the journalists' union, NUJ, had already voted to support the move to the new plant with the few dissenting voices sacked by Murdoch). Some 5,500 men and women working on Fleet Street were dismissed as they struck against plans to shift newspaper production (of *The Times, The Sun* and the *News of the World*) to the new plant in London's East End docklands which was fully geared to using new technology. The solidarity picketing at night near the gates of the plant proved unsuccessful in stopping Murdoch as he brought in scab labour with support from the electricians' union EETPU. Disputes such as this one, which followed the defeat of the miners a year earlier, proved to be defining moments in creating new ways of producing and organising work. Spirited resistance from collectivised labour, however, was not always enough to prevent technological change.

So how can we further explain technology as a defining ingredient of the production regime?

Is digitalisation "special"?

We can observe that technology has always been used in the workplace to measure, record and control as a means to maximise value creation and extraction. But commentators from both within and without the Marxist tradition often view digitalisation as a *distinct* form of innovation that produces qualitatively different outcomes on the world of work and value creation. So is digitalisation different from other forms of technical innovation? To answer we must first review the history of the technology itself.

The birth of computerisation

In the late 1960s the first computer-based information systems began to enter the workplace. Computerisation was presented by many as a fundamental break with old technology, allowing for a different world of work based on cybernetics and its associated feedback loops which would enable more efficiency in decision making. Alvin Toffler's best-selling *Future Shock* predicted that the introduction of the new information and communication technology (ICT) would engender a massive transformation of work, entailing the deconstruction of the "traditional" job, or the introduction of more leisure time for workers in aggregate as work "collapsed" and the unemployed drifted into leisure.[10] During the 1970s the fashion for predicting a "leisure society" even infected sections of

10 Toffler, 1970.

the trade unions, most notoriously with the 1979 publication of *The Collapse of Work* by Clive Jenkins and Barry Sherman of the white collar union ASTMS.[11] Suggestions that a fundamental transformation was taking place in work also gathered pace in academic circles with the publication in 1973 of Daniel Bell's *The Coming of Post-Industrial Society*, which predicted a society dominated by service employment and driven by new "intellectual" technology with scientists and engineers in occupational ascendancy.[12] Bell's vision was expanded two decades later by Jeremy Rifkin who foretold the "end of work", and by André Gorz in his postulations of the end of a "wage-based society".[13] The common denominator in all these studies over a 30-year period was an emphasis on the rise of "knowledge work" and its replacement of manual labour and the "traditional" working class. Manuel Castells, in his monumental trilogy *The Information Age*, added grist to the mill of technological determinism and placed information technology as the root of modern social change, arguing that the net would replace the hierarchy as the dominant form of social organisation, and the individual would construct her self-identity within the same technologically based process.[14]

The turn to digital and "immaterial" labour

These debates have taken a new form in the new century to suggest that digitalisation has created a different model of capitalism based on "free" and "immaterial" labour. Tiziana Terranova, in an essay published in 2000, developed an argument that cultural and technical work is integral to the internet, and that much of such work, involving "the activity of building websites, modifying software packages, reading and participating in mailing lists, and building virtual spaces on MUDs and MOOs", is carried out for "free".[15] Digital labour is also identified with a:

> dominant capital accumulation model of contemporary corporate Internet platforms...based on the exploitation of users' unpaid labour, who engage in the creation of content and the use of blogs, social networking sites, wikis, micro-blogs, content sharing sites for fun and in these activities create value that is at the heart of profit generation.[16]

---

11 Jenkins and Sherman, 1979. ASTMS was the Association of Scientific, Technical and Managerial Staffs.

12 Bell, 1973.

13 Rifkin, 1995; Gorz, 1999.

14 See Castells, 1996.

15 Terranova, 2000, p33. MUDs and MOOs are online virtual reality systems to which multiple users (players) are connected at the same time.

16 Fuchs, 2010.

The onset of Facebook, for example, is said to rely on the free labour of individual posters to the site, enabling the owners of the site to the reap rewards from advertising sales and revenues. However, there is more to the concept of the digitalisation of work, which stretches beyond the "unpaid" aspects of digital labour. The suggestion is that capitalism has shifted from a system of capital accumulation based on the factory and the collective workplace to one based on the accumulation and dissemination of knowledge through the internet. Hence a shift from "material" to "immaterial" labour.

Some mainstream management theorists have similarly interpreted the rise of networks based on the internet and digitalisation as an opportunity to re-invent organisational decision making structures in the workplace to the advantage of capital. The internet, it is argued, both facilitates and expands the horizons of digitalisation by offering opportunities to "flatten hierarchies and promote open and egalitarian workplace arrangements".[17] Such arrangements are not, however, designed to challenge management prerogative, but are rather intended to tap into worker creativity in the interests of corporate competitiveness. The model is taken further by others, from a left perspective, who champion the levelling effects of digitalisation. Some claim that digital labour, and "prosumption"—production by consumers—will enable a "shared" economy in which consumers create value for companies without receiving wages.

The emphasis on the perceived need to break down binaries and focus on "networks" is rooted in earlier autonomist and Italian *operaismo* (workerism) traditions. This tradition emphasised the primacy of the network and cultural discourse praxis over the economic power of the organised working class. Some, otherwise sympathetic commentators, have tempered this "post-*operaismo*" approach. Nick Dyer-Witheford, in his excellently researched book *Cyber-Proletariat*, for example, proposes a "post post-*operaismo*" perspective. Dyer-Witheford takes as his starting point "neither 'worker' nor 'multitude' but 'proletariat' whereby the proletariat, induced by cybernetics, embraces workers beyond the workplace as the key transformative agency".[18] When combined with robotics and AI the claims for the future become even more gargantuan. Human labour, in this utopian scenario, would be redundant, freeing us all for a life of leisure and a form of anarcho-communism based on cyber networks and shared digital creativity.

If knowledge sharing drives the system then the regime of capital accumulation is fundamentally altered. Most crucially, it is alleged that Marx's labour theory of value would be redundant as machines, computers, robots and AI take over all production. This is the core of the digital labour thesis offered in popular

17 Attwood-Charles and Schor, 2015

18 Dyer-Witheford, 2015

form by Paul Mason in his book *PostCapitalism* (critiqued in earlier issues of this journal), when he suggests that "knowledge-driven production tends towards the unlimited creation of wealth, independent of the labour expended".[19] This is because of a prediction that the marginal cost of production will be driven towards zero, as "stuff that can be made with tiny amounts of human labour is probably going to end up being free, shared and commonly owned".[20] The "post-capitalist" utopia (or dystopia) that would arise would be a world where the organic composition of capital (enshrined in robot and AI form) had risen so much that the creation of surplus value would shrink towards zero. Carl Shapiro and Hal Varian offer an orthodox economic explanation for this phenomenon suggesting that information is costly to produce but subsequently cheap to reproduce.[21] So the cost of producing the first copy of information may be substantial, but the cost of producing (or reproducing) additional copies is negligible. It is in this "reproduction" phase that the marginal costs associated with digitalisation may tend towards zero as "economics of abundance".

Proponents of the digital labour thesis often refer to Marx's "Fragment on Machines" in the *Grundrisse* whereby he conceptualises the tendency for capitalism to develop productive forces continually through the use of technology. Marx referred specifically to the potential of mechanisation to dominate the production process. The machine appears as an all-powerful force, both in fragmenting the input of the individual worker and engendering a subservient relationship to technology through division of labour:

> But, once adopted into the production process of capital, the means of labour passes through different metamorphoses, whose culmination is the machine, or rather, an automatic system of machinery (system of machinery: the automatic one is merely its most complete, most adequate form, and alone transforms machinery into a system), set in motion by an automaton, a moving power that moves itself; this automaton consisting of numerous mechanical and intellectual organs, so that the workers themselves are cast merely as its conscious linkages.[22]

Marx, however, foresaw mechanisation of the production process not only as a conceptual endpoint of the logic of capital accumulation but also as a driver of alienation, after which liberation could only be achieved by workers taking back power and control of production. Many in the autonomist tradition interpret this endpoint deterministically as the "inevitable" collapse of capitalism, and

19 Mason, 2015, p136. See also Choonara, 2015, and Green, 2016.
20 Mason, 2015, p164.
21 Shapiro and Varian, 1998.
22 Marx, 1973.

specifically refer to Marx's premise of "communal production", which emerges within this autonomist approach as a particular phase of capitalism where anarcho-communism is enabled by digital artisans. In this interpretation the power of capital, rather than being challenged directly as Marx intimated, is subverted in diffuse forms through networks of the dispossessed. In this supposed nirvana power is assumed without taking power.

Again we can trace the origins of this approach to the Italian workerist movement of the 1970s, which portrayed society as a "social factory" where work had shifted out of the factory, "thereby setting in motion a truly complex machine".[23] Michael Hardt and Toni Negri in *Empire* take the concept further and describe an epoch of "postmodernisation" in which material production has evaporated into a weightless world.[24] Digital communication as an alternative source of information (and the potential power that goes with such information) makes it possible to challenge dominant power structures. Again they argue that there are now no fixed boundaries or territorial centres of power. Instead we are bounded by a world where power lies "both everywhere and nowhere", one dominated by service work and immaterial labour embracing universal cultural "products", knowledge and communication. In this vision intensified use of information technology is once again used as a predictor of a more relaxed, leisure oriented society where menial work is done by machines, labour is collectivised and the division of labour dominant in the era of Fordist mass production is overcome. Marx in the *Grundrisse* is once again misleadingly used to justify such a position.[25]

Of course, we need to be cautious about accepting the idea of postmodernisation without examining the evidence of what has actually been happening in the contemporary world of work. If we simply look at the information technology industry itself, for example, rather than a disaggregated networked form of capitalism, as Castells and others predicted, we find instead a highly concentrated form of capitalism with giant corporations such as Microsoft and Google dominating the industry through processes of exclusivity and buying-up of smaller competitors. The legal regulation of information-sharing favours capital and corporate interests, and laws on intellectual property and corporate confidentiality restrict the ability of dissenters to expose corporate misbehaviour. Facebook is now owned by venture capitalists, while Google has bought YouTube.[26]

23 Negri, 1989, p92.

24 Hardt and Negri, 2000.

25 See the critique of Hardt's and Negri's use of the "Fragment on Machines" in Callinicos, 2014, pp198-204.

26 Go to http://whoownsfacebook.com/

This fact that reality is divorced from the rhetoric of the networked and disaggregated form of capitalism is especially highlighted in the case of the so-called "app economy" whereby we have the largest taxi company (Uber) which neither owns nor drives taxis, a holiday accommodation agency (Airbnb) which owns no holiday accommodation and a travel agency (booking.com) that arranges no holidays. Furthermore, when it comes to software reproduction we find that Microsoft software updates, for example, are designed deliberately to keep the consumer constantly compulsorily dissatisfied, without choice as to whether or not the older versions should be discarded. Rather than power being distributed, it appears more concentrated in huge corporations in time-honoured fashion as the industry develops.

The concepts of both weightlessness and immateriality have met critiques from the left. Ursula Huws, writing in 1999, questioned the concept of weightlessness, pointing out that: "perhaps one of the most dangerous illusions fostered here is the notion that the new information technologies mean that anything can now be done by anyone, anywhere: that the entire population of the globe has become a potential virtual workforce".[27] The danger referred to is the false notion that work is becoming entirely independent of space, that capital is footloose and super-powerful as a result, and that the collective worker is consequently emasculated. Such notions are suspect even when applied to new phenomena such as the "app economy". Recent disputes involving Uber taxi drivers and Deliveroo's cycle-based delivery agents in London, show us that the material is very real, and that collective strike action can deliver improvements in workers' conditions. Kevin Doogan pursues this point and similarly describes the weightless world scenario as a fallacious concept. The supposed death of distance and time engendered by the ICT revolution has, he suggests, led to an entirely false separation of motion and matter. He argues that in such a vision we appear to move beyond techno-centrism into a world where the transmission of knowledge becomes a fetish in itself. This is despite the important fact that "the production and consumption of knowledge remains materialist even if its circulation is immaterial".[28]

The concept of "free labour" associated with the digital economy has also come under some criticism. Of course, we can all point to *unpaid* time associated with our working lives; simply getting to work by public or private transport is an example. Professional work such as that in education, medicine and the law involves reading documents and learned articles and so on outside of scheduled work hours. It is also true that many features of civil society simply would not exist without volunteer activity: running scouts and guides, organising sports

27 Huws, 1999, p47.

28 Doogan, 2009, p50 refers here to "dematerialisation".

clubs and societies, etc. Much of this involves human exertion, which can be considered work in a general sense, but it is more akin to a labour of love—a hobby, rather than "free labour" in a postmodern world. More tellingly, as Diane van den Broek has argued in her critique of "free labour":

> digital labour is neither free or immaterial, because it is not the content of labour itself, but rather its relationship with capital that gives it "weight" and value... labour remains heavily bound by an employment relationship and a labour process, whether work is performed in cyberspace or other more "grounded" locations. Indeed, given the mutual dependency between wage labour and capital, both concepts become meaningless without the other.[29]

Let us now move from some of the theoretical disputes and examine the evidence for the transformation of work associated with digitalisation, AI and robotics.

Evidence?

Digital technology, just like previous technological advances, has the power to displace workers. But we need to consider the overall impact of technological innovation in aggregate before we can accept that digital technology will mean the end of work. First, computerisation, while decimating the jobs of typists and hot metal print workers, has expanded work and manufacturing jobs not only in computer hardware and software, but also in mobile phones and games consoles. Second, even the largest operators of the "prosumer" economy, such as Google, Facebook or Amazon, will rely on real-time exploitation of their workforces. In Amazon's case this exploitation is intense within its semi-automated warehouses and outsourced "crowd-workers", whereby workers undertake bite-sized tasks for Amazon on piece rate schemes from home via computer links.[30] Google may rely on advertising revenues from enterprises in the "real" economy for its survival, but at the same time will need to exploit its own workforce in order to compete with rival search engine and email providers such as Yahoo or Baidu.

Third, when we examine the empirical evidence we find that the data do not bear out either the "leisure class" or "end of work" scenarios. In 1975 the industrial sociologist John Child reviewed the available evidence. He rejected the outcome of a leisured or structurally transformed society and concluded that the "logic" of advanced information systems "would appear to extend the routinisation, indeed bureaucratisation of work to clerical and even managerial levels where this may hitherto have been absent".[31] In other words, rather than see the elimination of

29 Van den Broek, 2010, pp123-124.

30 For a description of Amazon's crowd-working see Knaebel, 2016.

31 Child, 1975, p149.

menial office and manual work we would come to see instead a routinisation of work abetted by computerisation. Such a scenario was eloquently exposed by Harry Braverman in *Labour and Monopoly Capital* in 1974, in which he describes the processes of deskilling and Taylorisation of office work.[32] Indeed, the introduction of word processors and the commercialisation of robots in the 1970s sparked concerns not only over routinisation but also over whether or not a "machine was taking your job". A pamphlet on this question written by Chris Harman for the British Socialist Workers Party in 1979 had this to say:

> It is easy to see how the same process of deskilling and increasing managerial control takes place in the store with the introduction of the computerised check-out system. The cash register operator no longer has the excuse when he or she feels tired of taking a "natural break" while they delay to check up on a price; the skilled warehouseman is no longer needed once a computer is keeping a check on stocks and makes out new orders; all the accounts clerk has to do is to read off figures from a computer terminal or print-out. All of them will be left with tasks which are boring and repetitious—and which will get harder as management increases the speed of the computerised parts of the work process.[33]

The onset of mass clerical factories, tied to the computer rather than the filing cabinet, was nigh.

Later historical overviews of the period since computerisation was introduced also point to the same conclusions regarding the falsity of a leisure-based utopia. After conducting a long review of the amassed evidence Peter Bramham found: "with hindsight, the original project around the mission to develop and manage 'leisure society' can be dismissed as naïve".[34] This apparent naivety was undoubtedly driven by a misunderstanding of employer motives for, and consequences of, introducing new forms of technology. From a Marxist perspective, any technical innovation, including ICT and other forms of digitalisation of work, should not be considered as a neutral agent of change within the labour process. Capital will be tempted to invest in new technology not because it may improve the public good, but because it can increase profit ratios. As a result, the utopia of a leisured society under capitalism is illusory. Capital needs innovation to have a pernicious rather than benign effect by intensifying work and increasing the rate of exploitation, not only because of the costs involved, but also because of the necessity for capital to create countervailing tendencies in the workplace to stagnation in productivity growth. Thus, rather than seeing a

32 Braverman, 1974.

33 Harman, 1979.

34 Bramham, 2006, p379. See also Veal, 2009, for an additional historical overview of the debates.

reduction in working hours in recent decades (in parallel with the rise in digitalisation and ICT) in advanced industrial societies the average hours worked by an employee has tended to increase. This trend sits alongside a general increase in both unemployment and in-work poverty.[35]

Fourth, it is not the case that computerisation and digitalisation have led to a long-term qualitative and quantitative upward shift in aggregate labour productivity (which might give space for the arrival of a leisure society). There will certainly be an initial leap in organisational productivity as a result of the introduction, for example, of newer forms of ICT such as web 2.0. However, such boosts to productivity are not sustained.[36] A study of companies in two countries for the UK-based National Institute for Economic and Social Research confirmed the conclusions from similar studies, that "it seems that the decision of going online does not have by itself long-lasting effects on productivity".[37]

The US-based economist Robert J Gordon is a long-term and mainstream critic of the position that ICT has substantially raised overall productivity. In his latest major study of the US economy he pours cold water on the claim that ICT has had a fundamental effect in raising productivity in the decades since it entered the workplace. Gordon's argument is directed at the "techno-optimists". He states that the IT revolution led to less significant changes in productivity than a host of other technologies including the telegraph, the electric light, or indoor plumbing and urban sanitation.[38] A major point to consider is that computers are a relatively small proportion of capital stock, and that, more significantly, investment in computers has been declining since the height of the "IT Revolution" of the 1990s.[39] The management specialist Michael Porter suggests that, "as all companies come to embrace internet technology, the internet itself will be neutralised as a source of advantage".[40] While upgrades in software and hardware are always likely to occur, the aggregate effect of such upgrading is likely to be small compared to the initial investment. Individual capitals must also consider what Marx described as the "lifespan of fixed capital". As Harman argued:

> Capitalists rarely replace existing machinery the moment technological advance takes place. They try to wait until they have recovered and made a profit on what they spent on that machinery—which usually takes them a number of years. This tendency to wait is increased by risks inherent in being the first to use untried

35 Pradella, 2015.

36 See UKCES, 2014, for a contemporary review of the evidence.

37 Domenech, Rizov and Vecchi, 2015, p24.

38 Gordon, 2016, pp441-461.

39 Goodridge, Haskel and Wallis, 2009, p34.

40 Porter, 2001, p62.

technology: the chance of scooping the market by a massive reduction in costs can be outweighed by the dangers of the technology simply not working.[41]

Such false dawns of technological change suggest that we need to apply caution to claims of universalism in application.

Robotics and artificial intelligence

Indeed, when examining the evidence, we also find that technical innovation in the form of robotics and AI is similarly restricted in its potential impact on the world of work. Evidence published in 2015 from a dataset of companies in 17 countries gathered between 1993 and 2007 suggests that, while productivity increases with robotic innovation and some semi-skilled and lower skilled jobs are abandoned, "there is some evidence of diminishing marginal returns to robot use—'congestion effects'—so they are not a panacea for growth". Indeed, the researchers suggest further that "this makes robots' contribution to the aggregate economy roughly on a par with previous important technologies, such as the railroads in the 19th century and the US highways in the 20th century".[42]

This is not to say that capital is not investing in robotics. The opposite is the case, as a process of robotic automation is taking place involving artificial cognition and machine learning.[43] Japan and South Korea are leading the way, with over 300 robots per 10,000 manufacturing employees. However, their job replacement value also remains limited, especially given the substantial cost of investment associated with robots. Another problem with investment in robots is that the tasks they can do effectively remain limited. For more complex tasks, robots have to be minded by humans lest they break down or miscalculate precision movements, which once again reduces their potential contribution to productivity enhancement. Mercedes-Benz, for example, has now begun replacing its robots with humans as they are more flexible.[44] Indeed, part of the reason for the limitation of robots in advanced technical processes is their lack of flexibility. A 2016 study of German automotive factories found that instead of providing a panacea for productivity enhancement, the use of robots meant that humans performed extra work which involved constant monitoring of the robots: "during a normal and otherwise smooth shift, a worker responsible for the ballet of eight welding and handling robots intervenes 20 to 30 times per shift—not because of technical

---

41 Harman, 1991.

42 Michaels and Graetz, 2015.

43 According to the International Federation of Robotics (IFR), the total number of industrial robots in operation worldwide was 1.5 million in 2014, while the IFR expects 1.3 million more to come online in the next two years.

44 See Gibbs, 2016.

incidents but in order to prevent them. Although human work declined quantitatively over the years, its qualitative role increased with automation".[45] Efforts by a leading robotics manufacturer—Rethink Robots—to create an affordable "plug and play" robot capable of mimicking human movement for widespread use in industry appear to have stalled. The company has recently downsized, announcing redundancies of nearly a quarter of its staff.[46] Moves are now afoot to develop "cobots" as an alternative to robots. These operate side by side with humans to enable flexibility and creativity to flourish.[47]

A second problem, as the Marxist economist Michael Roberts has reminded us, is that robots remain a machine, and as such:

> Robots do not do away with the contradictions within capitalist accumulation...a capital-bias or labour shedding means less new value is created (as labour is the only form of value) relative to the cost of invested capital. There is a tendency for profitability to fall as productivity rises... So an economy increasingly dominated by the internet of things and robots under capitalism will mean more intense crises and greater inequality rather than super-abundance and prosperity.[48]

Furthermore, "a vacuum-cleaning robot, a Roomba, will clean the floor quickly and cheaply and increasingly well, but it will never book a holiday for itself with my credit card".[49] While seemingly trivial, Roberts's comments further highlight the limitations on predictions of a world dominated by robotic innovation. For example, if it were possible to move to a world where robots reproduced themselves (robots making robots making robots) then we would have experienced the mother of transformations to a world of zero profits (as there would be no value creation through human labour), combined with superabundance and leisure with robots akin to slaves. The implications for a contest between capital and labour *en route* to this nirvana would be enormous. As Michael Roberts puts it, "we stand facing a future which might resemble either a hyper-capitalist dystopia or a socialist paradise, the second option doesn't get a mention".[50]

The question of consciousness is also problematic in that we must ask if consciousness transcends artificial "intelligence". When a human looks into a mirror she sees herself; when a monkey looks into a mirror it sees a monkey. But what does a robot "see" and what does it "recognise"? In fact, the robot does not "see" unless it is pre-programmed by human intelligence to record a specific

45 Pfeiffer, 2016, p16.
46 Tobe, 2013.
47 Paul-Choudhury, 2016, p18.
48 Roberts, 2015.
49 Roberts, 2016a.
50 Roberts, 2016b, p10.

image in distinction from other images. A robot may be programmed to perform new tasks, but it cannot transfer knowledge gained in one task to another. The robot has no imagination, emotion or consciousness and remains a machine. In *Consciousness Explained* Daniel Dennett rehearses this conundrum and argues that computers work very differently from the human mind—computers process increasingly large amounts of information serially, while the mind involves the simultaneous interaction of different mechanisms and processes.[51] The real challenge for AI becomes one of achieving the latter kind of complexity.

What about consumption?

Of course, it is not only in the world of production that automation appears to be gathering pace. As consumers we are constantly bombarded with advertising for new technological products which will supposedly enhance our lifestyle in a "barcode" or "app" society. This may include smart watches, fitness trackers, smart glasses and smart clothing.[52] Google's driverless car has now recorded more than one million miles on Nevada and Californian roads since its launch in 2012, and the UK government, according to media claims, is in the forefront of creating a deregulated approach to their use and actively examining how they may be insured.[53] Driverless cars are not without problems, they are pre-programmed for sets of traffic lights but do not currently recognise temporary lights at road works, nor do they recognise a police officer asking them to stop! Neither are they technically driverless as to date they are only allowed on public roads with a responsible driver with a full licence behind the "wheel". Despite these problems Google estimate they will be clear of such issues by 2020 (or rather that all regulatory hurdles will be dispensed with), while other predatory "sharing" economy companies such as Uber have expressed their willingness to introduce (actually) driverless taxis, clearly on the basis that the need to pay for a taxi driver as well as the taxi can be circumvented.

We are also now able to measure every aspect of our body movements and even our vital signs such as blood pressure and heart rate with wearable devices or via smartphone apps. A whole movement (the "Quantified Self") of people who share and swap such data on a mutual basis has arisen.[54] On a commercial level such quantification and recording of our body movements has, of course, further potential for commodification. In the kitchen a domestic robot may sweep the floor or even record the calorie intake of our food. A sex robot may be of use in the

51 Dennett, 1991, p431.
52 Fordham, 2015.
53 Titcomb, 2015.
54 See Moore, 2014, for a review and Nafus, 2016.

bedroom while for the completely self-obsessed male there is now an app called SexFit which "is worn on the male genitalia to help provide a stronger erection, and connects to a companion smartphone app via Bluetooth or WiFi so that you can measure the important things about a romantic moment, like calories burned and thrusts per minute. The information collected gets sent to your phone".[55]

All of this suggests that we may be moving rapidly to a world where robots, AI and computers become dominant over human inspired activity. However, predictions of the coming of the singularity (when artificial intelligence surpasses human intelligence) are often based on extensions and extrapolations from Moore's "law", named after Intel co-founder Gordon Moore, according to which the number of transistors that can be inserted into a computer doubles every two years, both lowering the cost and vastly increasing computing power. However, there is a finite supply of the rare earth metals used in the manufacture of computers,[56] and Moore has himself acknowledged that there will also be a physical limit to how many transistors you can squeeze into an integrated circuit.

The prospects of reaching the singularity as a result of the application of digitalisation, robotics and AI thus appears a long way off. This is due to the passage of technology that still needs to be undertaken fully to realise the potential of these innovations, but also because of the contradiction between the search for increased productivity and the crisis of profitability that it would entail. These limitations appear confirmed by the evidence. In a major study conducted to assess how likely the singularity is, seven significant tests for its onset observed within the last 50 years were tested. The tests in the study are focused on economic data recording the rates of acceleration in the supply and demand of information technology products such as computer software and related applications, as well as labour related issues of wage growth and productivity in key ICT sectors. The author of the study concluded that "five of the seven tests are negative for singularity while two are positive... Using simple extrapolation for the two positive tests, the time at which the economy might plausibly cross the singularity is 100 years or more".[57] Most significantly, the tests failed on the most important measures of increasing overall productivity and rising wage growth.

In summary we can discern that there appears to be no marked difference between ICT and digitalisation in its effects on productivity, performance and employment within the workplace (and the economy in general) and previous forms of technical innovation. Technology is introduced within the capitalist dynamic precisely to boost labour productivity and reduce unit labour costs, but

55 Amlen, 2014.

56 Go to www.techradar.com/news/computing-components/the-pc-rare-metals-crisis-921363

57 Nordhaus, 2015, p28.

tensions will inevitably arise which mitigate the immediate effects. Most importantly, the contradictions of the capitalist mode of production, seen through Marx's lens of the labour theory of value and the long-term tendency of the rate of profit to fall, still appear to pertain in the new world of digital work. We may well be in the storm of a process of deep automation within the workplace but it is not the case that productivity has been enhanced to a degree that we can foresee either the end of work or a communal utopia of digital artisans in a weightless world of immaterial labour. So can we identify any difference in the world of work as digitalisation gathers pace?

Towards the measurement of everything?

The clue to understanding the real impact of digitalisation upon work and the working class is to re-analyse the effects through Marx's concept of socially necessary labour time. Marx developed the concept of socially necessary labour time to help explain the dynamic of competition between capitals. To succeed in competition with rival capitalists, the individual capitalist is forced to utilise labour to the extent that output per person per unit of time does not fall below the average for the sector or occupation in which the capitalist operates. This average is expressed as the socially necessary labour time required to produce the commodity in question. It is subject to constant change as new applications of technology or new ways to organise and exploit labour power are introduced. Marx explains the relationship between socially necessary labour time and the market value common to all commodities of the same type: "the different individual values must be equalised at one social value, the above-mentioned market value, and this implies competition among producers of the same kind of commodities and, likewise, the existence of a common market in which they offer their articles for sale".[58]

Constant pressure is thus placed on the capitalist to keep up with competitors by revising work procedures and checking that workers are as productive as those of the competitors. The process is all embracing within the dynamic of capitalism. Most importantly, the introduction of new technologies is central to the process not only of increasing individual productivity, but also as a key mechanism to control the worker by enhancing the employer's ability to monitor work outputs in real time. To create maximum efficiency, and to extract the greatest surplus value from our labour, the input and output of all aspects of our physical and mental labour needs to be monitored and controlled by capital.

Marx further conceptualised the process of extracting value from the worker in terms of both concrete and abstract labour. Concrete or useful labour is the

58 Marx, 1966.

act of working itself to produce a particular kind of useful thing or effect, whereas abstract labour is the process whereby value is created through the equalisation of concrete acts of labour under the discipline of competition (within the dynamic of socially necessary labour time). In identifying abstract labour it is important to understand that Marx proposed that all labour has a dual character and exists simultaneously in both concrete and abstract form. It is abstract labour, however, through which the fruits of our labour are marketised, that is the root of estrangement of the product of labour from the individual labourer. Abstract labour is thus a source of alienation.

So we can expect an ever-increasing drive from employers to monitor, record and control our work, and to establish targets which are standardised across the factory, office, sector and occupation. The ever-increasing quantification of work output which flows from the above dynamic is no doubt the root of the target culture, and other alienative experiences that embrace modern working life, not only in the production process on the factory floor, but also in service and administrative functions. The employers' hunger for measurement stretches into all aspects of our labour whereby no job or occupation seems to escape. Targets are set into our work schedules, and monitored and controlled through competency assessments, appraisals and capability and disciplinary procedures.

The quantification of work is the holy grail of modern human resource practice. It stretches beyond the measurement of physical inputs and outputs into the realm of the psychological, social and attitudinal. In the education sector, for example, Microsoft has prepared a programme that includes a matrix of 39 competencies for "teachers and school leaders". These "competencies" are available to be measured which include such exotic names as "learning on the fly", "organisational agility" and "dealing with ambiguity". For "learning on the fly" alone there are four separate levels of competence from "basic" to "expert" that range over four further sub-competencies.

In this classical perspective we can foresee how the new information technologies are absorbed by capital to pursue its interests through the subordination of labour to its desire for profit maximisation. Thus we can predict that digitalisation will be utilised by capital to extend its ability to survey, monitor, measure and control the work of the individual worker. There is a parallel pathway, encapsulated in the turn towards neoliberal capitalism, which reinforces trends to a more intense dominance of capital by way of its ability to further atomise and individualise the worker so that her "value added" is left exposed and measurable. This neoliberal turn encourages, for example, the abandonment of collectively determined rates of pay, and introduces the prescription of individual performance related pay attached to ever harsher indicators of assessment, capability and discipline. For some commentators, this process of differentiation and atomisation has deep social, corporeal and cultural implications whereby we are measured not just in terms of our physical work output but also in terms of our psychological and social inputs.[59]

For others, such as Dyer-Witheford, it may have created the necessity to redefine the boundaries of work and labour by creating a new "cybertariat"[60] or "cyber-proletariat" in which the collectivised worker is subjugated and tempered by the existence of a non-waged pool of potential competitors that expands beyond the factory and office.[61] However, in many ways, of course, such a prognosis is not dissimilar from Marx's and Frederick Engels's original understanding of the reserve army of labour or rather the "surplus population", which may include not only the unemployed and under-employed, but also those who are outside of wage labour or involved at home in the social reproduction of labour. The similarity in concepts thus casts doubt on the uniqueness of the cyber-proletariat vision. Similarly, the "collective worker" is also a concept put forward by Marx as a result of the immediate processes of production. Workers are both subjugated by the employer and collectivised by the process of production at the same time. It is this double dynamic which Marx defined as the essence of the capitalist labour process, and which remains unchallenged by the "digital worker" while the employer continually seeks to exploit and extract surplus value from our labour.

But that is not to say that there are not some aspects of digitalisation that make work different from a pre-digital age. Capital has always sought to measure and control. The first time and motion studies, flowing from the work of Lillian and Frank Gilbreth and Frederick Winslow Taylor in the early 1900s, sought to standardise physical movements within the production process. The Gilbreths even used technological devices such as an electric motor-driven camera and a micro-chronometer to record and pre-determine the "necessary" time needed to undertake a task. Taylor and others such as Charles Bedaux took measurement further, by delving into the physiological and even psychological aspects of matching individual workers to specified work tasks. The movement continued throughout the 1920s and 1930s.

Such forms of measurement rapidly expanded into service and clerical work in the post-war period. Even the simplest work tasks were time measured against banks of photographs created under the Methods-Time Measurement system established in the United States in 1948. These banks of photographs recorded everyday clerical operations, such as lifting a biro or putting a file in a folder, and attached an average expected time to the task. But digitalisation allows for ever

59 See, for example, Moore, 2014.
60 Huws, 2003.
61 Dyer-Witheford, 2015.

wider and deeper forms of measurement not only in terms of accuracy of our physical output measurable as concrete labour but also as parallel proxies for our value added through abstract labour. These proxies also absorb our *propensity* to add value in the social, physiological and psychological spheres.

For immediate measurement we can list a host of "measurables" that lend themselves to digital recording and instant feedback to the employer. Radio frequency identification (RFID) is utilised by supermarkets to track the movements of warehouse workers, with some companies even insisting on implanting chips into employees.[62] The American analytics firm Sociometric Solutions has supplied some 20 companies with employee ID badges fitted with microphone, location sensor, and accelerometer.[63] Wearable accelerometers or smartphone apps can track individual body movements and even record body language in company meetings for the purposes of "emotional" feedback. These sometimes hidden accelerometers measure your body language and track how often you push away from your desk: "at the end of each day, the wearable badge will have collected roughly four gigabytes worth of data about your office behaviour".[64]

Microphones can record tone and volume of voice and record body language in company meetings for the same purpose. All of these and many other self-tracking devices such as FitBit and Jawbone are available to employers and are being used in increasing numbers.[65] Employers are also using new technologies to record our physical and mental health as an adjunct to predicting levels of performance, but often dressed up under the cloak of "employee wellbeing". Private insurance companies are, of course, itching to structure insurance pricing schedules to such data. Discreet recording systems such as Google Glass may be used at candidates' interviews for jobs meaning the interviewer can record and review the interview and scrutinise responses to questions to assess suitability for specific roles.

As employers search for things to measure and record (consultants are willing to satisfy these desires for a fee) new forms of "competency" assessment allow for psychological assessment and collection of bio-medical scores of neuroendrocine functioning. This, allegedly, makes possible predictions of good "emotional intelligence", ie emotional self-awareness and control.[66] Google has developed a contact lens that will monitor diabetes and glaucoma and has recently submitted a patent for a device that will test blood without a needle. The device works by "sending a surge of gas into a barrel containing a micro-particle that pierces the skin. Once

62 Cellan-Jones, 2015.

63 Go to http://slidingdoorcom.blogspot.co.uk/2015/09/spying-in-office-walls-have-ears.html

64 Kimura, 2015.

65 See Moore and Upchurch, 2015, for a fuller exposition of these trends.

66 Boyatzis and Akrivou, 2006.

blood is released from the skin, it's sucked up into the negative pressure barrel".[67] The device is wearable and intended to test for glucose. It could potentially be used by employers to monitor employee health. It is in this field of the corporeal that digitalisation could be utilised by capital to intensify employer dominance, allowing, as Peter Fleming suggests, for corporations to express newer forms of "biopower" over employees.[68] Of course, much of this new technology must be considered within the realm of employer fantasy; workers will always resist the tag, the needle or the contact lens in the same way that they have long resisted the time and motion clipboard and the stopwatch. One only has to think back to the introduction of pagers for workers such as telecom engineers as a way of monitoring their "on-call" whereabouts. Many of the pagers "accidentally" ended up in the washing machine and failed to work the next day. The point to understand is that no new technology is "neutral" in its effects once in the hands of the employer, but that its introduction can be resisted.

The intensification of employer dominance over our bodies and selves outlined in this article is a source of our alienation. The control we have over our thoughts and actions is subverted by capital in its own interests. It expands from the physical to the psychological and social, and intensifies the processes of attempted control that began with the time and motion movement over 100 years ago. Such subversion and appropriation will not be left unchallenged as resistance to the imperatives of capital is part and parcel of the structured antagonism of the workplace. Indeed, resistance to management control through technological means has often defined industrial and labour relations throughout history, whether it be auto workers' opposition to Taylorism in the 1930s, or struggles over employer efforts to reduce the "porosity" of the working day ever since. Most importantly, it is important to recognise that the struggle over technology cannot be divorced from the struggle over the control of work. Technology will always be used by capital to reinforce its domination, but can equally be used by workers to create a society not based on profit but on the requirements and needs of society. The battle for control may well, as Marx stated, be the key to human liberation, but rather than being located in the "immaterial", such struggles are firmly rooted in the material challenge to capitalism.

67 Duhaime-Ross, 2015.

68 Fleming, 2015.

References

Amlen, Deb, 2014, "SexFit: Because We Don't Have Enough Things to Measure", www.yahoo.com/tech/sexfit-because-we-dont-have-enough-things-to-measure-94172149719.html

Attwood-Charles, Will, and Juliet B Schor, 2015, "The Tyranny of Levelled Workplaces", American Sociological Association (17 August), http://workinprogress.oowsection.org/2015/08/17/the-tyranny-of-leveled-workplaces/#more-3152

Barbrook, Richard, 1998, "The Hi-tech Gift Economy", *First Monday*, issue 3, www.firstmonday.org/ojs/index.php/fm/article/view/631/552

Bell, Daniel, 1973, *The Coming of Post-Industrial Society* (Basic Books).

Boyatzis, Richard, and Kleio Akrivou, 2006, "The Ideal Self as the Driver of Intentional Change", *Journal of Management Development*, volume 25, issue 7.

Bramham, Peter, 2006, "Hard and Disappearing Work: Making Sense of the Leisure Project", *Leisure Studies*, volume 25, number 4.

Braverman, Harry, 1974, *Labor and Monopoly Capital: The Degradation of Work in the Twentieth Century* (Monthly Review).

Callinicos, Alex, 2014, *Deciphering Capital: Marx's Capital and Its Destiny* (Bookmarks).

Castells, Manuel, 1996, *The Rise of the Network Society: The Information Age: Economy, Society and Culture,* Volume 1 (Blackwell).

Cellan-Jones, Rory, 2015, "Office Puts Chips Under Staff's Skin", BBC News (29 January), www.bbc.co.uk/news/technology-31042477

Child, John, 1975, "Technical Progress", in Brian Barrett, Rhodes Beishon, and John Beishon (eds), *Industrial Relations and the Wider Society* (Open University Press).

Choonara, Joseph, 2015, "Brand New, You're Retro", *International Socialism 148* (autumn), http://isj.org.uk/brand-new-youre-retro

Darlington, Ralph, 2016, "Official and Unofficial Action in the Fight Against Anti-union Laws", *International Socialism 151* (summer), http://isj.org.uk/the-fight-against-anti-union-laws/

Dean, Jodi, 2005, "Communicative Capitalism: Circulation and the Foreclosure of Politics", *Cultural Politics*, volume 1, issue 1, https://commonconf.files.wordpress.com/2010/09/proofs-of-tech-fetish.pdf

Dennett, Daniel, 1991, *Consciousness Explained* (Penguin).

Domenech, Josep, Marian Rizov, and Michela Vecchi, 2015, "The Impact of Companies' Websites on Competitiveness and Productivity Performance" (Conference Paper: First International Conference on Advanced Research Methods and Analytics).

Doogan, Kevin, 2009, *New Capitalism? The Transformation of Work* (Polity).

Duhaime-Ross, Arielle, 2015, "Google Wants your Blood", *The Verge* (3 December), www.theverge.com/2015/12/3/9846088/google-needle-free-blood-draw-patent

Dyer-Witheford, Nick, 2015, *Cyber-Proletariat: Global Labour In The Digital Vortex* (Pluto).

El-Sahli, Zouheir, and Richard Upward, 2015, "Off the Waterfront: The Long-run Impact of Technological Change on Dock Workers", Working Paper 2015:11, Department of Economics, Lund University.

Fleming, Peter, 2015, *Resisting Work: The Corporatization of Life and Its Discontents* (Temple University Press).

Fordham, Louise, 2015, "What Place does Wearable Technology Have in Workplace Health Strategies?", Employee Benefits (15 September), www.employeebenefits.co.uk/what-place-does-wearable-technology-have-in-workplace-health-strategies/

Fuchs, Christian, 2010, "Labor in Informational Capitalism and on the Internet", *The Information Society*, volume 26, issue 3.

Gibbs, Samuel, 2016, "Mercedes-Benz Swaps Robots for People on its Assembly Lines", *Guardian* (26 February), www.theguardian.com/technology/2016/feb/26/mercedes-benz-robots-people-assembly-lines

Goodridge, Peter, Jonathan Haskel, and Gavin Wallis, 2009, "UK Innovation Index: Productivity and Growth in UK Industries", Nesta Working Paper 12/09.

Gordon, Robert J, 2016, *The Rise and Fall of American Growth* (Princeton University Press)

Gorz, André, 1999, *Reclaiming Work: Beyond the Wage-Based Society London* (Polity).

Green, Pete, 2016, "Paul Mason's *PostCapitalism*: A Response to Joseph Choonara", *International Socialism 149* (winter), http://isj.org.uk/paul-masons-postcapitalism-a-response-to-joseph-choonara/

Hardt, Michael, and Antonio Negri, 2000, *Empire* (Harvard University Press).

Harman, Chris, 1979, "Is a Machine After Your Job?" (SWP), www.marxists.org/archive/harman/1979/machine/index.htm

Harman, Chris, 1991, "A Class of Robots?", *Socialist Review* (November), www.marxists.org/archive/harman/1991/11/robots.htm

Huws, Ursula, 1999, "Material World: The Myth of the Weightless Economy", *Socialist Register 1999: Global Capitalism vs Democracy*.

Huws, Ursula, 2003, *The Making of a Cybertariat: Virtual Work in a Real World* (Monthly Review).

Jenkins, Clive, and Barry Sherman, 1979, *The Collapse of Work* (Eyre Methuen).

Kimura, Tara, 2015, "How New Data-collection Technology Might Change Office Culture", CBC News (14 September), www.cbc.ca/news/technology/how-new-data-collection-technology-might-change-office-culture-1.3196065

Kirkup, James, 2016, "Strike All You Like, Doctors—Technology will Soon Take Away your Power", *Daily Telegraph* (12 January), http://tinyurl.com/zkh78bq

Knaebel, Rachel, 2016, "Germany Looking for Ways to Defend the Workers of the Digital Age", Equal Times (9 May), www.equaltimes.org/germany-looking-for-ways-to-defend

Kurzweil, Raymond, 2005, *The Singularity Is Near* (Viking).

Marx, Karl, 1977 [1859], Preface to *A Contribution to the Critique of Political Economy* (Progress Publishers), www.marxists.org/archive/marx/works/1859/critique-pol-economy/preface.htm

Marx, Karl, 1966, *Capital*, Volume 3 (Penguin), www.marxists.org/archive/marx/works/1894-c3/

Marx, Karl, 1973 [1857], *Grundrisse: Foundations of the Critique of Political Economy* (Penguin), www.marxists.org/archive/marx/works/download/Marx_Grundrisse.pdf

Mason, Paul, 2015, *PostCapitalism: A Guide to Our Future* (Allen Lane).

Michaels, Guy, and Georg Graetz, 2015, "Industrial Robots have Boosted Productivity and Growth, but their Effect on Jobs Remains an Open Question", http://blogs.lse.ac.uk/politicsandpolicy/robots-at-work-the-impact-on-productivity-and-jobs

Moore, Phoebe, 2014, "Tracking Bodies, the 'Quantified Self' and the Corporeal Turn", in Kees van der Pijl (ed), *Handbook of the International Political Economy of Production* (Edward Elgar).

Moore, Phoebe, and Martin Upchurch, 2015, "Feedback, Performance and the Quantified Self", unpublished paper available from the authors.

Moulier Boutang, Yann, 2012, *Cognitive Capitalism* (Polity).

Negri, Antonio, 1989, *The Politics of Subversion: A Manifesto for the Twenty-first Century* (Polity).

Nafus, Dawn (ed), 2016, *Quantified: Biosensing Technologies in Everyday Life* (MIT Press).

Nordhaus, William, 2015, "Are We Approaching an Economic Singularity? Information Technology and the Future of Economic Growth", Cowles Foundation Discussion Paper number 2021, Yale University, http://papers.ssrn.com/sol3/papers.cfm?abstract_id=2658259

Paul-Choudhury, Sumit, 2016, "Outsmarted?'", *New Scientist* (25 June).

Pfeiffer, Sabine, 2016, "Robots, Industry 4.0 and Humans, or Why Assembly Work is more than Routine Work", *Societies*, volume 6, issue 2, www.mdpi.com/2075-4698/6/2/16/htm

Porter, Michael, 2001, "Strategy and the Internet", *Harvard Business Review* (March), https://hbr.org/2001/03/strategy-and-the-internet

Pradella, Lucia, 2015, "The Working Poor in Western Europe: Labour, Poverty and Global Capitalism", *Comparative European Politics*, volume 13, issue 5.

Rifkin, Jeremy, 1995, *The End of Work: The Decline of the Global Labor Force and the Dawn of the Post-Market Era* (Putnam).

Roberts, Michael, 2015, "Robots and AI: Utopia or Dystopia? Part One", (23 August), https://thenextrecession.wordpress.com/2015/08/23/robots-and-ai-utopia-or-dystopia-part-one/

Roberts, Michael, 2016a, "Robert J Gordon and the Rise and Fall of American Capitalism" (14 February), https://thenextrecession.wordpress.com/2016/02/14/robert-j-gordon-and-the-rise-and-fall-of-american-capitalism/

Roberts, Michael, 2016b, "Can Robots Usher in a Socialist Utopia or only a Capitalist Dystopia?", *Socialist Review* (July-August), http://socialistreview.org.uk/415/can-robots-usher-socialist-utopia-or-only-capitalist-dystopia

Shapiro, Carl, and Hal Varian, 1998, *Information Rules: A Strategic Guide to the Network Economy* (Harvard Business School Press).

Terranova, Tiziana, 2000, "Free Labor: Producing Culture for the Digital Economy", *Social Text*, volume 18, number 2.

Thompson, E P, 1982 [1963], *The Making of the English Working Class* (Penguin).

Titcomb, James, 2015, "Google's Meetings with UK Government over Driverless Cars Revealed", *Telegraph* (12 December), www.telegraph.co.uk/technology/2016/01/21/googles-meetings-with-uk-government-over-driverless-cars-reveale/

Tobe, Frank, 2013, "Rethink Robotics is Downsizing", http://robohub.org/rethink-robotics-is-downsizing/

Toffler, Alvin, 1970, *Future Shock* (Bodley Head).

UKCES (UK Commission for Employment and Skills), 2014, "The Future of Work: Jobs and Skills in 2030", Evidence Report 84 (February), www.gov.uk/government/uploads/system/uploads/attachment_data/file/303334/er84-the-future-of-work-evidence-report.pdf

van den Broek, Diane, 2010, "From Terranova to Terra Firma: A Critique of the Role of Free Labour and the Digital Economy", *The Economic and Labour Relations Review*, volume 20, number 2.

Veal, Anthony, 2009, "The Elusive Leisure Society, 4th Edition", School of Leisure, Sport and Tourism Working Paper 9, Sydney University of Technology, https://opus.lib.uts.edu.au/handle/10453/19821

Marx deflated
Alex Callinicos

A review of *Karl Marx: Greatness and Illusion*
Gareth Stedman Jones
Penguin (2016), £35

In 1972 the Cambridge historian Gareth Stedman Jones wrote a foreword to the English edition of Werner Blumenberg's useful biography of Karl Marx. Here he criticised Blumenberg's "Social Democratic interpretation", complaining that for Blumenberg "Marx's importance today stems not from his creation of a new revolutionary theory, but the grandeur of his humanism and the wealth of insights scattered throughout his works".[1]

Yet, nearly 45 years later, Stedman Jones, in his own massive and already highly praised biography of Marx, argues that "Karl" (as he rather shy-makingly insists on calling Marx) was at his most politically effective when he forged a "new social-democratic language in the mid-1860s" through his role in the First International, and supposedly distanced himself from his revolutionary communist youth.[2] Whereas in 1972 Stedman Jones criticised Blumenberg for accusing Marx of mythologising the Paris Commune of 1871, now he agrees that *The Civil*

1 Blumenberg, 1972, ppviii, x.
2 Stedman Jones, 2016, p466.

War in France was "in part an imaginary projection" and regrets the political isolation from British progressive opinion to which his defence of the Commune condemned Marx.[3]

These differences are easy enough to explain. In 1972 Stedman Jones was a revolutionary Marxist and one of the more intellectually interesting members of the editorial committee of *New Left Review* (*NLR*). But in the 1980s he broke with *NLR* and embraced poststructuralism. He made a splash in 1983 with a book, *Languages of Class*, that argued that class was not an objective social relation but a construct of the discourses prevailing in particular social and political movements.[4] Stedman Jones repeats this conception of class in *Karl Marx*, perhaps not realising that the idea that class is just talk must seem quaint to a generation for whom the Occupy slogan of the 1 percent vs the 99 percent captures the stark economic inequalities forged in the neoliberal era.

Happily Stedman Jones now spares us the fancy philosophy used to justify poststructuralist reductions of everything to discourse. His approach in *Karl Marx* is indistinguishable from the so-called "Cambridge school" in the history of political thought inspired by the work of scholars such as Quentin Skinner and John Dunn, who treat theoretical texts as (in Stedman Jones's own words) "the interventions of an author within particular political and philosophical contexts that the historian must carefully reconstruct".[5] He is himself a distinguished intellectual historian, and he makes a thorough and competent job of showing the contexts—the relatively liberal Rhineland, the counter-revolutionary Prussian regime of the 1830s and 1840s and the break up of Hegel's philosophy—in which Marx's own ideas germinated. We get good, detailed accounts of, for example, Paris in the lead-up to 1848, the revolutions of that year and the developments in the British working class movement and in European radical politics that made the First International possible.

There is, however, something a bit lifeless about the book. Maybe because of his past Stedman Jones has conflicted feelings about Marx, despite his insistence on getting on first name terms with him. He assiduously cites Marx's immediate relations' complaints about his lack of family feeling and, without any substantiation, accuses him of getting deported from France in 1845 thanks to his own "arrogance or incompetence".[6] Elsewhere he suggests Marx suffered in the late 1850s from "mood changes ranging from real euphoria through uncontrolled

3 Stedman Jones, 2016, p502.

4 Stedman Jones is one of Ellen Meiksins Wood's main targets in her critique of the intellectual retreat from Marxism—Wood, 1986.

5 Stedman Jones, 2016, pxv.

6 Stedman Jones, 2016, p165.

paranoia to fantasies of revenge".[7] More seriously, Stedman Jones cites Marx's 1844 essay "On the Jewish Question" as an example of "socialist anti-Semitism", ignoring the extensive (and by no means uncritical) discussions of this text by Hal Draper and David Leopold.[8] Stedman Jones demonstrates considerable sympathy for Marx's target in "On the Jewish Question", the left Hegelian philosopher Bruno Bauer, but somehow omits to mention the latter's subsequent evolution into a virulent anti-Semite.

I would recommend anyone looking for an up to date academic biography of Marx to try Jonathan Sperber's 2013 book instead. Although Sperber is much weaker theoretically than Stedman Jones, he doesn't suffer from the latter's mixed feelings about Marx. Moreover, as a historian of 19th century German radicalism he is very good on Marx's German context and also gets him as a person, warts and all, much better than Stedman Jones does.[9]

Stedman Jones's book is more ambitious than Sperber's, as its subtitle indicates. He argues that the real Marx has got lost behind the mythical figure of the founder of a science of history allegedly constructed by Friedrich Engels and the Second International after his death in 1883. (Stedman Jones is not a fan of Engels and indeed suggests, without any evidence, that Marx and his family concealed disagreements between the two because of their financial dependence on him.) There is nothing especially original about this idea, which has been expressed in different ways by Marxist and non-Marxist scholars for many decades. How interesting the divergence is between the official "Marxism"[10] fabricated after Marx's death and his own thought depends on the content one finds in the latter.

It is here that Stedman Jones claims the distinctiveness of his book lies, in correcting the posthumous "inflation in Marx's reputation".[11] The real Marx's lifework, the critique of political economy culminating in the three volumes of *Capital*, was of course incomplete, with only Volume I appearing in his lifetime. Stedman Jones argues that Marx in his last years abandoned the project out of a sense of intellectual impasse. He claims the much-awaited publication of Volume III by Engels shortly before his death in 1895 was greeted with disappointment because the book offered no proof that capitalism would inevitably break down economically. As for Marx himself, Stedman Jones contends that in his last years his main interest was in anthropological and historical studies of communal social forms, whose survivals—notably the peasant *mir* in Tsarist Russia—could provide the

7 Stedman Jones, 2016, p405.
8 Stedman Jones, 2016, p626-627, note 74.
9 Sperber, 2013.
10 Or "Marxisms"—for example, German Social Democracy's version is different from the Stalinist variant.
11 Stedman Jones, 2016, p3.

basis for a transition to socialism that bypassed capitalism. But these speculations were ignored even by Marx's own followers in Russia. This is how Stedman Jones finishes the book. He avoids any discussion of the contemporary relevance of Marx's critique of capitalism, presumably to underline the gap between what he regards as the illusory political hopes placed in Marx and the intellectual failure of his actual project.

But if Stedman Jones seeks to offer an original intellectual biography, his treatment of Marx's critique of political economy does not meet the standards of contemporary scholarship. This has developed considerably in recent decades thanks to the much greater availability of his notes and drafts through the giant Marx-Engels *Completed Works* (*MEGA*). Stedman Jones largely ignores this research. Marx's critique developed first through periods of intensive study of political economy in Paris and Brussels in the mid-1840s and in London in the early 1850s, and then through a succession of manuscripts written mainly, though not exclusively, between 1857 and 1867. Stedman Jones focuses on the first of these manuscripts, the *Grundrisse* (1857-8), and devotes little attention to two subsequent ones, the vast and in many ways crucial *1861-63 Manuscript,* and the *1864-65 Manuscript* from which Engels edited *Capital,* Volume III. This is a critical mistake because it means he fails to grasp the intensive process of conceptual refinement, reformulation and development that takes place across successive manuscripts.[12]

Thus Stedman Jones makes a great song and dance over the fact that Marx in the mid-1840s read the French translation of the first (1817) edition of David Ricardo's *On the Principles of Political Economy and Taxation* and therefore failed in his Paris writings to address the doubts Ricardo expressed about the labour theory of value in the third edition (1821). In fact, the problem—the apparent contradiction between the labour theory of value and the existence of a general rate of profit—was already posed by Ricardo in the first edition.[13] In any case this would not have interested Marx when he first read Ricardo, because in his Paris writings he rejected the labour theory of value. But the problem is central to the *1861-63 Manuscript,* as Enrique Dussel shows in his superb commentary.[14] It is here that, while seeking to overcome Ricardo's theory of rent, Marx formulates his solution to the problem, showing how the (labour) values of commodities are transformed into prices of production that govern the fluctuations of market prices (for more detail, see Michael Roberts's article elsewhere in this issue).

12 See Callinicos, 2014.

13 Oddly Stedman Jones's relatively scant citations of secondary literature seem to come mainly from the works of his colleagues published by Cambridge University Press. But he ignores one great piece of Cambridge scholarship, Piero Sraffa's edition of Ricardo's *Works and Correspondence* (1951-2), which shows why Ricardo never abandoned the labour theory of value.

14 Dussel, 2001. See also Callinicos, 2014, chapters 2 and 3.

But Stedman Jones ignores both this manuscript and Dussel's work on *Capital* and its drafts, merely repeating the old saw that there is a contradiction between Volume I and Volume III.

Stedman Jones argues Marx abandoned his critique of political economy because "he had not been able to sustain his original depiction of capital as an organism whose continuous and unstoppable spiral of growth from inconspicuous beginnings in antiquity to global supremacy would soon encounter world-wide collapse".[15] But nowhere in Marx's writings of the critical period 1857-67 does he claim that capitalism is heading towards economic breakdown. His initial six-book plan of the *Critique of Political Economy* culminated in a volume on "World Market and Crises"—crises are not the same as collapse. Marx actually wrote: "*Permanent crises do not exist*".[16] His fullest discussion, in *Capital*, Volume III (dismissed in a sentence by Stedman Jones), portrays a spiral movement in which the tendency of the rate of profit to fall interacts with financial busts and economic slumps thanks to which capital is destroyed and exploitation increased sufficiently to allow the engine of accumulation to resume. Marx's discussion of the tendency of the rate of profit to fall concludes in the original manuscript with the sentence, cut by Engels: "Hence crises". The "vicious circle" of boom and bust will continue as long as capitalism exists.[17]

One of Stedman Jones's oddest suggestions is that Marx supposedly abandoned his economic studies after the publication of *Capital*, Volume I, in 1867 because he was unable to address the development of capitalism as a global system. Recent research (naturally ignored by Stedman Jones) has shown that from the 1840s onwards Marx analysed bourgeois society as a transnational nexus of relationships.[18] One of his main preoccupations in the 1870s was to ensure that *Capital* was not simply a study of Victorian Britain. In the French edition of Volume I he included more material on colonialism and the world market. He also sought to extend the analysis of crises and financial markets to cover developments in the United States, which Marx was quick to recognise as a new centre of global capitalism.

Marx's interest in the Russian commune was connected in that he also sought to deepen his analysis of rent and landed property in Volume III by studying American and Russian agriculture. It was the unending pursuit of these studies, amid the distractions of politics and illness, combined with Marx's

15 Stedman Jones, 2016, p430.

16 Marx and Engels, 1975-2005, volume 32, p128n*.

17 Marx, 2016, pp375, 364. For more discussion of Marx's theory of crises, see Callinicos, 2014, chapter 6.

18 Pradella, 2014.

perfectionism, what he called in a letter to Ferdinand Lassalle of 28 April 1862 "that quirk I have of finding fault with anything I have written and not looked at for a month, so that I have to revise it completely", that explains why he left *Capital* unfinished.[19] But closer acquaintance with Marx's drafts leaves one with a strong sense of the grandeur and the contemporaneity of his project.

This doesn't mean he was always right. He argues that the overthrow of capitalism will occur, not through economic breakdown, but by the political action of the working class, stimulated by the cumulative effects of economic crises and class polarisation. What is genuinely problematic here is that he sees this movement developing "with the inexorability of a natural process".[20] Stedman Jones doesn't pay much attention to this, perhaps because it doesn't fit his portrayal of a Marx ignored and misrepresented by the Second International: the inevitability of socialist revolution was an idea eagerly embraced by theorists such as Karl Kautsky and Georgi Plekhanov.

But it was an idea that, under the inspiration of the Russian Revolution and of the experience of the Bolsheviks, much more creative figures such as Georg Lukács and Antonio Gramsci rejected in the 1920s. This generation of revolutionary Marxists were encouraged by Lenin to return to Marx's writings on the Paris Commune and the vision they offered of socialist revolution as an active process of self-emancipation directed at the destruction of the capitalist state. The Stedman Jones of 1972 also shared this vision. Maybe the unsuccessful efforts of the Stedman Jones of 2016 to cut Marx down to size reveal him at war with this past self.

---

19 Marx and Engels, 1975-2005, volume 41, p357.
20 Marx, 1976, p929.

References

Blumenberg, Werner, 1972 [1962], *Karl Marx: An Illustrated Biography* (NLB).

Callinicos, Alex, 2014, *Deciphering Capital: Marx's Capital and Its Destiny* (Bookmarks).

Dussel, Enrique, 2001, *Towards an Unknown Marx: A Commentary on The Manuscript of 1861-63* (Routledge).

Marx, Karl, 1976, *Capital*, Volume I (Penguin).

Marx, Karl, 2016, *The Economic Manuscript of 1864-1865: Capital Book Three: Forms of the Process as a Whole* (Brill).

Marx, Karl, and Frederick Engels, 1975-2005, *Collected Works*, 50 vols (Progress).

Pradella, Lucia, 2014, *Globalisation and the Critique of Political Economy: New Insights from Marx's Writings* (Routledge).

Sperber, Jonathan, 2013, *Karl Marx: A Nineteenth-Century Life* (Liveright).

Stedman Jones, Gareth, 2016, *Karl Marx: Greatness and Illusion* (Penguin).

Wood, Ellen Meiksins, 1986, *The Retreat from Class: The New "True" Socialism* (Verso).

Marie Equi, Wobbly
John Newsinger

A review of *Marie Equi: Radical Politics and Outlaw Passions*
Michael Helquist
Oregon State University Press (2015), £19

On May Day 1950 the dockers' union in Portland, Oregon, presented a bouquet of 13 red roses and a poem to 78-year-old Doctor Marie Equi in honour of her years of service to the working class and the socialist cause, service that included time in San Quentin. The poem read in part:

These are for you, thirteen red roses, Doc;
Your lucky number in the old cell block
Chalked on cold stone. This day is ours
To honour heroes, mark the labour gain,
we who have suffered have our special flowers,
Deep as our blood and dark with Portland rain.
Thirteen red roses.[1]

Who was Marie Equi and why was she deserving of this tribute? She was born in 1872, the daughter of working class parents, of an Italian immigrant father and an Irish immigrant mother. Her first job was working in a textile factory, but

1 Munk, 2007, p58.

she went on to go to college and to become a medical doctor. A working class woman becoming a doctor was remarkable then (it still is today!), but Equi was also a lesbian who was quite open and unashamed about her sexuality and her same sex relationships. She was a campaigner for women's suffrage, a champion of birth control and of a woman's right to abortion and, as we shall see, in 1913 was won over to the struggle for socialism by her involvement in a cannery workers' strike in Portland. She became an active supporter of the Industrial Workers of the World (IWW) and when war came took a strong stand against it, a stand that was to earn her a three-year prison term. According to Elizabeth Gurley Flynn, a leading Wobbly, later one of the leaders of the Communist Party, and who lived with her for nine years, she was:

> a stormy petrel...a fiery personality...among the most feared and hated women in the Northwest because of her outspoken criticisms of politicians, industrialists, so-called civic leaders and all who oppressed the poor. She was loved and cherished by masses of plain people.[2]

And yet, until recently this remarkable woman has been all but forgotten. She does not get a mention in the standard histories of the IWW,[3] not even in Eric Thomas Chester's invaluable recent book *The Wobblies in their Heyday*.[4] She was celebrated in a path-breaking article by Nancy Krieger, "Queen of the Bolsheviks: The Hidden History of Dr Marie Equi", that appeared in the much missed US journal, *Radical America*, back in 1983.[5] But it is only with the publication of Michael Helquist's new biography that a giant step has at last been taken towards remedying the neglect of this remarkable woman and fighter for socialism.

Strike

In July 1913 some 200 women working for the Oregon Packing Company walked out on strike. They were overwhelmingly young women, the majority aged between 12 and 20, working up to 12 hours a day, seven days a week, canning fruit in appalling conditions, for a wage that averaged less than 10 cents an hour.

2 Flynn 1973, pp197-198. According to Lillian Faderman, Flynn's relationship with Equi was "very disturbing" for the Communist Party leadership, especially when Flynn "revealed her lesbianism in a draft of her 1955 memoir, *Alderson Story*, but according to one source, the party not only censored the chapter but even insisted on 'substituting an anti-gay chapter' in its place". As Faderman notes, "most historians...until recently omitted discussing the nature of Flynn's relationship with Marie Equi from accounts of Flynn's life"—Faderman 1999, p162.

3 Foner, 1965; Dubofsky, 1969; Thompson and Bekken, 2006.

4 Chester, 2014.

5 Krieger, 1983.

They turned to the Portland IWW for support. Some of the strikers were Equi's patients so she knew the exploitation they endured and decided to give them her support on the picket line. The strikers attempted to rally popular support for their cause with demonstrations and street meetings that soon involved clashes with the sheriff and his deputies. At one street meeting the deputies arrested and roughed up everyone who tried to mount the soap box and speak, including the pregnant Agnes O'Connor, one of Equi's patients. Outraged at this behaviour, Equi began abusing the deputies, swapping blows with them that left her badly bruised. She then led a march on the jail to demand the prisoners be released. Here, according to the newspapers, she punched two deputies in the face and maintained such a torrent of abuse that the sheriff ordered O'Connor's release. Equi's involvement in the struggle continued and she was herself later arrested, accused of stabbing a deputy with a hat pin. She was held for three days, roughed up (when she was released her friends "noticed bruises all over her body"[6]), abused and threatened with incarceration in an asylum if she did not leave Portland. She remained defiant. Before the strike was over she was to be trampled by a police horse when a demonstration was violently broken up, but she never faltered in her active support for the strikers. The strike went down to defeat with the workers replaced by scabs provided by "a local religious group".[7] For Equi though, it taught a clear lesson: "It was my experiences during that strike that made me a socialist... Any betterment of conditions must come about by direct action, in other words militancy".[8]

Her involvement with the IWW continued. Towards the end of 1913 she was active in the Wobbly-sponsored Unemployed League, protesting against the use of the vagrancy laws to drive the unemployed homeless out of the town. In February 1914, she was the Unemployed League's delegate to the National Conference on Unemployment in New York where she defended the IWW and proclaimed herself a "radical socialist".[9] When the massacre of Wobbly members trying to land in the port of Everett to reinforce a Free Speech campaign took place on 5 November 1916, she rushed to give medical assistance to the wounded. Indeed, her standing in the IWW was such that when Oregon received its envelope of Joe Hill's ashes, she was given the honour of dispersing them on 19 November 1916.[10]

---

6 Helquist, 2015, p121.

7 Chandler, 2013, p177.

8 Krieger, 1983, p60.

9 Helquist, 2015, p125.

10 IWW member and union organiser Joe Hill had been framed for murder, tried and then executed by firing squad on 19 November 1915. A year later to the day his ashes were dispersed in every state except Utah—where he had been judicially lynched—and across much of the world.

Birth control and abortion

One often neglected campaign that the IWW fought was in favour of birth control. Margaret Sanger, a nurse, was the most active and vocal birth control advocate of the time. She was to become a strong IWW supporter and activist, won over during a laundry workers' strike in New York. Sanger was actively involved in the victorious 1912 Lawrence textile strike, was to be arrested twice during the less successful silk workers' strike in Hazelton and played an important role in the 1913 Paterson strike. She was outraged by the defeat in Paterson and in March 1914 started her own magazine, *The Woman Rebel*. It was while discussing the launch of the magazine that one of her friends, Otto Bobsein, actually first coined the term "birth control". *The Woman Rebel* had a decidedly anarchist tone, advocating among other things: "The right to be an umarried mother. The right to destroy. The right to create. The right to live. The right to love". It proclaimed as its watchword the slogan: "No Gods, No Masters". As far as Sanger was concerned, "woman is enslaved by the world machine, by sex conventions, by motherhood and its present necessary childrearing, by wage-slavery, by middle class morality, by customs, laws and superstitions". Women had to look "the whole world in the face with a go-to-hell look in the eyes; to have an ideal; to speak and act in defiance of convention". *The Woman Rebel* certainly lived up to this expectation.

On 20 April 1914, state militia and company guards attacked a tent encampment erected at Ludlow, Colorado by striking miners. They had been evicted from their company houses by John D Rockefeller's Colorado Fuel and Iron Company. The camp was machine-gunned and set on fire. By the time the attack was over there were more than 20 miners and family members dead including two women and 11 children. A number of miners who were taken prisoner were summarily executed by their captors. This episode was part of what was, in effect, a small-scale war between strikers and scabs, company guards and the state militia. There were furious protests against this particularly brutal act of class war. Some months later, on 4 July 1914, an anarchist bomb, intended to blow up John D Rockefeller's New York mansion in retaliation for the Ludlow massacre, exploded prematurely killing the conspirators instead, including one IWW member, Arthur Caron. Sanger celebrated them for having "courage, determination, conviction, a spirit of defiance". The magazine published a defence of the assassination of tyrants and urged its readers to always "Remember Ludlow". At this point, the US government moved to suppress the magazine. In August, Sanger was indicted on four counts, three of indecency and one of incitement to "murder and assassination". The charges carried a maximum sentence of 45 years.[11]

11 Chesler, 2007, pp75-76 and 97-102.

While awaiting trial, she wrote her pamphlet, *Family Limitation*, which, as her biographer puts it, not only provided birth control information, but also embraced the rhetoric of revolution. When the pamphlet was finished, she disguised herself and using a false name, crossed into Canada, shipping out from there to safety in Liverpool. Once safely on board ship, she cabled Bill Shatoff,[12] the Wobbly, "who was waiting to release 100,000 copies of *Family Limitation*, already addressed and bundled and awaiting distribution through IWW locals and other sympathetic groups".[13]

Sanger was to return to the United States in February 1916, by which time the charges against her had been dropped. Once back home, she toured the country, lecturing on birth control. She spoke in Portland, where Equi was one of the leading figures in the local Birth Control League, on 19 June. The police arrested three men selling copies of *Family Limitation*, whereupon Equi climbed on a table and began giving copies away for free. Not to be intimidated, another lecture was planned. Meanwhile, Equi revised the pamphlet, which was rushed into print. When Sanger returned to Portland for another lecture on 29 June it was this revised edition that was on sale. When she began speaking to a packed hall, the police arrested her, Equi and two other women. A large crowd followed the police to the jail and demonstrated outside, "calling out in solidarity and defiance, 'We have also broken the law'". They were subsequently tried along with the three men arrested at the earlier meeting and all were found guilty of circulating a "lewd, obscene and indecent book".[14] The men received a suspended $10 fine and the women a caution. Equi's response to this led to her being threatened with contempt of court. Later meetings took place without interference.

Equi's commitment to birth control education was accompanied by her belief in a woman's right to abortion, a right that she actively facilitated in Portland, providing abortions for both the wealthy and the poor, the former subsidising the latter. And, of course, she was an open lesbian. Indeed, in April 1915, she and her partner of 15 years, Harriet Speckart, even adopted a daughter, Mary. At this time, adoption was often an informal procedure. While her sexuality was certainly used to turn public opinion against her, homosexual women were not subjected to the legal persecution that was inflicted on homosexual men. At this time, Oregon law punished sodomy with from two to five years in prison and the Oregon State Penitentiary "confined many men for these offences". In 1913, the

12 Bill Shatoff was a Russian anarchist who had emigrated to the US but later returned to Russia and became a Bolshevik. He disappeared during Stalin's Great Terror.

13 Chesler, 2007, p103.

14 Helquist, 2015, p150.

state's new Eugenics Law introduced castration as a punishment available "for the crime of sodomy. This law remained in effect until the 1960s".[15]

Imperialist war

As the US prepared to intervene in the European war that had began in 1914, Equi threw herself into anti-war activity. When Portland held its Preparedness Parade on 3 June 1916, the assembled patriots were confronted by Equi with a banner: "Prepare to Die, Workingmen—J P Morgan and Co Want Preparedness for Profit". The banner was destroyed and she was roughed up and arrested. On another occasion, when the IWW tried to hold an anti-war meeting and everyone who mounted the soapbox was arrested one after another, she borrowed a telegraph lineman's spurs and climbed to the top of a telegraph pole. Once at the top she displayed her banner, "Down with the Imperialist War" and addressed the crowd while the police stood by helpless.

When the US went to war, any opposition was treated as treason and a ferocious wave of repression was unleashed against the left. The reformist Socialist Party bore the brunt of the assault. The IWW leadership tried to escape this repression by not participating in the anti-war movement. The intention was to concentrate on building up the union on the job. But many rank and file members ignored this strategy and threw themselves into anti-war activity. As IWW militant and anti-war activist Frank Little later pointed out, the strategy was futile because the government was going to come after the IWW leadership anyway. He was absolutely right.

Equi herself was finally arrested on 30 June 1918 for an anti-war speech she had made at the IWW hall a few days earlier. She was charged with insulting the flag, US soldiers and Britain (she had spoken in wholehearted support of the Easter Rising).[16] This was the culmination of a large-scale operation by the Bureau of Investigation (later the FBI) involving eight agents who "tracked her every move" and installed "wiretaps in her rooms". The Bureau had also successfully placed an informer, Margaret Lowell Paul, posing as a member of Sinn Féin, in her circle of friends. According to the Bureau's Portland chief, William Bryon, Equi was "one of the most dangerous anarchists and plotters against constituted authority in the United States". She was "an anarchist, a degenerate and an abortionist".[17]

15 Chandler, 2013, p168.

16 Equi was a strong supporter of the Irish republican struggle and had many friends in the republican movement. For a while, she had a relationship with Kathleen O'Brennan, an Irish republican and IWW member, who helped organise the New York dockers' boycott of British ships in 1920. Hanna Sheehy-Skeffington, whose husband had been murdered by the British in 1916, was also a life-long friend.

17 Helquist, 2015, pp163, 168; Krieger, 1983, p67.

Her trial did not begin until 12 November, the day after the war ended. The reality was that she was not being prosecuted for her opposition to the war, but because she was a Red, a Wobbly and a radical socialist. Her trial was part of the Red scare that had been launched against the left during the war but was actually intensified in the post-war years. In Equi's particular case, the authorities also felt that they were dealing with "the embodiment of the liberated woman as monster" and called on the jury "to re-establish control over such disorderly women".[18] At her trial, the prosecutor, Bert Haney, described Equi as an "unsexed woman". He revealed what the trial was all about in his summing up when he told the jury that "The red flag is floating over Russia, Germany and a great part of Europe. Unless you put this woman in jail, I tell you it will float over the world".[19] She was found guilty and sentenced to three years.

While her case was going through the appeal process, Equi continued to be politically active. She was arrested on 13 March 1919 because her IWW membership violated Oregon's anti-syndicalism law, but was never prosecuted. In a speech she made in Portland on 31 October 1919 she told her audience: "We may think we live in a free country, but we are in reality nothing but slaves. When President Wilson recently said we are at war he spoke the truth for once. But it is not a war against another nation, but a never-ending class war within our own country".[20]

Her appeals were all unsuccessful and on 19 October 1920 she finally surrendered herself at San Quentin prison where she remained for ten months. She was released on 10 September 1921. By now she was unwell, her health damaged by her prison experience, and the left had been defeated. She remained on the left, but was only episodically involved in political activity. In February 1929 she spoke at a meeting demanding justice for IWW activist Tom Mooney. Earlier, in 1926, Elizabeth Gurley Flynn, in a state of nervous collapse after the failure to save Sacco and Vanzetti,[21] had come to live with her in Portland, and they remained together for nearly ten years.

The great dock strike of 1934, one of the class battles that heralded the revival of working class struggle and militancy in the US, saw Equi leave their home to stand on the dockers' picket line. It was the first time in two years that she had gone out, such was her health. She donated $250 to the strike fund. When the Portland police issued a "Red List" of dangerous subversives living in the area that same year, she was outraged at being left off the list and threatened to sue. Marie Equi deserves, indeed demands, to be remembered.

18 Kennedy, 1999, p97.

19 Helquist, 2015, p176.

20 Krieger, 1983.

21 Nicola Sacco and Bartolomeo Vanzetti were two US anarchists who were framed for murder in 1920 and executed seven years later.

References

Chandler, J D, 2013, *Hidden History of Portland Oregon* (The History Press).

Chesler, Ellen, 2007, *Woman of Valor: Margaret Sanger and the Birth Control Movement in America* (Simon and Schuster).

Chester, Eric Thomas, 2014, *The Wobblies in their Heyday: The Rise and Destruction of the Industrial Workers of the World During the World War 1 Era* (Praeger).

Dubofsky, Melvyn, 1969, *We Shall Be All: A History of the Industrial Workers of the World* (Quadrangle Books).

Faderman, Lillian, 1999, *To Believe in Women: What Lesbians Have Done For America—A History* (Houghton Mifflin).

Foner, Philip S, 1973, *The Industrial Workers of the World 1905-1917* (International Publishers).

Flynn, Elizabeth Gurley, 1973, *The Rebel Girl: An Autobiography (1906-1926) (International Publishers).*

Helquist, Michael, 2015, *Marie Equi: Radical Politics and Outlaw Passions* (Oregon State University Press).

Kennedy, Kathleen, 1999, *Disloyal Mothers and Scurrilous Citizens: Women and Subversion During World War 1* (Indiana University Press).

Krieger, Nancy, 1983, "Queen of the Bolsheviks: The Hidden History of Dr Marie Equi", *Radical America*, volume 17, number 5.

Munk, Michael, 2011, *The Portland Red Guide* (Ooligan Press).

Thompson, Fred W and Jon Bekken, 2006, *The Industrial Workers of the World: The First 100 Years* (A K Press).

The new Cuba: myths and realities
Mike Gonzalez

A review of ***A Hidden History of the Cuban Revolution: How the Working Class Shaped the Guerrillas' Victory***
Steve Cushion
Monthly Review Press (2016), £20.42

Cuba and the US Empire: A Chronological History
Jane Franklin
Monthly Review Press (2016), £18.87

The last year and a half have left no doubt that the history of the Cuban Revolution will need to be revisited and probably rewritten. From the moment that Raúl Castro and Barack Obama met, and the American president visited the island, everything changed. The process had begun earlier, of course, with unannounced meetings between representatives of US government and business and their Cuban counterparts. But despite some claims that the rapprochement was a "victory for Cuban statecraft", it was clear that this was an ending as well as a new beginning. The Cuban Revolution was over, though the regime it had brought to power remained in place, astonishingly, 55 years later.

The Cuban state that emerged from the successful revolution that overthrew Fulgencio Batista's regime in January 1959 enjoyed, quite rightly, the support of radicals and socialists around the world. It was still the Cold War era, dominated by the economic and military power of the United States. That tiny Cuba, whose fate had been determined throughout its history by its northern neighbour, should have exposed the vulnerability of the imperialist giant was especially inspiring. Two years later Fidel Castro's declaration of the revolution's socialist nature gave an impetus to anti-imperialist resistance across the world, and particularly in Latin America. These two factors in their turn explain the virulence of the right in the US and their relentless lobbying against the revolution ever since. The powerful Miami lobby, swollen by half a million Cubans fleeing the revolution, found support and approval in each of the presidencies that have accompanied the history of the revolution. And yet, from the Bay of Pigs invasion in 1961 to the fall of the Berlin Wall in 1989, Cuba has survived every confident prediction of its imminent demise.

While Cuba had been a highly profitable colony for US capital, which dominated its sugar industry, it was small beer in the Latin American context. Its strategic location, however, as a gatekeeper to the Caribbean and to the southern continent as a whole, reinforced its significance for successive Washington regimes. It was the last Spanish colony in the Americas, but its war of independence in 1898, when a people's army took on the colonial troops and won, was immediately appropriated by the US, renamed the Spanish-American War and attributed to the skill of Theodore Roosevelt's Rough Riders. The new republic's constitution was then rewritten by its new masters with the introduction of the Platt Amendment, which gave the US control over key areas including customs and police. Segregation was introduced by the colonisers, who then crushed the 1912 rising of the Independent Party of Colour.[1] By the 1920s it was US interests that dominated Cuba's chief export, sugar, and the Mafia who controlled its hotels, its night life and its sex industry. The crash of 1929 exposed its vulnerability and inexorably led to economic collapse. The revolution of 1933, led by Havana's transport workers, briefly generated soviets but was ultimately diverted by the revolt of the sergeants, led by Batista, who quickly transformed his controlling role into a dictatorship.

Against that historical background, it becomes clear why the 1959 revolution took on such a symbolic significance. After all, Cuba was the US's safest ally in Latin America. But it was also perilously close to the Florida coast, so it was particularly ironic that this small island should expose the weakness of the imperial state. It lit a flame of hope for a Latin America baulking under the interests of

1 The Partido Independiente de Color was founded in 1908 by veterans of the War of Independence, in reaction to the new segregation imposed by the US-dominated government. Two years later the Liberal government banned parties based on race. The armed insurrection of 1912 was an attempt to gain recognition; 6,000 died in the repression that followed.

empire—provoking the "great fear" that John Gerassi addressed in his influential book on the role of the US in Latin America.[2] It is interesting to reflect on the first responses to the revolution, when figures like C Wright Mills called on the US government to negotiate with what they saw as a new nationalism. As was to be expected, Dwight D Eisenhower, then US president, responded instead with the imposition of an economic embargo that, given that the whole of Cuba's sugar production went to the US, was intended to cripple the island in months.

But Cuba survived; the Soviet government took delivery of Cuban sugar and subsidised Cuba's new regime. There was a price to pay, of course, and not just becoming a captive market for the far from satisfactory products of Eastern European industry. The missile crisis of 1962 was, for many of us, the threshold of nuclear Armageddon in a world dominated by the image of the mushroom cloud. Its resolution with a US-Soviet agreement after 13 tense days was bitterly resented by Fidel Castro and Che Guevara, who felt that Cuba was being used as a pawn in a great power game. For the rest of the 1960s Cuba seemed to be looking for alternative strategies, Third World anti-imperialist alliances summed up in the famous phrase from Guevara's last printed article—"to create one, two, three many Vietnams". The implication was a different kind of revolution, a liberation project not constrained by the limits of the Soviet economic and political model.

Cuba's reputation and its symbolic stature derive from those times. It was radical, unrestrained by political realism and anti-Stalinist, at least by implication, in the refusal to be bound by objective conditions, a refusal personified by Che Guevara.

The alternative revolutionary strategy was exported to Latin America, supported and legitimised by the Cuban Revolution—*or at least by a particular historical narrative*. The movement led by Fidel was very far from being Marxist-Leninist, as he defined it after the Bay of Pigs invasion of 1961. His 26 July Movement (MR-26-7) was radical nationalist, as his famous speech from the dock in 1953 ("History will absolve me") very clearly shows. In the accounts of the revolution written after 1959 the revolution is presented as the result of armed struggle against the Batista regime conducted by a small group of dedicated, professional revolutionaries. Its method is enshrined in Guevara's *Guerrilla Warfare*, a manual for the guerrilla fighter, and his subsequent *Remniscences of the Guerrilla War*. These were the texts that inspired a generation of young Latin American revolutionaries to abandon the development of mass working class organisations in favour of the armed "focos" or cells that were the basic organising units of guerrilla warfare. In fact the experience of those courageous groups of young revolutionaries was almost entirely tragic. Few survived the repression

2 Gerassi, 1963.

that their existence provoked. And the final victim was Guevara himself, whose death was the clearest manifestation of the inadequacy of the strategy.

Hidden from history: workers and the revolution

Steve Cushion's painstaking and perceptive research into the pre-revolutionary workers' movement in Cuba has recently been published by Monthly Review Press as *A Hidden History of the Cuban Revolution: How the Working Class Shaped the Guerrillas' Victory*.[3] He is right to describe it as a "hidden history", in the sense that, in the debates and discussions about the Cuban Revolution, and the interpretations of its origins, this issue has been largely ignored in favour of an account that places the impulse to revolution exclusively with the 26 July Movement. What Cushion demonstrates, by contrast, is the ambivalence of the 26 July Movement towards the working class movement in the period prior to the revolution. In fact, the Cuban working class in the 1950s had the highest percentage of union membership in Latin America. The trade union bureaucracy was dominated by Eusebio Mujal, the incarnation of a corrupt anti-communist leadership dedicated to the containment of workers' struggles. The result was the growth of a combative rank and file in key unions like the sugar workers in the early 1950s, and especially after the crisis in the sugar industry after 1953. With Mujal's support, Batista attacked the strongest unions one by one—sugar, transport and banking in particular—after bitter strikes and confrontations, culminating in the strike of 500,000 sugar workers in late 1955.

The role of two organisations becomes important at this point. The Revolutionary Directorate (originally a student group), under José Antonio Echeverría, were active participants in the strike movements. Echeverría would eventually be killed in a failed attempt to assassinate Batista. Surviving members of the directorate, however, moved towards armed struggle with cells active in central Cuba during and after the revolution. The Communist Party, for its part, had a very questionable history, especially in collaborating with Batista during the Second World War; and it was, as Cushion details, conservative in its exclusive concern with concrete demands. Yet many of the rank and file leaders were Communists and, especially in the Guantánamo area, Trotskyists. What was emerging through the 1950s was a rank and file network, opposed to the bureaucracy and advocating a "combative workers' movement" that combined sabotage and mass action. At the same time the 26 July Movement was beginning to draw workers towards it who had suffered defeat at the hands of the state, as well as sections of the most militant rank and file—especially in Santiago, where Frank País, a teachers' leader, was working with the guerrillas.

3 Cushion, 2016.

Repression grew after the landing of the *Granma*, the motor vessel carrying the 82 guerrillas led by Fidel Castro, on 3 December 1956. Only 18 people survived the landing. Batista's troops were expecting them. In the aftermath a number of MR-26-7 militants around the country were tortured and killed. The strikes continued in the following years, but were brutally put down. In that environment the 26 July Movement, offering armed confrontation with the state, began to attract some of the best workers' leaders who employed their organisational methods. But Cushion several times makes a key point: "The MR-26-7 was a cross-class organisation whose founding leaders had little understanding of the day-to-day practicalities of organising in the workplace".[4] The Communist Party leadership, however, which had considerable experience in those practicalities, was wary of the growing MR-26-7, and often clashed with its most combative base.

The two general strikes prior to the revolution were defining. In August 1957 a general strike called in Santiago after the murder of the charismatic Frank País was highly successful, though mainly in the east of the island. País had argued fiercely within the movement for more active engagement with workers—but even he lacked understanding of the concrete demands around which they could be mobilised. The demands of the guerrillas were still general and exclusively political. This won them working class recruits, of course; but it did not actively strengthen the working class movement itself. The call for another general strike in April 1958 proved to be a failure, probably for the same reasons—though repression was also intensifying. In the aftermath of April the Communists and the guerrillas agreed to cooperate which, in Cushion's view, "probably ensured a revolutionary victory". And by January 1959 Batista had fled.

At the same time there was, I believe, a political cost. The armed struggle discourse prevailed and the leadership of the resistance to Batista shifted definitively to the mountains. While the "combative workers' movement" actively supported the guerrillas, their role became secondary.

Among the first decisions of the new government was the removal of Mujal and his replacement by the long standing MR-26-7 workers' leader David Salvador. But Salvador, like many in this "cross-class" movement, was bitterly hostile to the Communists and was soon replaced by Lázaro Peña, a leading Communist. Cushion's account makes it forcefully clear that the most militant and most courageous rank and file activists in the workers' movement were key to the weakening of the Batista regime. Yet that involvement has been underplayed in the subsequent histories of the revolution, in favour of the military victory. This is more than just an oversight that should now be adjusted. Its repercussions can be seen in the character of the new Cuban state, built around a command

4 Cushion, 2016, p145.

structure rather than in the encouragement of active grassroots involvement. Its longer-term consequences will take us back to Cuba in the present.

The special period and beyond

After 1970, and marked by Fidel's speech to the Non-Aligned Conference in Algiers, Cuba fully entered the Soviet ambit, not just economically but also politically. The Guevara years faded into memory, and with them both the voluntarism and the guerrilla method associated with Che. The Cuban Communist Party was the sole and unchallenged authority, and Eastern Europe the source of all consumer goods and industrial products as well as virtually the sole market for what remained Cuba's main export—sugar. Cuba's contribution to the liberation struggles in southern Africa and more controversially its military support for the Ethiopian Derg were also expressions of its supporting role in Soviet foreign policy—though this is not to deny the courage of its fighters or the sacrifices many of them made.

In Latin America, Cuba retained its symbolic significance as an anti-imperialist icon. Yet Cuban realpolitik was moving away from confrontation—as Fidel's praise for the Chilean Road to socialism in 1971, and his encouragement of a strategy of negotiation in Central America in the late 1970s, made very clear. And when the US invaded Grenada in 1983, citing the Cuban presence (the Cuban construction workers were building an extended airport runway commissioned by Maurice Bishop, Grenada's radical leader), Cuba kept its distance.

But hard-won reputations sometimes survive beyond their moments of origin. Thus Cuba's anti-imperialist credentials were sustained by the relentless campaign waged by the right wing Cuban lobby in Miami and its many friends in Washington. Certainly their votes were important, though the Nixon connections with the Cuban-American lobby, for example, went well beyond vote-catching! The unstinting hostility of successive US administrations to Castro's Cuba ensured an uncritical response from its supporters abroad. The recently issued volume *Cuba and the US Empire* by Jane Franklin illustrates the problem.[5] It is a strange work of history, a chronology from the early 20th century until the 1990s (the period after 1995 to the present merits only 20 pages—of 456). The succession of dates and names gives no sense of the forces and movements that have shaped history, beyond the US government and the CIA. Most importantly, there is very little to explain the shifts and changes within Cuba, let alone the character of the regime. Fidel's state visits are carefully listed, but there is nothing on internal events. It is significant that one of the heroes of the Angolan war, Arnaldo Ochoa, later minister of the interior, was summarily executed in 1989, together with others—this is noted but not explained. The

5 Franklin, 2016.

introduction of mixed enterprises in 1991 by new economics minister Carlos Lage appears out of the blue, as does the later authorisation of private enterprise. But they are simply noted. Dates and times can be useful, but in this case they are limited by the filter through which they are viewed—the Cuban state.

The problem is that the literature on Cuba from the left offers no explanation for the sudden emergence of the new Cuba with its doors opened wide to foreign capital. Nor can it shed any light on the absence of critical voices in this or previous moments of dramatic change. One exception to that, though this was not its original intention, is Antoni Kapcia's 2014 *Leadership in the Cuban Revolution*.[6] The title is especially revealing in a book whose final chapter is entitled "A revolutionary corporatism?" For socialists committed to participatory democracy—what Hal Draper called "socialism from below"—the question mark is all-important. And it begs a question. How did Cuba move, apparently effortlessly, from revolutionary icon to a new and promising market place in a neoliberal world?—because that is what it has become.

Behind the curtain

1991 was the beginning of what was called the "special period in time of peace", when the full effects of the withdrawal of Soviet support and the fall of the Berlin Wall left an impoverished and denuded Cuba on the brink of collapse. The accounts of hardship at the time are legion—but they tell a contradictory story. On the one hand, the generation of the revolution accepted conditions of extreme hardship, the rationing, the lack of food—a mark of the level of commitment to the revolution. The younger generation, however, were less convinced. But the lack of anything more than minor acts of rebellion is testimony to the effectiveness of the Cuban regime. It survived with its structures of control intact. The command structure that Fidel had built from the beginning, and which remained under the control of a tiny group whose authority derived from the pre-revolutionary sierra, held out. As Kapcia put it, "however weak the Cuban state might have been in its institutional structure...it has always demonstrated a remarkable degree of effectiveness in its various mechanisms of defence".[7] He is, of course, describing the defence of *the state*, and mechanisms which included the Rapid Response Brigades that pursued dissent wherever it arose. So the regime held through the special period; but apart from the state itself, what was it defending?

To understand recent events, it is critical to recognise that what was being protected and defended was not an egalitarian state or a communism in which

6 Kapcia, 2014.

7 Kapcia, 2014, p18.

the majority of Cubans were the subjects of their own history. By the mid-1990s an important shift was taking place. The core leadership positions—political, economic and military—were now increasingly occupied by the military, placed and distributed by Fidel's brother Raúl Castro. He had already brought in Japanese management consultants in the late 1980s and sent high ranking personnel to learn entrepreneurial skills in the next decade. In the face of the post-Stalinist crisis, new concessions to private enterprise allowed small businesses to be set up, in the tourist sector, for example. But the beneficiaries of these changes were in their majority state functionaries, who had already attained a degree of material and political privilege (the two largely went together) within the system through corruption and the traffic of influence. These were the sectors which were in a position to offer bed and breakfast, meals and services as the tourist industry was relaunched later in the 1990s—*under the aegis of the armed forces*. Fidel had acted on the increasingly obvious corruption within the state with the "rectification" campaign of 1986. But the campaign could do very little in the face of the "special period". Although it would not become official for another decade, it was clear that by any criteria Cuba was no longer the socialist state it claimed to be—though its definition of socialism had always embraced authoritarian structures, the repression of dissent and the absence of formal democracy; party congress delegates and National Assembly candidates were nominated from above. The "negotiation" that Kapcia insists replaced the institutions of open grassroots democracy could hardly claim to be an adequate substitute for the self-emancipation of the working class.

The impact of the "special period", furthermore, was not equally distributed. The remittances from family members in the US reached $2.5 billion by 2013. In real terms they sustained the economy from the late 1990s onwards. But the family members from which they came were the middle classes who left Cuba after the revolution. None of that money reached Alamar, the almost wholly black housing scheme on the outskirts of Havana. Nor did it alleviate the high unemployment levels among that section of the population. These were the marginals of Cuban society—living on the minimal rations and social welfare that held off starvation. But they were severely under-represented in the new private sector, let alone in the state or the government, whose upper echelons—including the party leadership—were overwhelmingly white and male.

When you spoke with anyone from the Cuba Solidarity Campaign, the starting position in any conversation was to point to the high levels of educational achievement in Cuba and its health service. Until the special period they were extremely good, but from then on spending on those sectors began to decline. The graduates of the higher education system have found themselves locked in a society of few opportunities; some 40,000 Cuban doctors are outside the island now and many will never return. In fact the medical service itself, beyond basic health provision, has become a dollar earner, both by commercialising its facilities and marketing its most innovative pharmaceutical products like its anti-meningitis vaccine and its highly respected ophthalmology.

In fact the process that led towards the meeting between Raúl Castro and Obama began during this phase. The Law of Foreign Investment of 1995 permitted mixed enterprises with foreign capital. Only health, education and the press were closed to that investment. At the same time, a resolution of the National Assembly in 2001 made it absolutely clear that Cuba would remain a "one-party system"—a party which had sustained a high level of centralisation and control of every social space.

Effectively the model of the new Cuba was being shaped throughout those years under Raúl and with the collusion of a new "modernising" bureaucracy appointed by Fidel and later summarily dismissed by Raúl—men like economics minister Carlos Lage. That modernisation was explicitly an opening to the market. To put it in context, this was accompanied by a fall in social spending and a fall in the real value of wages to 27 percent of their 1989 value by 2008. Pensions for an ageing population fell from 100 percent in 1989 to 16 percent in 1993 returning to only 50 percent of the 1989 value in 2013. At the same time the retirement age was raised, the level of personal contribution raised and 500,000 state employees dismissed.

The new model, then, combined a one-party state with privatisation ("modernisation") of the economy and a reduction in the welfare spending which had virtually defined Cuban socialism until the assumption of power by Raúl. I don't mean to suggest for a moment that Raúl removed Fidel in a power struggle. They had led the Cuban Revolution in combination for 55 years. Fidel was clearly both aware and approving of these changes. In any event, he was infirm and quickly moved sideways into a symbolic niche.

It might be argued that the revolution was beaten by the fall of Eastern Europe and the rise of neoliberalism. If that is the case, then it would be the responsibility of socialists to say that and to seek strategies in Cuba, as elsewhere, to allow the majority of working class people to develop methods to defend themselves against the effects of the crisis and to evolve a new strategy for socialism. For that to happen, knowledge of the history of the Cuban working class movement—the kind of research that Cushion has produced—would have been indispensable; but it was not available. Ironically, the questions about power, democracy and the anti-capitalist struggle that in the same period, from 2000 onwards, were being publicly posed by the new social movements in Latin America passed Cuba by. That could happen because travel beyond the island remained difficult for ordinary Cubans (in other words, those who were not bureaucrats) beyond a handful of musicians who were a new area of Cuban exports. Cuba remained sealed off from most political developments abroad by the non-availability of the internet and by strict censorship. The slight relaxation of the early 1990s was followed by a new wave of repression in the early 2000s. Dissidents—the few that there were—were represented as agents of US imperialism or the Miami Mafia. The serious critical writing of people like Haroldo Dilla, who was analysing the new emerging managerial class, was rapidly suppressed, just as the serious Marxist debates around the magazine *Pensamiento Crítico* in the early 1970s were shut down.

By the time Raúl Castro assumed full control he had put in place the economic instruments of the transition to the new Cuba. Under the control of his son in law, a military conglomerate called La Gaviota had taken control of much of Cuba's industrial and tourist sector—sugar having declined to a shadow of its former self. The directors of these companies were interwoven with the upper echelons of the state and the military—ensuring that the coming move into the global market would benefit but not threaten the state bureaucracy or its political system.

The Venezuela factor

This reorganisation was in many ways made possible by the rise of Hugo Chávez to power in Venezuela in 1999. The guarantee of cheap oil almost certainly saved the Cuban economy, given that Cuba in the late 1990s had no reliable suppliers and insufficient foreign currency to pay for oil. Chávez's commitment to Cuba, and to Fidel in particular, was unconditional and total. It was the policy of the Bolivarian Revolution to divert oil revenues towards social programmes—the first of which, Barrio Adentro, brought health provision to Venezuela's poor *barrios*. Since most of the Venezuelan medical profession was hostile to Chávez, the gap was filled by Cuban doctors. Cuban personnel also filled posts in education, sport, some state departments and, critically, in the military—particularly in military intelligence. These services were all paid for—so that Cuba benefitted twice from Venezuelan oil. Cubans were also politically influential; the main political party in Venezuela, the United Venezuelan Socialist Party (PSUV)—created by Chávez in 2006—was quite clearly modelled on the Cuban Communist Party, a party whose high levels of centralisation and command structures were in direct contradiction to the participatory democracy promised by Chávez's "21st century socialism". The only country permitted to own 100 percent of shares in a Cuban enterprise was Venezuela—and it is undoubtedly the case that many members of the new chavista bureaucracy have "invested" state funds there. This is an issue to be developed elsewhere.

In this context, the timing of the public acknowledgment of Cuba's new relationship with Washington was significant. Chávez died, in Cuba, in March 2013. Three months later, the first formal meetings took place between Cuban and

US officials. While nothing changed at the level of rhetoric, Cuban-Venezuelan relations deteriorated from then on. Venezuela's oil shipments were reduced as the world price fell. But although Cuban influences remain significant within the Venezuelan state, relations between the two countries started to cool noticeably, just as they warmed between Havana and Washington.

The conditions for Cuba's opening to the market, and particularly US capital, had already been laid down. The port of Mariel, from which yachts and makeshift rafts once took refugees across the Florida Straits, is now emblematic of this new engagement. Declared a Special Economic Zone, where normal labour and economic legislation are suspended for foreign investors, its port development is run by Odebrecht, the giant Brazilian engineering firm (now in some trouble as its director has been jailed for corruption) as well as Malaysian and other firms. An Israeli construction company will have a central role in the development of Havana's Malecón esplanade and seawall (despite Israel's 100 percent record of supporting US calls for a continuation of the Cuban embargo at the United Nations!). US wheat producers lobbied fiercely for the lifting of that embargo and have been exporting food to the island for some time. *The Economist* felt secure enough to mount an international seminar in New York in December 2015 on economic opportunities in Cuba. Visa, among others, have already declared their intention to move into the Cuban market.

Some conclusions and a glimpse of the future

The economic structures for a capitalist Cuba already exist, from the privatisation of small commerce to the control of state finance and investment in a "mixed" sector. It will be "mixed" in the sense that the state will remain a controlling actor in the development of a new Cuban capitalism. To ensure a smooth transition the shape of state power, the role of the party and the concentration of economic, political and military power in a small leadership group will continue just as it was throughout the revolutionary period. This group and its associates today comprise a clear bureaucratic class, a nomenklatura who will be the beneficiaries of the new economic environment. But there are others, the well-known and often dissolute children of the generals, as they are called, who will want power but may not inherit it.

At the grassroots level, ordinary Cubans will find the expectations that they have grown up with are not met. Social spending has been cut, as have pensions; higher education will no longer be free and universally available; and differentials within the health sector will strike at one of the most cherished achievements of the revolution. The position of Cuba's black population is a time-bomb. The figures given in a wide-ranging 2008 report by Esteban Morales Domínguez on "The Challenge of the Racial Problem in Cuba"—a problem denied for decades—are fantastically telling (Morales has since been dismissed from his post). Of the 131 members of the leading state committees, 114 are white and five black; 34.2 percent of black people have jobs as opposed to 63.8 percent of whites; 73 percent of scientists and technicians are white; and there are few black faces in the burgeoning tourist industry. In a "free market" situation, where over half of the economy is already effectively privatised, the inequalities will grow and the shiny new products global capital will deliver will be inaccessible to a majority population already resentful of the "dollar shops" to which they cannot gain entry.

It is several years since Raúl warned in a BBC interview of what was to come when he explained that Cuba was not seeking equality but "equality of opportunity". The meaning of this must be clear to all in a neoliberal world. The critical question politically, then, is how those left behind by these new "opportunities" can organise themselves independently, as workers, to fight discrimination, inequality and exploitation. Marxism and the history of working class struggle will be key tools in building that response. Sadly, Marxism has been devalued for many Cubans as an ideology of power—and the wide range of debates around Marxist ideas have not been available where often the best that could be obtained, at least until the slow opening of the internet, were dusty Soviet manuals. And as Steve Cushion's careful research has shown, the history of the struggles of the Cuban working class will need to be rediscovered—to inspire a new generation and open the road to socialism again.

References

Cushion, Steve, 2016, *A Hidden History of the Cuban Revolution: How the Working Class Shaped the Guerrillas' Victory* (Monthly Review Press).

Franklin, Jane, 2016, *Cuba and the US Empire: A Chronological History* (Monthly Review Press).

Gerassi, John, 1963, *The Great Fear in Latin America* (Macmillan).

Kapcia, Antoni, 2014, *Leadership in the Cuban Revolution: The Unseen Story* (Zed Books).

Is disability different? A reply to Rob Murthwaite

Roddy Slorach

Rob Murthwaite's review of my book *A Very Capitalist Condition: A History and Politics of Disability* endorses its general approach that disability discrimination is rooted in the development and continued existence of capitalist society.[1] However, I want to respond to two criticisms Rob raises.

His first, objecting to the lack of space given to an analysis of the biopsychosocial (BPS) model of disability, is well made. As the name implies, the BPS model emphasises negative attitudes among benefit claimants rather than social factors in explaining poverty among disabled people. The BPS model was developed by successive governments from 2008 onwards to justify stricter assessment regimes and tighten eligibility criteria for ESA and other disability benefits, with the aim of reducing what were seen as unacceptably high levels of claims. It has been analysed at length elsewhere, so won't be discussed further here.[2] Rob's main disagreement concerns the book's analysis of the nature of disability discrimination—specifically a passage from the section on disability identity in Chapter 13:

> The point, however, remains that their more fragmented experiences of oppression means disabled people are less likely to identify with each other than other

1 Slorach, 2015, reviewed in the previous issue of *International Socialism*—Murthwaite, 2016.

2 See in particular Jolly, 2012, and Shakespeare and others, 2016.

> groups of the oppressed. The social model's assumption that disabled people can find common cause first and foremost with other disabled people is therefore problematic.[3]

After quoting this passage, Rob goes on to say: "The idea that the oppression of disabled people is somehow fundamentally different from oppression based on race or gender runs throughout this section without a convincing argument being made in support of this contention".[4]

Any political account of a type of oppression must examine its particularities. But at no point does the book state that disability discrimination is "fundamentally" different from other forms of oppression. It starts from the insights of the social model of disability, but goes on to argue that impairment is central to a more rounded and explicitly Marxist account of disability as a form of oppression. The core arguments in the book were developed from an article written for this journal five years ago, where I wrote that impairment is "the raw material on which disability discrimination works".[5]

It is important to acknowledge that this is a controversial subject among disabled people. Disability discrimination works by constantly reducing people to their particular "deficits", or diagnostic labels—or by denying the significance or presence of these in the first place. But that's precisely why I think it necessary to discuss impairment.

Most of those familiar with the term "disability" tend to confuse it with limitations in someone's physical, sensory or functioning; in other words, impairments. But for 40 years disability activists (particularly in the UK) have insisted on a sharp distinction between the concept of disability and that of impairment. The social model of disability shows how people with impairments are marginalised, excluded and scapegoated by a society that refuses to take account of their needs. Very few people, however, understand this distinction. The disadvantages faced by disabled people are commonly seen to be inevitable, arising directly from their particular impairment. So the meaning of disability is highly contested.

To summarise the arguments from the book:

- Impairment is a hugely diverse and heterogeneous category, and different impairment groups may not recognise any common disability identity. Blind people and wheelchair users might, for example, find it easier to draw parallels with each other's experiences than with those of someone with dyslexia or who has a progressive or chronic disease.

3 Slorach, 2015, p256.
4 Murthwaite, 2016, p195.
5 Slorach, 2011, p127.

- Unlike wheelchair users, whose symbol is instantly recognisable for signifying disability across the world, most people's impairments—for example, various kinds of learning difficulties or forms of mental distress—are neither visible nor obvious to others.
- We are much more likely to acquire an impairment over the course of our lives than to be born with one: one in 20 UK children are disabled, with that proportion rising to almost one in two people over state pension age. Therefore saying "disability is just something that hasn't happened to you yet" makes a lot of sense.
- Some groups commonly considered to be disabled by others may reject the label. Many deaf, neurodiversity and mental health activists don't see themselves as having any impairment or disadvantage. These approaches shouldn't be mutually exclusive. Disability is about discrimination on the grounds of perceived disadvantage or inferiority, so not identifying as disabled yourself doesn't make you any less subject to discrimination by others.
- Despite the passage of anti-discrimination legislation, only a minority of disabled people see themselves as such. This is clearly influenced by wider political factors. Research by the Department for Work and Pensions shows that, of those who met the legal definition of disability in the UK in 2012, only 25 percent said they were disabled.[6] This represents a steep drop from an equivalent figure of 48 percent in 2001. The period in between saw escalating attacks on disability "fraudsters" and "scroungers", with huge cuts and reforms removing many thousands of people's entitlement to disability benefits. Many people believe that to be disabled is to be a burden on the state or their loved ones.

Rob objects to my stating that the experience of oppression is "more fragmented" among disabled people than among other oppressed groups, but he is wrong to say that I don't explain why. Besides the arguments repeated above, I explore this in the chapters on deafness and disabled war veterans, in the sections on neurodiversity and mental health and in discussing the impact of institutionalisation and segregation on particular impairment groups. I also show how disabled people are more marginalised than other oppressed groups in one particular area: fully half of all disabled people of working age in the UK are unemployed—a proportion largely unchanged for 50 years.

Analysing these differences isn't, of course, about saying that disability matters more or less than other forms of oppression. Neither is identifying its high degree of internal differentiation and subjectivity intended to suggest that it

6 DWP, 2013.

cannot be overcome. Just as the causes of disability are social and economic, so are the causes of impairment—such as pollution, war, poverty, or the mental or physical stresses of work. These factors dictate that a large majority of disabled people belong to the working class. Socialists are in favour of both individual and collective interventions to address impairment and disability alike: we want better services and treatment as well as wider social change. The principles of self-emancipation apply here as elsewhere—disabled people must be the subjects of change alongside their fellow workers, not passive objects of the good or bad intentions of others.

The book's central argument is that disability is rooted in a society based on wage labour and profit, because the labour power of disabled people is more expensive to purchase and to reproduce (though less so than popularly believed). This is the basis for mythical notions of normality and what appear to be arbitrary distinctions between disabled and non-disabled people. The millions of disabled people who do work are more likely than their peers to join trade unions, but there is nothing inevitable in seeing their fellow workers as allies, or capitalism as their enemy.

References

Department for Work and Pensions, 2013, "Building a Deeper Understanding of Disability in the UK Today" (February), www.gov.uk/government/uploads/system/uploads/attachment_data/file/320509/building-understanding-main-report.pdf

Jolly, Debbie, 2012, "A Tale of Two Models: Disabled People versus UNUM, ATOS, Government and Disability Charities", http://disability-studies.leeds.ac.uk/files/library/A-Tale-of-two-Models-Leeds1.pdf

Murthwaite, Rob, 2016, "Disability, Resistance and Revolution", *International Socialism 151* (summer), http://isj.org.uk/disability-resistance-and-revolution/

Shakespeare, Tom, Nicholas Watson, and Ola Abu Alghaib, 2016, "Blaming the Victim, All Over Again: Waddell and Aylward's Biopsychosocial (BPS) Model of Disability", *Critical Social Policy*, volume 36, number 4.

Slorach, Roddy, 2011, "Marxism and Disability", *International Socialism 129* (winter), http://isj.org.uk/marxism-and-disability/

Slorach, Roddy, 2015, *A Very Capitalist Condition: A History and Politics of Disability* (Bookmarks).

The Kapp Putsch and the German October: a reply to John Rose

Tony Phillips

My previous piece on the German Revolution in *International Socialism 149*[1] was prompted by John Rose's argument at his meeting at Marxism 2014 that the revolution was effectively over by January 1919.[2] My article was not an attempt to provide a potted history of the entire period, only a response to the areas of John's talk with which I disagreed. There is no need for a new history given the existence of the two classic accounts by Pierre Broué and Chris Harman which are easily available in English.[3] Although both books are decades old, I do not believe that the account and interpretations of the events contained in them have been superseded from a revolutionary socialist perspective by subsequent scholarship. However, contrary to John's claim, I do not regard the works of Chris Harman (or any other Marxist) as holy writ and therefore beyond criticism. I do maintain on the basis of my study of the period (not just Harman and Broué) that John's argument that the prospects for victory after January 1919 were non-existent is not borne out by the facts.

In his response to my piece in *International Socialism 150* John accused me of giving a misleading account of his talk. I do not accept that. I included all the

1 Rose, 2016.

2 Phillips, 2016.

3 Harman, 1982; Broué, 2006.

quotations from John's talk that I disagreed with in response to his complaints about an earlier draft. Readers can judge for themselves by listening to the recording of John's talk (you can hear my intervention at the end of the discussion just before he sums up in which I first raised my disagreements with him) and reading my *International Socialism* article.[4] Readers can also listen to our debates at Marxism 2015 and 2016 (the latter also with Ian Birchall).[5]

John's talk focused on the role of workers' councils in the November Revolution and the weeks immediately afterwards. I argued at the meeting and in *International Socialism* that a victorious workers' revolution was objectively possible right up until October 1923, referring to the civil war of 1919, the mass strike wave of that year, the general strike in response to the Kapp Putsch in 1920 and finally the revolutionary crisis of 1923.

John chides me for ignoring John Riddell's article in *International Socialism 130*[6] and claims that "Riddell's emphasis...on the 1920 Kapp Putsch is very different from Tony's".[7] In fact I agree totally with Riddell's assessment. I did not claim in my piece that the Kapp Putsch represented a direct opportunity for workers to take power. I argued only that it offered the potential to turn the tables on the bourgeoisie in a similar way to the defeat of the Kornilov coup in Russia in August 1917 which radically changed the balance of class forces while defending the gains of the February Revolution.

John appears to have retreated from his claim in his Marxism talk that the defeat of the Kapp Putsch strengthened the Weimar Republic. However, his statement that "the strategic and tactical initiative was with Carl Legien, the notorious right wing trade union leader," does not do justice to the revolutionary potential of this event.[8] It is true that Legien, the man who said before the war that "the general strike is general nonsense" was forced, faced with a military coup, to call, yes, a general strike to save the skins of the union bureaucracy and the SPD leadership. It is also true that he did not call off the strike even when the generals had been routed in order to strengthen the hand of the ADGB (the national confederation of trade unions) in determining the government that would follow, although it is also doubtful that many workers would have taken any notice of a call for an immediate return to work.

However, the strike cannot be reduced to a bureaucratic mass strike controlled by the union leadership from start to finish. It was completely solid from

4 I do however accept John's criticism in footnote 2 of his *International Socialism* article.

5 Phillips and Rose, 2015; Birchall, Phillips and Rose, 2016.

6 Riddell, 2011.

7 Rose, 2016, p192.

8 Rose, 2016, p192.

the Rhine to the Elbe. Given the level of military repression, this was only possible through rank and file initiative even in politically backward areas such as rural East Prussia, where the unions were weak but the farm labourers nonetheless armed themselves against the coup and joined in. As John rightly mentions, in Saxony there was a revival of the workers' councils led by the KPD leading to dual power. As I pointed out in my previous article, the workers also took control of the Ruhr, Germany's most important industrial area, where a red army was set up with mass workers' support that routed General von Watter's regular Reichswehr troops.

The strike was only allowed to peter out thanks to the vacillation of the KPD and USPD leaderships. It was the USPD that had real control of the strike, not Legien, as that organisation contained many of the militants who were leading it on the ground. But its leadership was divided between reformists whose politics were no different to the SPD and left wingers such as Ernst Daumig who were confused over how to respond to Legien's proposal of a workers' government. As Broué writes, "the real decision on stopping the general strike was in the hands of the Independents [the USPD]".[9] Ralf Hoffrogge writes that revolutionary shop stewards' leader Richard Müller "accused the [USPD] party leadership of abandoning the struggling workers in the Ruhr region by calling off the strike".[10]

As it was, the defeat of the coup and the defence of the gains of the November Revolution were a great victory despite the army being allowed to take revenge on the Ruhr workers. But the most important outcome was less tangible. As Riddell argues, "the successful resistance to the Kapp Putsch increased the confidence of working people in Germany, giving the revolutionary left new energy".[11] KPD leader Ruth Fischer recalled that the lost opportunity represented by the sell-out of the general strike by the right wing USPD leaders had a huge impact on the hundreds of thousands of party members, which included the cream of working class militants in the factories and pits: "The Kapp Putsch stimulated new impulses in the USPD... The mood prevailing in the spring of 1920 was 'We need an organisation able to cope with...the Freikorps and their allies in the army'".[12] That is what enabled Communist International president Grigori Zinoviev to persuade the USPD congress a few months later to vote to affiliate to the Comintern and merge with the KPD.

I fully concur with John's discussion of the problem of the demand for a workers' government. As Harman argues, the slogan of the workers' government

9 Broué, 2006, p367.
10 Hoffrogge, 2015, p138.
11 Riddell, 2011, p119.
12 Fischer, 1948, p134.

is highly ambiguous. It can mean different things to different political forces in the same situation and different things in different situations.[13]

In November and December 1918 the SPD-USPD government had acted as cover for the right wing SPD leaders Philipp Scheidemann and Gustav Noske to outmanoeuvre the revolutionary workers and work with the army high command to repress the revolution. Lenin argued that the KPD should adopt the workers' government slogan following the Kapp Putsch to put pressure on the SPD, USPD and ADGB leaders to form a government to take measures to repress the army generals who had supported the coup attempt. He believed that they should use any backsliding by the government to expose the reformist parties and trade union bureaucrats such as Legien and grow the influence of the KPD. The Communists should avoid adding to illusions in the reformists by arguing for the strengthening of the workers' councils and workers' militias as the only way to ensure that action was actually taken against the leaders of the putsch.[14] Lenin was arguing for essentially the same approach as used in June 1917 when Bolshevik workers demonstrated in the streets of Petrograd carrying banners saying "Down with the Ten Minister-Capitalists".[15] The fourth congress of the Communist International also correctly supported the use of the slogan during 1922 to help increase the influence of the KPD.[16]

I only referred to the March action of 1921 in passing in my previous article because John did not mention it in his talk. I agree with his verdict that it was an unmitigated disaster. It cost the KPD thousands of the worker militants it had just won over and led to the departure of some of its most able leaders such as Paul Levi and Daumig. KPD leaders such as Heinrich Brandler who had supported the March action were clearly scarred by the experience and the harsh criticism they received from Lenin and Trotsky at the subsequent Comintern congress. They lost confidence in their ability to make independent judgements which was to prove disastrous in 1923.

However, I do not believe that the March action meant that victory two and a half years later was impossible. Fischer argues that: "During the latter part of 1922 the Communist Party of Germany was gaining in influence and membership. In the third quarter of 1922 it had 218,555 members. This contrasts with a membership figure of a year earlier, just after the March action, of 180,443".[17] Harman states that "there is little doubt that [the united front policy] built the party up again in 1922

13 Harman and Potter, 2007.
14 Lenin, 1977, pp579-580.
15 Trotsky, 1977, pp462-463.
16 Riddell, 2012, p1,167.
17 Fischer, 1948, p222.

after the near devastation of 1921".[18] Broué shows that during 1923 all indicators show the spectacular growth in size and influence of the KPD in the mass organisations of the working class including the trade unions, factory councils and proletarian hundreds and that the influence of the SPD and the trade union bureaucracy was draining away. Circulation of *Die Rote Fahne*, the KPD national daily paper, outstripped the SPD's *Vorwärts*, despite raging inflation and dire poverty.[19]

John rightly goes through some of the things that went wrong in 1923 including the failings of the Brandler leadership. However, he persists in his efforts to play down the importance of the factory councils. John refers to Broué's discussion of their role in 1920, but by 1923 they had developed dramatically and were now led by the KPD at national level, spreading their power beyond the workplaces through the proletarian hundreds (armed workers' battalions) and the control committees that sought to control food prices. As Victor Serge, in Germany at the time working as a Comintern official, points out, "the factory committees have in the present situation a role which is in some ways reminiscent of the Soviets at the beginning of the February Revolution in Russia...they constitute a genuine proletarian power in the face of the government".[20] John does correctly describe the leading role of the factory councils in the Cuno general strike of August 1923 and rightly calls the outcome of the strike "a tremendous disappointment".[21] However, he implies that the limitations of the factory councils were in some way partly responsible for both this and the final defeat of the revolution in October but does not explain why.

The Cuno strike did not achieve its full potential outcome, not because of the limitations of the factory councils or the predictable betrayal of the SPD leadership, but because of the wrong perspective of the KPD leadership and the Executive Committee of the Communist International (ECCI) up to that point. By the beginning of August only the KPD did not recognise that a revolutionary situation now existed in Germany. On 26 July the Prussian conservative *Kreuz-Zeitung* paper, which carried the Iron Cross on its masthead, wrote that: "Without doubt we are on the eve of another revolution—who could be mistaken after seeing what is unfolding before our eyes." The Catholic Zentrum Party's *Germania* drew similar conclusions.[22] On 29 July the KPD had called an anti-fascist day of demonstrations across the country in response to the rise of the far right. It then cancelled outdoor protests in many regions due to fear of

18 Harman, 1982, p239.

19 Broué, 2006, pp713-720.

20 Serge, 2000, p52.

21 Rose, 2016, p196.

22 Quoted in Broué, 2006, p742.

state repression. But the response was still massive, with 200,000 workers joining indoor meetings in Berlin, for example.

The fact that two weeks later the KPD, through the factory councils and against the opposition of the official ADGB bureaucrats, called a nationwide general strike that toppled the Cuno government showed that workers' power was on the agenda. At this point the slogan of a workers' government was lagging behind the movement. In a fast developing revolutionary situation with the KPD now hegemonic in the working class, the Cuno strike should have been turned into a struggle for workers' power. Harman asks: "Would things not have been a little different if the party had moved (as Brandler had himself suggested) from the defensive to the offensive two or three weeks before the strike broke—if it had not retreated on the anti-fascist day of demonstrations—and if it had raised a clearer slogan than for the 'workers' government'".[23] The central slogan of the strike should have been "Down with the Cuno government—all power to the factory councils!"

But it was only with the fall of the Cuno government that the ECCI in Moscow woke up to the situation in Germany and started urging the KPD to go onto the offensive and start preparing for an insurrection. Drawn out planning for the rising began in Moscow accompanied by detailed military preparations in Germany. But all this should have started months earlier. The presence of key KPD leaders, such as Brandler, in Moscow for weeks in August and September contributed to the failure of the KPD to give a positive lead to continuing workers' struggles. Fischer, who was also in Moscow for much of this time, later argued that too great an emphasis was placed on technical military preparations and that political preparation of the mass organisations of working class for the rising was neglected. She believed that a correct strategy would have involved the "occupation of factories by workers' committees, open military organisation in all industrial centres, armed demonstrations and finally the formation of a dual government—regional and Reich committees of factory councils proclaiming their aspiration to rule Germany from now on".[24] This particular view is supported by August Thalheimer, a leader of the rival Brandler faction in the KPD leadership otherwise very hostile to Fischer.[25]

John writes, "Brandler's doubts must have been increased by the foul atmosphere in Moscow. It is inconceivable that he didn't have some sense of just how bitter and explosive was the showdown, in particular, between Zinoviev and Trotsky".[26] But as Brandler told Isaac Deutscher many years later: "In the

23 Harman, 1982, p273.
24 Fischer, 1948, p322.
25 Thalheimer, 1931.
26 Rose, 2016, p197.

Executive of the Comintern, these differences between him [Trotsky] and the rest of the Soviet delegation were concealed".[27] Deutscher reports that Brandler told him that "the Soviet delegation to the Comintern presented outwardly a united front so that other members knew little or nothing about the disagreements among the Russians...the whole Soviet delegation considered the situation in Germany a revolutionary one".[28]

As John argues, the decision to rely on the support of the local leaders of the left wing of the SPD at the Chemnitz conference of the workers' councils for a general strike as the trigger for the insurrection was a huge mistake. But an even bigger mistake was for the KPD leadership to then call off the insurrection. The delegates at Chemnitz were from Saxony only. The government had banned a national conference of the factory councils but the Cuno strike had been launched by a delegate conference of factory councils in the Berlin area. Failing that, the factory councils' leading national body, the Council of Fifteen, could have called a general strike. Fischer points to the growing involvement of SPD supporters in the proletarian hundreds in the key industrial areas, which suggests that, unlike in 1921, the KPD would not have been isolated if the rising had gone ahead on 21 October, the date of the Chemnitz conference.

Of course, there was no guarantee of success but, unlike in March 1921, Germany was in deep crisis and the rising could have galvanised the whole working class. Hitler's and Erich Ludendorff's bid for power in Munich in early November was a total flop. The ruling class had driven the majority of the population into desperate poverty and, in mortal fear of revolution, it had appealed to British, French and US imperialism for help. The KPD had marched the most militant sections of the working class up to the top of the hill; marching them back down again led to huge demoralisation and loss of faith in the party. It did not even live to fight another day as a revolutionary party. The crisis passed and within months the bureaucratisation of the Comintern under the direction of Zinoviev—and later Stalin—was under way.

Ten years later the KPD would allow Hitler to come to power over a divided working class without a shot being fired. It would have been better to have fought and lost in 1923 than to miss an opportunity that could have changed history. In hindsight defeat can either be seen as inevitable or we can look at how things could have been different. This period is so fascinating because the stakes were so high and the lessons for revolutionary socialists today are so important and so numerous. But the key lesson that stands out is the need to build the revolutionary party now.

27 Quoted in Deutscher, 1977.

28 Deutscher, 1977.

References

Birchall, Ian, Tony Phillips and John Rose, 2016, "Debating the German Revolution 1918-23", talk at Marxism 2016, http://swpradiocast.bandcamp.com/track/debating-the-german-revolution-1918-23

Broué, Pierre, 2006, *The German Revolution 1917-1923* (Haymarket).

Deutscher, Isaac, 1977, "Record of a Discussion with Heinrich Brandler", *New Left Review*, I/105.

Fischer, Ruth, 1948, *Stalin and German Communism: A Study in the Origins of the State Party* (Harvard University Press).

Harman, Chris, and Tim Potter, 2007 [1977], "The Workers' Government", *International Socialism* (online only), http://isj.org.uk/the-workers-government/

Harman, Chris, 1982, *The Lost Revolution, Germany 1918-1923* (Bookmarks).

Hoffrogge, Ralf, 2015, *Working Class Politics in the German Revolution: Richard Müller, the Revolutionary Shop Stewards and the Origins of the Council Movement* (Haymarket).

Lenin, V I, 1977 [1920], "'Left-wing Communism': An Infantile Disorder", in *Selected Works* (Progress Publishers), www.marxists.org/archive/lenin/works/1920/lwc/index.htm

Phillips, Tony, 2016, "Was the German Revolution Defeated by January 1919?", *International Socialism 149* (winter), http://isj.org.uk/was-the-german-revolution-defeated-by-january-1919/

Phillips, Tony, and John Rose, 2015, "Workers' and Soldiers' Councils of Germany 1918: The High Point of the Revolution?" talk at Marxism 2015, http://swpradiocast.bandcamp.com/track/workers-soldiers-councils-of-germany-1918-the-high-point-of-the-revolution-marxism-2015

Riddell, John, 2011, "The Origins of the United Front Policy", *International Socialism 130* (spring), http://isj.org.uk/the-origins-of-the-united-front-policy/

Riddell, John (ed), 2012, *Toward the United Front: Proceedings of the Fourth Conference of the Communist International, 1922* (Haymarket).

Rose, John, 2016, "Revolutionary Workers' Movements and Parliaments in Germany 1918-23: A Reply to Tony Phillips", *International Socialism 150* (spring), http://isj.org.uk/revolutionary-workers-movements-and-parliaments-in-germany-1918-23-a-reply-to-tony-phillips/

Serge, Victor, 2000, *Witness to the German Revolution: Writings from Germany 1923* (Redwords).

Thalheimer, August, 1931, *A Missed Opportunity? The German October Legend and the Real History of 1923* (Marken Press), www.marxists.org/archive/thalheimer/works/missed/index.htm

Trotsky, Leon, 1977, *The History of the Russian Revolution* (Pluto Press).

Book reviews

Egypt: In the heart of the struggle

Philip Marfleet

Egypt's Long Revolution: Protest Movements and Uprisings
Maha Abdelrahman
Routledge (2015), £34.99

This book was written as the Egyptian Revolution unfolded. Its author experienced the hopes and anxieties of tens of millions of people, sharing "moments of soaring elation, periods of uncertainty and self-doubt, instances of retreat and dark days of potential defeat" (pvii). Her analysis of rising opposition to the Hosni Mubarak regime, of the mass uprising that began in 2011 and of the military coup of 2013 is especially important for activists seeking to understand these tumultuous events. Her conclusion is notable: quoting Lenin, she observes that despite all difficulties, those prepared to "preserve their strength and flexibility", learning from experience and pursuing their aims with vigour, can anticipate new opportunities to effect change (p142).

When the uprising against Mubarak began in January 2011 most journalists and many academics expressed surprise, even astonishment. It seemed to them that an Egyptian population they viewed as docile and compliant had overnight discovered an appetite for change—for what millions were already calling a "revolution". The uprising promptly deposed Egypt's dictator but when the dictatorship proved more resilient these pundits were quick to assert that the movement had failed. There were soon many obituaries for the revolution, reflecting on its abrupt rise and fall. Maha Abdelrahman takes a different approach, seeing Egypt's revolution as a process—part of a struggle for change that began long before the uprising in Tahrir Square and one that continues as the regime of Abdel-Fattah el-Sisi grapples with economic crisis and popular hostility to its own intense repression.

Abdelrahman is precise, asserting that: the revolution "did not start in

Tahrir" (p29). She rightly identifies the solidarity demonstrations launched in September 2000 by supporters of the Palestinian intifada as a key development. These protests created space for public action soon occupied by anti-globalisation and anti-war activists, then by the Egyptian Movement for Change (the democracy movement known by its slogan *Kifaya!*—Enough!), and in 2006 by workers' struggles on a scale not seen for 60 years. Abdelrahman describes the cumulative impact of "a tidal wave of protests" (p55) that set the scene for the uprising of 2011.

These struggles were invisible to most academic experts. Concentrating on institutional matters and above all on the apparent resilience of authoritarian regimes in the Middle East, they ignored politics from below. This approach reproduced the policies of colonial and post-colonial regimes that for decades practised a politics of denial. British rulers of Egypt maintained that Egyptians were passive and incapable of organising for change. Gamal Abdel Nasser, first president of an independent Egypt, saw slothfulness and lassitude among the masses who, he said, required to be led. His successors Anwar Sadat and Mubarak were contemptuous of the people, viewing them as bystanders to their projects of personal enrichment and monopolisation of power.

Abdelrahman is focused on the mass of people and their creative energies. She addresses the innovative methods of the pro-democracy movement and the "organisational ingenuity and professionalism" of workers in struggle (p61). Tracing in detail the interlocking struggles of 2000 to 2010, she identifies a "normalisation of protest", as struggles in workplaces, campuses, schools and neighbourhoods embraced millions of people, so that subversive action became "part of everyday lived reality" (p69).

Unlike almost every other academic analyst Abdelrahman is interested in relationships between activist groups and political organisations including nationalists, Islamists, Communists of the old left, and a new generation of revolutionary socialists. She notes that most activists rejected the established parties of the left: rigid and highly centralised, these inhibited mobilisation against the regime. The most effective campaigns against Mubarak "aimed to be everything these formal groups were not" (p49), operating with fluid structures, participatory decision-making and forms of public protest that proved effective in the face of the regime's clumsy methods of repression.

Abdelrahman examines the problems faced by activist networks under Mubarak and the innovative means used to maintain the momentum of the movement. She highlights the role of the Cairo Conference, an event held annually between 2002 and 2008, at which Egyptian activists coordinated with anti-war movements in North America, Europe, Africa and Asia, and which served as what she calls "a network of networks" for dissident Egyptians (p35).

The conference was indeed significant, not least because it provided a rare opportunity for members of the Muslim Brotherhood to engage systematically in debate with the secular left. Some readers of *International Socialism* who attended these events will recall unprecedented discussions in which young women and men of the Brotherhood engaged with revolutionary Marxists on subjects including the meaning of democracy, the labour theory of value, women's rights and the difference between anti-Zionism and anti-Semitism.

Abdelrahman is not wide-eyed about the activists of 2011. Unlike some recent assessments influenced by autonomist and libertarian traditions, she addresses the limitations of their networks, especially after the fall of Mubarak. The key issue at stake, she suggests, was that of finding a means to facilitate self-expression and, at the same time, to ensure "sustainability" (p83)—to provide coherence and leadership. The ingenuity of activists who challenged Mubarak was not enough, she suggests, to provide a focal point for a revolutionary movement that, after February 2011, confronted the core of the state apparatus in the form of the Supreme Council of the Armed Forces (SCAF). In order to resist the generals' repression and to advance the movement's aim of achieving social justice, activists urgently required new forms of coordination; their failure to collaborate, she maintains, undermined the whole revolutionary project.

The revolution did indeed require coordinated leadership—but why was this not forthcoming? Abdelrahman does not address this question directly. She highlights issues of party loyalty and practical problems of coordination but does not get to the heart of the matter—the tortured history of the established left in Egypt and its willingness to accommodate to the state and to capitalist agendas.

Egypt's Communists had played a significant role in struggles against the colonial power, Britain. However, inhibited by Stalinist obsessions with the search for "progressive" bourgeois allies, they failed to accept opportunities to challenge the colonial state and the pro-British monarchy. When the army under Nasser seized power in 1952 most Communists celebrated a "revolutionary" initiative. Although they experienced severe repression under Nasser, they later joined his state capitalist regime. In 1965 the Egyptian Communist Party dissolved itself on the basis that Nasser had met its aspirations for change. Deserting the workers' and students' movements, it handed the initiative to Islamist currents, soon established as a key pole of attraction for activists.

Presidents Sadat and Mubarak adopted neoliberal policies, supervising the transfer of public assets to private hands, greatly increasing inequality and making the apparatus of the state—*al-nizam* ("the order" or "the system")—an object of hatred for most Egyptians. The established left remained a tame reformist lobby, joining the regime in its assaults on the Islamists, whom Communists dubbed a "fascist" menace. When it became clear that the uprising of 2011 might challenge the state itself, the left—including Communists and radical nationalists of the Nasserist current—joined the generals in an outright assault on the Muslim Brotherhood and subsequently upon the revolutionary movement.

The failure of the popular movement to coordinate an effective leadership was less an organisational matter than an outcome of an orientation by ostensibly radical currents upon the state itself. In 2013 Communists and radical nationalists joined with liberals, social democrats, bourgeois parties and *feloul* ("leftovers" or remnants" of the Mubarak regime) in an alliance with the generals. Some, used and abused by the el-Sisi regime, have since come to regret their naivety as they too are swept up by the current repression.

These largely secular parties were not alone in their embrace of the generals, however. In 2011 leaders of the Muslim Brotherhood entered what Abdelrahman calls an "uneasy marriage of convenience" with SCAF (p79)—one that led not merely to divorce but to a murderous assault on the Brotherhood's members. Abdelrahman might have analysed these developments more closely. The Brotherhood was not the iron-clad organisation described by many analysts of Egyptian affairs, in which the blind obedience of members guaranteed support for the leadership. Nor was it ideologically homogenous and unaffected by changes in wider society. As with her treatment of the left, Abdelrahman might have used historical materials to contextualise the agendas of the organisation's leaders. Why were they so firmly oriented on the state? What were their political aspirations? How did they envisage their relationship with the mass of people?

The Muslim Brotherhood, says Abdelrahman, had long been largely stable—a closely knit group held together by complex economic and social ties. It was in fact deeply affected by the uprising of 2011, experiencing a series of splits and losing a number of high profile figures and some of its most determined young activists. Its relationship with the armed forces and crude attempts to control the movement resulted in a huge loss of support among those who earlier backed the organisation against Mubarak—the latest chapter in the Brotherhood's history of complex shifts and changes in fortune.

Notwithstanding these reservations *Egypt's Long Revolution* is an important assessment of the revolutionary process by an acute and supportive observer of struggles for change. It draws extensively on the testimony of activists and provides key insights into their motivations, dilemmas and successes. It concludes persuasively that millions of people eager for social justice will continue to challenge the prevailing order.

For a right not to work

Chris Newlove

Inventing the Future: Postcapitalism and a World Without Work
Nick Srnicek and Alex Williams
Verso (2015), £12.99

Inventing the Future is a welcome intervention into the growing debate about how we can move beyond capitalism. The authors are previously known for their "#Accelerate: Manifesto for an Accelerationist Politics" published in 2013. Many of the same themes in the Manifesto are expanded upon in the book. *Inventing the Future* starts with a critique of current anti-capitalist practice which the authors call "folk politics" and what we in this journal's tradition would refer to as "autonomism". The book traces the rise of "folk politics" through the Zapatistas, the anti-capitalist movement of the mid to late 1990s to more recent movements such as Occupy, Spain's 15-M and the student occupations in Britain in 2010 to the present.

Growing from a rejection of a rightward moving social democracy, the collapse of the Soviet Union, the defeats of organised workers in the 1980s, folk politics became attractive to those who want to fight the system. But it ultimately reflects pessimism about winning the majority of people over to anti-capitalism. Srnicek and Williams skilfully outline some of the problems: the fetishisation of local actions, horizontalism and autonomous zones and the general emphasis on personal experience rather than systematic thinking. Instead they emphasise the importance of strategy and the building of a counter-hegemonic project. Part of this project will be the outlining of a "utopian vision" to move beyond capitalism. This is summarised in the authors' four main demands: full automation; the reduction of the working week; universal basic income and the diminishment of the work ethic. As Owen Hatherley points out in the *London Review of Books*, the authors base their demands and vision of a future society on what they see as the potential within the current tendencies of capitalism. The authors largely avoid the celebratory technological determinism of, for example, Paul Mason's recent book *PostCapitalism: A Guide to our Future* or Michael Hardt and Antonio Negri's *Commonwealth*.

The demands themselves are seen as beginning to move away from a system driven by the profit motive. Full automation is about replacing as many jobs in the economy as possible with technology, in particular robots. The demand is seen as "accelerating" the existing tendency within capitalism for replacing labour power with technology. The authors point to research that suggests between 47 and 80 percent of today's jobs could be automated (p112). Of course they also note that for some jobs, for example in the care industry, it would be undesirable or impossible to replace workers with machines. Automation could reduce the working week and add an extra day to the weekend. A basic income that workers could live on would mean they could choose to avoid low paid or arduous work. Jobs that are seen as menial or difficult would have to be paid more than others. This would increase the bargaining power of workers as they would no longer be compelled to work for capitalists in the same way as they are presently.

However, some of the tendencies the book mentions seem to reflect current anti-capitalist "common sense". Srnicek and Williams see the working class as too weak to be the agent of social change. They largely assume ideas around widespread precarity to be true without much empirical evidence. And, as is the case with much anti-capitalist literature, the objective power of workers and the subjective factors of organisation and confidence are not delineated.

The book discusses the usefulness of Antonio Gramsci's concept of hegemony but later adopts Ernesto Laclau's version of it. This is problematic for two reasons. Firstly, Laclau's work represents the wider Eurocommunist movement's shift away from class struggle in the 1980s. When the authors discuss winning anti-capitalist hegemony their focus is on creating think tanks, making use of the mass media and reinvigorating leftist economics in academia. They use the example of how neoliberal economics went from being a marginalised set of ideas to having a dominant influence on governments as something the left should try to emulate. But this downplays the extent to which right wing economists like Milton Friedman had the resources to set up an international network of think tanks and greater access to the media as well as the differing audiences of the two projects. By contrast, Gramsci's version of hegemony emphasises struggle at the time when workers' practice and their old "common sense" ideas come into conflict. The conscious intervention of revolutionaries can help to generalise from the best experience of workers' struggle. For example, the journal *L'Ordine Nuovo* (*New Order*) that Gramsci helped set up aimed to become the voice of the factory council movement during the "two red years" (1919-20) in Italy.

The second problem with adopting Laclau's version of hegemony is the taking on of the idea of left populism. In the formation of Podemos, Pablo Iglesias and the team around him consciously sought to implement Laclau's idea of building hegemony, replacing talk of the working class or capitalists with "the caste" versus "the people". The limits to this ambiguous approach were seen when a section of Podemos voters switched to the right wing populist Ciudadanos (Citizens) party. Higher levels of class struggle were the source of the popularity of Syriza and Podemos rather than the adoption of left populism.

The latter parts of the book discuss organisation and strategy. The authors point out that many anti-capitalists today see lasting organisation as authoritarian or open to co-option. They point out that for effective long-term action to be built from movements, permanent organisation is necessary. Taking an agnostic approach to what such organisation will look like, they state that they want a "healthy and diverse ecosystem of organisations". They point out that organisation has to be based on context. However, they go on to reject the idea of a Leninist or vanguard party without serious discussion. And they skirt over the crucial question of reform or revolution with statements like: "Greece and Spain are showing the potential that arises when social movements engage in a dual strategy both within and outside the party system. If a major transformation as the post work project is to occur, it will come on the back of a mass movement rather than simply decreed on high" (p164).

Inventing the Future is likely to become an increasingly influential work in anti-capitalist politics today. The People's Assembly demonstration against austerity in April this year had a "No Jobs Bloc" inspired by the book. Its critique of "folk politics"/autonomism and its call for organisation and strategy deserve to get a wide resonance. However, the Syriza and Podemos model seems to be becoming increasingly discredited just as the demands in the book gain in popularity. As Hatherley notes "post-capitalism" seems vague compared with socialism, communism and anarchism despite the differing interpretations of these traditions. The way to a truely post-capitalist future remains through socialist revolution and an organisation based on this goal.

Incorporation and exclusion: Israel's Palestinian citizens

Miriam Scharf

Stateless Citizenship: The Palestinian-Arab Citizens of Israel
Shourideh C Molavi
Haymarket (2014), £20

Israel defines itself as a Jewish State although many of its citizens are not Jewish. It is the state of all Jews worldwide rather than those who live within its territories; the only state in the world that defines itself in this way.

In *Stateless Citizenship* Shourideh Molavi focuses on the '48 Palestinians, those who were living in Israel when the state was founded in 1948, and who remained after the Nakba, the expulsion of about 750,000 Palestinians. The book concentrates more on how these Palestinian citizens of Israel cause a legal problem, rather than a political problem. The Zionist project demands that Jewish dominance is maintained, that the ethnic cleansing begun in 1947-8 is continued, and that those Palestinians who stay are kept as a suppressed minority. This book makes the case that the Palestinians within the 1948 Green Line, 20.5 percent (1.6 million) of the Israeli population, have been controlled through their incorporation as "stateless citizens".

These Palestinians hold Israeli citizenship and have some rights, but they do not have a Jewish national identity. Most are Muslim, including 200,000 Bedouins, some are Druze and some Christian. Molavi says that "the State of Israel continues to deny the existence of its Palestinian-Arab citizenry as an indigenous population, a national group, or even as a national minority... Israeli (ab)uses of citizenship...have situated these people on the periphery of both Israeli and Palestinian society" (p3).

At a time when the refugee and migrant crisis is showing democratic states to be all too ready to deny or diminish rights to whole groups of people, a discussion of citizenship is useful. Each European state is harbouring or promoting forms of racism. But comparisons with racism in Europe are limited as in Israel the Palestinians are the indigenous group and Zionism, the enforcement of Jewish hegemony over Palestinians by colonisation (nowhere in the book is this called a racist ideology), is the founding ideology of the state. So in Israel the content of citizenship from the beginning has been a key political question. The fact is that "access to the home, the city, the state and the land itself in the State of Israel in the form of civic identification, claims, rights and membership, is deliberately designed to exclude the non-Jewish community" (p4). As Molavi points out repeatedly, the Israeli state allows no separation of Jewish identity and national identity. Legal challenges or petitions calling for an Israeli national identity, or for legal amendments referring to Israel as "a state of all its citizens", are rejected. Conceding an Israeli national identity or equal citizenship would allow the idea of Palestinian Israelis being included as equals; this is not to be.

How does Israel square this inequality with its claim to be a democracy? Molavi cites court cases and government policies to show that, where this contradiction arises, it was always the practice, and is now enshrined in law, that maintaining the Jewish character of the state outweighs democratic criteria.

Molavi reviews some of the key critical scholarship on the exclusionary nature of Palestinian citizenship, examining various formulations. She uses these as a springboard for her thesis that "it is through inclusion within the Israeli citizenship regime that they are excluded" (p181). The idea of an incorporation regime is a conceptual framework increasingly accepted in academic circles. Molavi develops this with a chapter on Yasemin Soysal's work (see *Limits of Citizenship, Migration and Post-national Citizenship In Europe*), though she insists her own idea of "stateless citizenship" is a different conceptual tool.

Molavi says that "the historical matrix of colonialism within which the Jewish national movement burgeoned is explained as a main source of the Israeli incorporation regime and the multi-faceted discrimination faced by Arab citizens today", ie that Zionism is the problem. Included among the plethora of discriminatory legislation she describes are the recently passed laws banning citizens from organising or promoting boycotts of Israeli goods or services and the Loyalty Oath (Bill at the time of writing). The latter requires citizens to declare an oath to Israel as a "Jewish, Zionist, and democratic state, to its symbols and values, and to serve the state in any way demanded", a substantial change from the previous, "I declare I will be a loyal citizen of the State of Israel." The laws target all areas of life and force concessions to the dominance of Zionism, strengthening the Jewish character of state institutions and weakening their democratic features. An important aspect of this is the denial of collective in addition to individual rights for Palestinians. An example is rewriting of Arab village names in Hebrew characters—a measure claimed by the government as an example of inclusion! If any doubts remain as to Israel's lack of legitimacy as a democratic state then Molavi cites the 2002 electoral law amendment, which prevents any person or political party standing, "if their aims and actions either explicitly or implicitly deny or challenge the Jewish and democratic nature of the State of Israel" (p71).

The book contains a summary of key events following the Nakba: the "Military Administration" restrictions and land confiscations, the beginning of minimal spaces for political participation in the 1970s, the establishment of Land Day, and the development of the High Follow-Up Committee to represent the interests of Arab citizens of Israel culminating in support for the first intifada of 1987. The results of the Oslo Accords fed the Israeli Palestinians solidarity with the second intifada 2000-2002. Since then Molavi notes there has been "increased securitisation and isolation of Arab citizens in what had become a heavily polarised Israeli society" (p13). It would have been helpful to use the historical framework to contextualise developments in Zionist practice and laws. For example the batch of aggressive laws introduced by the Israeli State in 2002 surely parallels its brutal military response to the second intifada.

Some of Molavi's reviews of previous scholarship seem solely for academic consumption. However, she does take on the "liberal" Zionist argument in Alexander Yakobson and Amnon Rubinstein's 2009 book *Israel and the Family of Nations*, a text worth critiquing. The formula used to legitimise a Jewish State is that any denial of this "undermines the principles of universal equality since it denies the right of the Jewish people to self-determination and national independence". Molavi points out that "even the most liberal Zionists consider exclusive Jewish democratic control as vital for the existence of a Jewish national home, regardless of its legal, political and human costs. And with these two factors as priorities, the liberal Zionist ideology proves incapable of implementing even the most basic principles of liberalism." Molavi concludes that Yakobson and Rubinstein "are trying to divert the reader from the devastating historical record to the myth of a basically virtuous colonial-settler project" (p146). Other contemporary liberal Zionist authors are also examined. But the focus being on present citizenship, surely Molavi did not need to include Theodor Herzl's Orientalist depictions of Arabs and Golda Meir's denial of the word "Palestinian"? A clear statement that Israel as a Jewish State has been built on the denial of Palestinians to self-determination would not have gone amiss.

It is disconcerting that Molavi uses the terms "Arab citizens" and "Arab Israelis" interchangeably with "Palestinian citizens" and "Palestinian Israelis", ignoring both Jews of Arab origin, and the Druze, neither of whom identify as Palestinian. This aside, she has lifted some interesting questions from other scholars as to naming citizens: Anton Shammas asks for a new definition of being Israeli, one that includes Arabs, while Baruch Kimmerling suggests that, if in France you can have a French Jew, can you have, in the Jewish State, a Muslim Jew or a Christian Jew? This conundrum arises because "neither Jewish nationalism...nor the Israeli State were able to invent a purely secular or a civil national identity" (p149). Molavi looks at various ideas of Palestinian citizenship; Miloon Kothari, writing on the right to adequate housing, explains: "Nationality status in Israel is not linked to origin from, or residence in a certain territory, as is the norm in international law...ethnic criteria [are] the grounds for the employment of full rights" (p149).

Molavi uses many studies to show that the constitutional definition of the state as Jewish, bolstered by structural and institutional policies of dominance and control, essentially prevents Palestinian Israelis from having any meaningful citizenship. *The Arabs in Israel* by Sabri Jiryis (1976) is referenced as giving a useful history of the systematic expropriation and oppression of the colonial project from 1948. Elia Zureik's *The Palestinians in Israel: A Study of Internal Colonialism* states the "primacy of Israeli political economy, its class structure and Jewish-Arab relations" in defining the situation of Palestinians in Israel as an "internal colony" (p161). Ian Lustick's *Arabs in the Jewish State: Israel's Control of a National Minority* focuses on how the quiescence of the Palestinian minority has been obtained, the aim being "to control the Arab community in Israel rather than to eliminate, integrate, absorb or develop it" (p163). Finally, Ilan Pappé adopts a systematic view of Israel as a settler-colonial society (p166), showing how Palestinians are viewed as part of a group outside Israel, not as part of Israel. Molavi also emphasises the importance of independent Arab scholars.

Although chapters can appear like a collection of separate essays, this sampling of scholarship gives the reader a range of analytical and conceptual frames, and outlines the practical and theoretical effects of the foisting of Jewish nationalism on Palestinian citizens.

It is disappointing that the author does not comment on or critique how Palestinian "statelessness" has fed the idea of a two-state solution. She does not mention the possibility of a single—secular and democratic—state although her analysis seems to support this as a way to challenge and resolve Palestinian "statelessness". It is impossible to divorce the treatment of Palestinians within the Green Line from actions of Palestinians outside, indeed from regional and global changes, yet Molavi avoids such wider analysis. With a text focused on academic debate and critique, any activist reader must work hard to get useful ammunition. Nevertheless, she has contributed to showing that the Israeli state, from its inception to the latest legislation, is far from being a democracy in its discriminatory treatment of its non-Jews.

Imperialism: novel forms, old problems

Adrian Budd

Imperialism in the Twenty-first Century: Globalization, Super-Exploitation, and Capitalism's Final Crisis
John Smith
Monthly Review Press (2016), £18.99

The significance of John Smith's book lies in his powerful critique of mainstream economics and official statistics as he attempts a renewal of dependency theory. Mobilising Marxist value theory to this end he argues that the Global South's formal independence masks an abiding economic and political subordination to the imperialist powers and powerful Northern capitals. The book's impact is reflected in the critical commentary that it has provoked, including on Michael Roberts's blog.*

Smith's opening chapters highlight the devastating impact of globalisation on Southern labour. His initial focus is on iconic global commodities—T-shirts, iPhones and coffee—and Smith emphasises the disparity between the wages of those producing values and the retail prices and profits in the advanced importing countries. Thus, while the numbers employed in iPod-related activities in

* Go to https://thenextrecession.wordpress.com/2016/03/07/imperialism-and-super-exploitation/

China and the United States are broadly similar, total wages in the former in 2006 were $19 million but $719 million in the latter (p28). Smith argues, therefore, that value produced in the South is disproportionately captured as profit in the North. Meanwhile, the horrors of globalisation, including environmental devastation and the deaths of workers in unsafe factories and dormitories, are concentrated in the Global South.

Smith argues that the scale of transnationalised production is understated by foreign direct investment (FDI) data since transnational corporations (TNCs) increasingly organise global production chains via arms-length relations with independent Southern firms, rather than investing directly in overseas production. These relations have grown dramatically in recent decades: export processing zones, home to much Southern manufacturing, now exist in over 130 countries and in 2010 there were 541 million industrial workers living in the Global South compared to 145 million in the imperialist countries (p101). The share of wages in national income is falling everywhere (more rapidly than official figures indicate since, as Smith points out, the stratospheric pay packages, bonuses and stock options of employers and managers are included as income to labour). But for Smith the low wages of workers in the Global South are at the heart of imperialism.

Global labour arbitrage involves the shift of production to low-wage economies, where it is reinforced by factors such as repressive labour regimes and huge flows of female workers and workers from the countryside into factories. The consequence is "super-exploitation", defined as the payment of wages below the value of labour power. Increases in absolute and relative surplus value (by extending working hours and increasing productivity respectively) persist, but Smith argues that "super-exploitation" is increasingly dominant in the Global South and key to explaining the changing form of imperialism.

However, while it is clear that powerful capitalist forces have restructured global capitalism to enable massive exploitation of huge numbers of new workers, the concept of "super-exploitation", and the political consequences that Smith sometimes suggests, are problematic. The value of labour power is the socially necessary labour time required to produce and reproduce that labour power. But how is social necessity defined? Smith rightly highlights the migration controls that keep Southern workers largely confined to national labour markets and maintain downward pressure on wages, and for most of the book it seems that national yardsticks of social necessity apply. Yet, rather late in his analysis, he quotes Andy Higginbottom—who has promoted the importance of "super-exploitation" in Marxist analysis—that Southern workers are super-exploited because they are "systematically paid below the value of labour power" of Northern workers. But despite deepening global economic integration, there is no international value of labour power; the production and reproduction of Southern labour power are not easily related to the value of labour power in the North. Meanwhile low wages, casualisation and youth unemployment continue to characterise advanced capitalism. What is more, Smith rightly argues that despite a gradual movement up the value chain, Southern manufacturing produces low value-added commodities and is heavily reliant on imports of high value technologically advanced inputs from the rich countries. This suggests that he should not rush to the conclusion that Southern workers' low wages confirm "super-exploitation".

The key political problem with Smith's analysis concerns the beneficiaries of Northern transnationals' profit capture. The equalisation of profit rates entails a transfer of value from less to more productive capitals, and at the global level Northern capitalists may gain at the expense of Southern. But it is difficult to discern benefits to Northern workers, particularly in industries where production has shifted to the South. Indeed, Southern manufacturing jobs, for example in Latin America and Africa, have also been lost as a result of Chinese competition. Yet Smith quotes Tony Norfield that there "is a direct economic benefit for the mass of people in the richer countries" (p14), and argues that there is a "distribution of some of outsourcing's bounty to increasingly wide sections of the working class through falling prices of consumer goods" (p41). Certainly, falling consumer prices cushion the blow of unemployment and wage restraint, and lower the value of Northern labour power, but if "super-exploitation" does exist it is better understood as involving a transfer of value to capital rather than to Northern workers.

Smith's work grapples with the contemporary dynamics of imperialism, which no longer centres primarily on advanced capitalist exploitation of Southern primary products. It is thought-provoking and should be widely read. But the key problems of dependency theory remain and cannot be side-stepped by disdainfully, and occasionally moralistically, labelling its Marxist critics as "Euro-Marxists" (writers from the Socialist Workers Party are among Smith's chief targets), as if the argument that Northern workers may be more exploited than Southern workers entails an insensitivity, or even blindness, to Southern labour's exploitation and associated horrors. If Marxism is adequately to grapple with contemporary imperialism, it is imperative to reject Smith's argument that since Lenin wrote on imperialism there have been no additions to the imperialist club (p226). China's role in Africa, for instance, demonstrates that imperialism cannot be reduced to the issue of Northern oppressor nations feeding off the oppressed of the South.

Changing the world, changing ourselves
Geoff Brown

Young Lives on the Left: Sixties Activism and the Liberation of the Self
Celia Hughes
Manchester University Press (2015), £70

For those who argue that women and men make history, it makes sense to assess the 1968 generation, those at the heart of "the fire last time", their strengths and weaknesses. What better way than oral history of capturing the extraordinary spirit of the last time the rulers of the world feared they were losing control? Celia Hughes is not the first to take this approach. In particular, Ronald Fraser's, *1968: A Student Generation in Revolt*, written nearly 30 years ago, is still worth reading. For Hughes's own book she interviewed 70 "68ers", mainly former members of the International Socialists (IS), forerunner of the SWP, and of the International Marxist Group (IMG), now Socialist Resistance. She has also talked to some who were "non-aligned", mainly North London activists who opposed the Vietnam War. All were decisively shaped by the political upturn of 1968, many are still active, a fair few are readers of this journal and indeed some are contributors.

Her questions have a wide scope. They include growing up during and after the war, family, school, the Campaign for Nuclear Disarmament (CND), the Young Socialists, university, work, political activities, branch life, organising, campaigning, living collectively, sex, family and childcare. Her central focus is what she calls the New Left, which grew out of the Vietnam Solidarity Campaign (VSC) 1967-9, and the "new politics" of the women's liberation movement, emerging a little later.

Her interviews show how individuals change, moving from feelings about what is wrong with the world to ideas about how to change it, how they become revolutionaries. For many, key moments included challenging their parents at home, their teachers at school and their colleagues and managers at work, going on a first demonstration, picketing or being thrown into a police van. But Hughes also demonstrates how people change through engaging with ideas such as workers' control, challenging the revisionism of Anthony Crosland in *The Future of Socialism*, reading Marxist literature, watching films such as Lindsay Anderson's 1968 film *if.....*

Much of the narrative is about intense collective struggles against the police, government, university authorities and employers as well as racists, fascists and male chauvinists. The interviewees were also aware of being part of an international movement against war and imperialism, racism and women's oppression. The outcome is a book with much fascinating detail of how times were a-changing, for example showing how CND, a movement from below, prepared the ground for campaigning over the Vietnam War.

Memory is often faulty and we have our own agendas when people ask us questions about our past. We forget and we "forget". We want to construct our histories in our own way and are sometimes afraid of challenging the interpretations of others. What is lost when some of those invited refuse to be interviewed? Hughes recognises the difficulties with oral history and is rigorous in dealing with them. While sometimes critical of her interviewees, for example in pointing out the failures of some to change chauvinist attitudes in relationships in the face of the women's liberation movement, she remains sympathetic towards the people she speaks to and their revolutionary aspirations.

The problem with the book lies not in Hughes's method but in her agenda. Her title refers to "the liberation of the self". But as she acknowledges, this wasn't how many of the interviewees saw their actions. To change the world people needed to change themselves—but this was a means to an end rather than their main objective. They certainly did change and the book captures many of these changes but why should this be the subject of investigation? For all involved, it was about collective agency: "How do we shape events? How do we organise? What works? Where did we get it wrong?" The key to these questions was (and is) politics.

The New Left of 1968 was divided in its answers. For those who joined the IS, the slogans "For workers' power" and "Neither Washington nor Moscow?" were of critical importance: Can workers run society? Is Russia socialist? How does capitalism work? When does it go into crisis? Hughes sees this but does not pursue it. Her interest is in subjectivity; her aim, to make "an informative contribution to the unfolding subjective turn in social history". Important as this might be, for those seeking to change the world, social history is not enough. The subjective needs its context, the circumstances "existing already, given and transmitted from the past". Events such as the long post-war boom, the Hungarian Revolution, the seafarers' strike of 1966 and the Vietnam War changed how people saw the world. If we are to make a judgment of the revolutionary left, these events and the arguments they generated need to be included in the history. In the meantime, it is far from clear how the concept of a "left subjectivity" should be used.

In itself, this shouldn't stop this book being something we might want to read or recommend to a younger generation. Sadly this book is not written for those starting to shape their lives in the struggle but for academics. The sometimes dense interpretation and academic referencing frequently obscure the narrative created by the interviews. Nevertheless, as Hughes points out, the history of the 1960s is still contested, its movements often labelled superficial or dangerous. While Chris Harman's *The Fire Last Time: 1968 and After* remains indispensable, there is still scope for assessing the '68ers.

Pick of the quarter

October's *Science and Society* (volume 80, number 4) is a special issue edited by Eduardo Albuquerque and Alex Callinicos entitled "Crises and Transformation of Capitalism: Marx's Investigations and Contemporary Analysis". Their reasons for revisiting Marx's writings on crises are twofold: there is a need for theoretical and empirical research into the economic crisis of 2007-9 and its aftermath, and previously unpublished work by Marx has now been made available thanks to the *MEGA* (*Marx-Engels Complete Works*) project.

Lucia Pradella makes use of some of the works included in the *MEGA* project as well as *Capital*, volume I. Pradella shows how Marx integrated an understanding of global politics into his analysis of capital accumulation rather than treating the British state as self-enclosed. His understanding of crisis was linked to his understanding of revolution. While it is often assumed that Marx saw economic crisis as leading to social upheaval, he also speculated about the reverse happening; an uprising in the colonies could trigger economic crisis in the imperialist countries.

In "How Not to Write About the Rate of Profit" Alex Callinicos and Joseph Choonara criticise David Harvey's attempts to discredit theorists of the tendency of the rate of profit to fall. Harvey accuses such theorists of ignoring other factors—such as financialisation—as causes of crisis. But for Callinicos and Choonara this is a basic misunderstanding of Marx's method, which, they note, involves starting from the abstract and "successively introducing more concrete determinations" and that "addresses apparent counter-examples by integrating them into the theory". Therefore Marx can introduce a discussion of finance and circulation into his overall analysis but without detracting from the centrality of the rate of profit.

By contrast Jan Toporowski says that "corporate finance has been largely overlooked in explanations of the 2008 crisis". Toporowski takes a more empirical approach using data from *The Economist* to argue that large companies cut back on expenditure to try to deal with their debt problems and that this, rather than the failings of the banks, was the mechanism behind the crisis. Other contributors to the special issue include Guglielmo Carchedi, Gérard Duménil and Dominique Lévy, Leonardo Gomes de Deus and Michael Roberts, who has also contributed a book review to this issue of *International Socialism*.

The latest issue of *New Left Review* (II/100) has a number of interesting articles. The editor, Susan Watkins, offers a detailed analysis of the Brexit referendum and its consequences. This cogently argued article confirms the dramatic shift that *NLR* has made from supporting European integration when Britain joined the European Common Market in the 1970s to opposing the European Union from the left today. Both were minority positions on the wider British left, but, amid the mourning over Brexit from the likes of the *Guardian*, Watkins's tough-minded assessment is refreshing:

> The Brexit vote doesn't mean state break-up, yet. Still less the downfall of Brussels. For now, though, it is plain that Blairised Britain has taken a hit, as has the Hayekianised EU. Critics of the neoliberal order have no reason to regret these knocks to it, against which the entire global establishment—Obama to Abe, Merkel to Modi, Juncker to Xi—has inveighed.

One of the most influential articles *NLR* published in the 1970s was Perry Anderson's "The Antinomies of Antonio Gramsci", a detailed examination of what he argued were the conceptual and political ambiguities in Gramsci's theory of hegemony. His interpretation has been challenged, notably by Peter Thomas in *The Gramscian Moment*. As far as we know, Anderson hasn't responded to these criticisms, but maybe he will in a forthcoming book on the concept of hegemony.

The current issue of *NLR* carries an extract in which Anderson discusses those he regards as the most creative continuers of Gramsci's explorations of hegemony—the cultural theorist Stuart Hall, the philosopher Ernesto Laclau, the postcolonialist historian Ranajit Guha and the political economist Giovanni Arrighi. Anderson's tone is generally neutral, though not uncritical. Although he's maybe a bit too kind about Hall, his justified admiration for Guha and Arrighi is clear. But he can't restrain himself when discussing Laclau, whose theory of populism was a major influence on the founders of Podemos. His judgement on Laclau's attempt, together with Chantal Mouffe, to fuse Gramsci and poststructuralism is definitive:

> The linguistic turn of the theory, in common with its late twentieth century vogue in general, proposed a discursive idealism severing significations from any stable connexion with referents. Here the result was to detach ideas and demands so completely from socio-economic moorings that they

could in principle be appropriated by any agency for any political construct. Inherently, the range of articulations knows no limit. All is contingency: expropriation of the expropriators could become the watchword of bankers, secularisation of church lands a goal of the Vatican, destruction of guilds the ideal of craftsmen, mass redundancies the call of a working class, enclosures the aim of a peasantry. The proposal defeated itself. Not only could anything be articulated in any direction: everything became articulation. First hegemony, then populism, were presented as a type of politics, among others. Then, in a characteristic inflationary move, they became the definition of all politics as such—thereby making themselves supernumerary.

AC & CR